GOLDSMITH
AS JOURNALIST

GOLDSMITH
AS JOURNALIST

Richard C. Taylor

Rutherford ● Madison ● Teaneck
Fairleigh Dickinson University Press
London and Toronto: Associated University Presses

92
G624t

Associated University Presses
440 Forsgate Drive
Cranbury, NJ 08512

Associated University Presses
25 Sicilian Avenue
London WC1A 2QH, England

Associated University Presses
P.O. Box 338, Port Credit
Mississauga, Ontario,
Canada L5G 4L8

The paper used in this publication meets the requirements of the American National Standard for Permanence of Paper for Printed Library Materials Z39.48-1984.

Library of Congress Cataloging-in-Publication Data

Taylor, Richard C., 1956–
    Goldsmith as journalist / Richard C. Taylor.
      p. cm.
    Includes bibliographical references and index.

MB

    ISBN 0-8386-3462-1 (alk. paper)
    1. Goldsmith, Oliver, 1728–1774—Knowledge—Communication.
2. Journalism—Great Britain—History—18th century. 3. Authors, Irish—18th century—Biography. 4. Journalists—Great Britain—Biography. I. Title.
PR3494.T38   1993
828'.609—dc20
[B]   91-58960
                                            CIP

PRINTED IN THE UNITED STATES OF AMERICA

to
Robert D. Hume

Contents

Works Frequently Cited

Basker   Basker, James G. *Tobias Smollett: Critic and Journalist.* Newark: University of Delaware Press, 1988.

Brewer   Brewer, John. *Party Ideology and Popular Politics at the Accession of George III.* Cambridge: Cambridge University Press, 1976.

Friedman   Friedman, Arthur, ed. *Collected Works of Oliver Goldsmith.* 5 vols. Oxford: Clarendon Press, 1966. Unless otherwise noted, all references to Goldsmith's work will be to this edition and will be cited parenthetically in the text by volume and page numbers.

Graham   Graham, Walter. *English Literary Periodicals.* New York: Thomas Nelson & Sons, 1930.

Hume, *Letters*   Greig, J. Y. T., ed. *The Letters of David Hume.* 2 vols. Oxford: Clarendon Press, 1932.

Letters   Balderston, Katharine C., ed. *The Collected Letters of Oliver Goldsmith.* Cambridge: Cambridge University Press, 1928.

Life of Johnson   Hill, George Birkbeck, and L. F. Powell, eds. *Boswell's Life of Johnson.* 6 vols. Oxford: Clarendon Press, 1934–1950.

Nangle   Nangle, Benjamin Christie. *The Monthly Review First Series, 1749–1789: Indexes of Contributors and Articles.* Oxford: Clarendon Press, 1934.

Percy's Memoir   Balderston, Katharine C. *The History and Sources of Percy's Memoir of Goldsmith.* Cambridge: Cambridge University Press, 1926.

Prior   Prior, James. *The Life of Oliver Goldsmith, M.B. from a Variety of Original Sources.* 2 vols. London: John Murray, 1837.

Smollett, *Letters*   Knapp, Lewis M., ed. *The Letters of Tobias Smollett.* Oxford: Clarendon Press, 1970.

Spector, *ELP*   Spector, Robert Donald. *English Literary Periodicals and the Climate of Opinion during the Seven Years' War.* The Hague: Mouton, 1966.

Wardle   Wardle, Ralph. *Oliver Goldsmith.* Lawrence: University of Kansas Press, 1957.

Preface

My aim in this study is to place the periodical work of Oliver Goldsmith in the contexts of journalism as a profession and of the literary and political history of the Seven Years' War period (1756–63). I will try to demonstrate how contemporary writers conceived of the emerging profession in which they were engaged. I use the term *profession* advisedly: when Goldsmith began his career in 1757, the idea of authorship—let alone journalism—as a profession was a heated issue, debated by journalists themselves in London newspapers and magazines. This conflict was part of a greater concern: the fear that England's status as an empire and center of learning was in jeopardy. The alarm that resulted from ministerial crises and military defeats early in the war gave rise to an unprecedented interest in London periodicals and largely determined their content. While most critics have thought Goldsmith aloof from politics, his career was profoundly influenced by the war, the changing demands of his readers, and the innovations and adaptations of an emerging profession.

Though much of Goldsmith's journalistic work has been analyzed as literary or biographical artifact, his journalistic career as a whole—as a reflection and product of a changing profession—has been overlooked. A study of this subject faces an imposing obstacle: periodical writing during the period was usually anonymous, and except for those essays Goldsmith himself selected for collected editions and the book reviews that his employer Ralph Griffiths attributed to him, few of Goldsmith's periodical writings can be assigned indisputably to him. The record of twentieth-century scholarship on Goldsmith is marked by efforts to expand or restrict the author's known canon. Arthur Friedman's cautious approach in his five-volume *Collected Works* (1966) held sway until James Basker, in his *Tobias Smollett: Critic and Journalist* (1988), proposed a significant expansion of the journalistic canons of both Smollett and Goldsmith.[1] Basker relies on the testimony of Isaac Reed, editor of the "Reed-Wright" collection of Goldsmith's essays (1798). Reed confirms that the printer Thomas Wright was involved with the *British Magazine* in 1760, when Goldsmith contributed heavily to that periodical, and that Wright kept a record of Goldsmith's essays.[2] This study will take account of the twenty-nine proposed additions, but with caution. Some of the pieces confirm the picture of Goldsmith that emerges from his well-accepted journalistic pieces; some of them are shockingly contradictory and further complicate the task of developing a unified picture of this "knight-

11

errant to the booksellers."[3] Goldsmith himself recognized the difficulty that accurate attribution of authorship posed and saw it as a barrier to his self-expressed desire for fame. Indeed, any study of the periodical authors of the period, even of Fielding and Johnson, must allow for doubt and varying degrees of uncertainty in confronting the veil of anonymity.

My purpose here, rather than to propose significant additions to the known canon, is the largely unassayed one of trying to place the first phase of Goldsmith's authorial career in the contexts of the journalists and book-sellers, periodicals and politics, and the controversies and change that vitalized the London periodical profession. The same forces that enabled Goldsmith to establish himself as a journalist became a principal focus of his work. In defining himself as a periodical contributor and carving a place for himself in a trade toward which he frequently expressed animosity, Goldsmith became an important commentator on the state of mid-eighteenth-century publishing. Taken as a whole, his reviews, essays, and short fiction form a narrative of conflict. He was the unknown yet ambitious outsider grappling with commercial and cultural forces that inhibited his talent and concealed him from public recognition; the arbiter of taste attacking an aesthetic wasteland; the self-proclaimed literary offspring of Addison, denied his rightful inheritance by a public no longer interested in the "moral" essay; the "foreign correspondent" confined to a bookseller's garret; and the "apolitical" essayist forced to confront political controversy.

This study will review details of Goldsmith's journalistic career and place particular emphasis on his work as a reviewer, a phase of his career much more neglected than his work as an essayist. It will also discuss, more generally, the nature of reviewing and magazine writing during the Seven Years' War to demonstrate some of the shaping influences on Goldsmith's periodical writing. Finally, it will assess his responses to the war, party politics, ministerial crises, the accession of George III, and the politicization of the press. The ultimate goal of this study is to show how personal factors, historical influences, and the vagaries of the profession converged to define Goldsmith as a journalist.

Except for those of Fielding, Smollett, Johnson, Arthur Murphy, and John Hawkesworth, the journalistic careers of the principal mid-eighteenth-century periodical writers have attracted little critical notice.[4] A number of factors contribute to this persistent neglect. One is the writers' own ambivalence about the seriousness of "hack" writing and the anonymity in which they worked. For many scholars, this "professional" writing has been relegated to the status of subliterary artifact. The venomous attacks on Grub Street by Alexander Pope, John Brown, and others, coupled with the frequent self-denigration of the "hacks" themselves, reinforce this view.

Another reason for the relative neglect of Goldsmith's journalistic work is the discouraging lack of documentary evidence. Most of the evidence relating to Goldsmith's life and career was uncovered in the half-century following his death in 1774 (though such twentieth-century studies as R. S. Crane's *New Essays* also addressed themselves to still-unresolved attribution problems).[5] Most of the biographies written since the middle of the nineteenth century, including the generally accepted standard study by Ralph Wardle (1957), have done little more than revise James Prior's two-volume *Life* (1837), a work remarkably dependable and well-researched for its time. Later nineteenth-century biographers should, however, be credited with challenging the "Poor Goldsmith" approach to his journalistic career.[6] Initiated by sympathetic nineteenth-century authors such as Washington Irving, this tendency to focus on the oppressiveness of Goldsmith's early career— especially on the supposedly tyrannical treatment he received at the hands of Ralph Griffiths and Griffiths' wife—prevented an objective analysis of the substance and contexts of Goldsmith's periodical work. Biographers such as John Forster (1877) and Austin Dobson (1888) took issue with this largely imaginative reconstruction which had defined both Goldsmith's early career and Griffiths' historical reputation.

Recent interest in Goldsmith's journalistic career has declined, along with his critical reputation. In fact, Goldsmith criticism may be nearly unique among that for major eighteenth-century authors, in that significantly more enduring scholarship was published between 1927 and 1966 than has been produced since. Actually, excepting Arthur Friedman's edition, the high point in twentieth-century Goldsmith scholarship occurred within a few years of the bicentennial of the author's birth—specifically, 1926–34.[7] In 1926 Katharine Balderston examined the first biographical account of Goldsmith, Thomas Percy's *Memoir,* and collected and published a census of the manuscript evidence relating to Goldsmith.[8] Following Crane's *New Essays* in 1927, Balderston published the *Collected Letters* (1928), a still-unsuperseded source, and Temple Scott furthered her work with a bibliographical study.[9] R. W. Seitz produced, in 1929, the last major revision of the canon to be accepted by Friedman,[10] and a year later Walter Graham published his ambitious survey *English Literary Periodicals,* dated and occasionally unreliable on Goldsmith, but valuable for Graham's observations on individual journals. In 1933, Elizabeth Eaton Kent published *Goldsmith and His Booksellers,* a scantily documented but a useful source of contextual information.[11] Finally, in 1934, Benjamin Nangle produced his *Monthly Review* index for the years 1749–89. Deciphering most of Griffiths' attribution inscriptions on the editor's file copies, Nangle provided a solid basis for analyzing the reviewing careers of Goldsmith and his colleagues.[12] After this flurry of scholarly activity, little of importance was published before Wardle's biography (1957) and Friedman's edition (1966).[13] Even Basker's daring study has yet to provoke much renewed interest.

Two works roughly coinciding with the appearance of Friedman's edition serve as points of departure for a full-length consideration of Goldsmith's journalistic career. Ricardo Quintana's *Oliver Goldsmith: A Georgian Study* (1967) distinguishes the "High Georgian" period to which Goldsmith belonged from an earlier era entertained and enlightened by the *Tatler* and *Spectator*. [14] Quintana offers some valuable commentary on individual reviews and essays, and a rare, appreciative treatment of Goldsmith's journalism, though his treatment of Goldsmith's periodical career and its contexts is relatively brief and general in scope. Robert Donald Spector's *English Literary Periodicals and the Climate of Opinion during the Seven Years' War* (1966) is perhaps the most impressive treatment of the development of periodicals and their historical influences during this period. As a sophisticated analysis of the politicization of the press, it invites a political interpretation of Goldsmith's journalistic work and provides a solid, historical frame for such a study.

Of the more recent biographical treatments, the most useful is John Ginger's *The Notable Man* (1977). Ginger recognizes Goldsmith as "the journalist who had given graceful expression to the liberal ideals of his age." [15] Though his narrative contains as much speculation and imaginative recreation as careful interpretation of evidence, his study is lively; steeped in the study of Goldsmith's historical milieu, his interpretations of the journalistic writing are usually provocative and well-founded. However, surprisingly little work has been done since Samuel Woods discussed "The Goldsmith 'Problem'" in an essay for *Studies in Burke and His Time* (1978). [16] Woods cited the view of Goldsmith as a "lesser Johnson" and the writer's "striking versatility" as barriers to serious scholarship. While he did not single out the journalistic career as needing further study, Woods did call for an approach to Goldsmith's career through "cultural history." [17] Though he provided a useful reference guide to Goldsmith studies in 1982, Woods's attempt to revitalize interest has, so far, failed to generate much scholarly enthusiasm. [18]

The present study aims to situate Goldsmith in discussions of journalism as an unstable genre and as an unrecognized but clearly emerging profession, practiced by frustrated, ambivalent, and anonymous authors, struggling to define themselves.

I am deeply indebted to Robert D. Hume for his inspiration and advice. I would also like to thank John Harwood, James West, Nicholas Joukovsky, Philip Jenkins, Antonia Forster, Michael McDonough, Nancy Mace, E. Thomson Shields, Jeffrey Williams, Trudy D. Butler, and Lisa Taylor for their assistance, encouragement, and criticism.

GOLDSMITH
AS JOURNALIST

1

Journalist by Profession

Mr. Johnson, Dr. Goldsmith, and I supped together at the Mitre. I had curious ideas when I considered that I was sitting with London authors by profession.

—Boswell's *London Journal*, 1 July 1763

As a phrase describing the careers of reviewers, essayists, and editors of periodicals in the 1750s and 1760s, "journalist by profession" represents a compromise—a term as fraught with political implications as its counterpart, "hack by trade." Throughout the years Goldsmith toiled for the London press, the legitimacy of professional authorship was hotly debated, and these two phrases express opposing attitudes toward careers still in the shadows of anonymity and a class of patronless authors adjusting slowly—and often bitterly—to a greater reliance on booksellers and the public.

The term *journalist,* as applied to periodical writers, was just beginning to come into currency during this period; Johnson's *Dictionary* defines it only as "a writer of journals." Its usage in the 1750s most frequently implied contempt. In the third number of Bonnell Thornton and George Colman's *Connoisseur,* a periodical that demonstrably influenced Goldsmith and his contemporaries, the narrator makes a typically pejorative remark: "Myself, and every petty journalist, affect to dignify our hasty performances by stiling them LUCUBRATIONS; by which we mean, if we mean any thing, that as the day is too short for our labours, we are obliged to call in the assistance of the night."[1] Goldsmith, too, echoed a popular attitude toward "The Trade" in a "Chinese Letter" for the *Public Ledger* (3 June 1760): "Should you look for the character of Voltaire among the journalists and illiterate writers of the age; you would find him there characterized as a monster" (II, 183).[2] By 1758 Johnson had discovered the term and defined it in his introductory essay for the *Universal Chronicle* (8 April 1758), "Of the Duty of a Journalist":

A Journalist is an Historian, not indeed of the highest Class, nor of the number of those whose works bestow immortality upon others or themselves; yet like other Historians, he distributes for a time Reputation or Infamy, relates the opinion of the week, raises hopes and terrors, inflames or allays the violence of the people.[3]

The steadily increasing usage of the term *journalist* coincided with a growing wariness of this group's influence—the appalling power of anonymous "hacks" to make or break reputations and to incite the masses. Johnson's rhetorical strategy, here, is typical: submerged in this attack on the power of second-class writers is the obvious fact of the writer's own participation in this system and the recognition that even for a superior practitioner, the barrier to fame as a journalist is almost insuperable. The work is as transient as public opinion, and the temporary and arbitrary authority it wields is as likely to be destructive as to be a positive social force. The attack serves, in part, to distance the author from the pernicious aspects of the profession; he presents himself as one aware of its dangers and one who, without hope of recognition, attempts to use this forum for the public good.

Johnson's definition in the *Universal* suggests a second semantic problem: the use of *professional* to describe the activities of editors, translators, reviewers, and essayists whose livelihoods depended on their work for the dozens of London periodicals of the late 1750s and early 1760s. Scholars generally do not treat authorship, and certainly not authorship of articles in periodicals, as a socially recognized profession before the nineteenth century. Magali S. Larson observes that even by the end of the eighteenth century, "the recognized gentlemanly professions were, in practice, only three: divinity, and its recent offshoot university teaching; the law, which filled, with the exception of architecture, most of the relatively prestigious specializations that could be considered 'professional' before the industrial revolution; and the profession of medicine."[4] However, authors of the period did not always confine their use of the word *professional* to the description of those working in divinity, law, and medicine. Even so particular a wordsmith as Johnson extended the term to other vocations. His *Rambler* Number 9 (17 April 1750), for instance, calls for those in all lines of work—drapers, soldiers, and manufacturers, as well as physicians and lawyers—to honor their "professions."[5]

By 1757, when Goldsmith entered the "profession" of journalism, the idea of periodical authorship as a pastime for the financially independent had become a thinly disguised fiction, maintained largely by struggling, anonymous authors like Goldsmith who adopted gentlemanly personae in their magazine work. Two influential treatises, published around the time of Goldsmith's initiation as a periodical apprentice, recognized the reality of a changing "profession," though their authors came to opposite conclusions about the changes involved.

Brown versus Ralph: Authorship as Profession

John Brown's *An Estimate of the Manners and Principles of the Times* (March 1757), a jeremiad on England's supposed moral collapse, focused its attack on the perfidies of booksellers and authors dependent on them.[6] Book reviewers, whose ranks Goldsmith joined just a month after publication of *An Estimate,* were depicted in reptilian terms. In wording Goldsmith later emulated in his *An Enquiry into the Present State of Polite Learning in Europe* (1759), Brown assailed London's

> two notorious Gangs of *monthly* and *critical* Book-Thieves, hackney'd in the Ways of Wickedness, who, in the Rage of Hunger and Malice, first *plunder,* and then *abuse, maim,* or *murder,* every honest Author who is possessed of ought worth their *carrying off;* yet by skulking among other Vermin in *Cellars* and *Garets,* keep their Persons tolerably out of Sight, and thus *escape* the Hands of *literary Justice.*[7]

Though Brown's complaints were hyperbolic, even hysterical—a point the book's reviewers duly noted—the book achieved phenomenal popularity.[8] Its six editions in 1757 generated debate in virtually all the London periodicals and prompted a flurry of replies and imitations.[9]

Complaints about the commercialization of authorship were not unique to the Seven Years' War period, though they were certainly more widespread than they had been in previous generations. Steele's *Tatler* Number 3 (16 April 1709) bemoaned London's dearth of wit, attributing it to a change in the status of authorship: "But it is wonderful there should be so few Writers, when the Art is become merely Mechanick, and Men may make themselves Great that Way, by as Certain and Infallible Rules, as you may be a Joyner or a Mason."[10] Steele's observation is remarkably similar to a complaint issued by the *Court Magazine* more than a half-century later:

> In the present age literature is much upon the decline in England, and the vast number of Magazines in which it is retailed, have not hitherto been able to repair the defect. Learning seems to be now become a trade, and amongst the variety of publications daily obtruded upon the town, there are few or none worthy the attention of a man of taste or discernment.[11]

Self-appointed guardians of English learning had warned against the perilous decline of literature and the "mechanization" and degradation of authorship since the beginning of the century. But the popularity of *An Estimate* galvanized the London press to an unprecedented level of self-analysis: the press itself became a principal topic in London books, pamphlets, and periodicals. For "Weekly Historians," as Steele referred to periodical authors, reporting the decline of English letters and attacking the malice and illiteracy of booksellers offered steady and reliable employment.[12] And for disappointed authors, the object of blame shifted in its personification from foppish aristocrats and their sycophants to profit-governed Fagins and their gangs of literary cutpurses.

Isaac Disraeli's study *The Calamities and Quarrels of Authors* (1867) erroneously traces the origin of the phrase "author by profession" to William Guthrie, a bookseller and political writer. In a letter of 3 June 1762, Guthrie wrote: "Your Lordship may possibly now suspect that *I am an Author by Profession:* you are not deceived." In fact, the phrase was certainly current in the late 1750s. Disraeli does, however, correctly identify a common contemporary implication: "literary taskwork, and political degradation."[13] His model of the author by profession is Smollett, whom he characterizes as being bled dry and impoverished by booksellers, who are "but commercial men. A trader can never be deemed a patron, for it would be romantic to purchase what is not saleable; and where no favour is conferred, there is no patronage."[14] Disraeli's study of "poor Smollett" and his fellow victims of a soulless commercial system captures, a half-century later, the tenor of a great deal of journalistic discourse in the late 1750s and 1760s.

Samuel Foote's successful farce *The Author,* first acted at Drury Lane on 5 February 1757, capitalized on the popular disdain for "The Trade." Foote's character "Cape," a young author, complained to his acquaintance, the rejected "Poet": "My Protectors are *Title-page,* the Publisher; *Vamp,* the Bookseller; and *Index,* the Printer. A most notable Triumvirate; and the Rascals are as proscriptive and arbitrary, as the famous *Roman* one, into the Bargain."[15] Even Brown's detractors, such as George Lyttleton, shared his concerns about the power of booksellers and the virtual disappearance of literary patronage. Dialogue XXVIII of Lyttleton's satiric *Dialogues of the Dead* (1760) imagined a newly deceased Bookseller encountering Charon and Plutarch:

> *Charon.* Take him under your care therefore, good Plutarch; you will easily awe
>   him into order and decency by the superiority an Author has over a Bookseller.
> *Bookseller.* Am I got into a world so absolutely the reverse of that I left, that here
>   *Authors* domineer over *Booksellers?* Dear Charon, let me go back, and I will pay
>   any price for my passage.[16]

Lyttleton's Bookseller "defends" the present system of authorship: "Our men of the world should read our New Books, which teach them to have no Virtue at all. No book is fit for a Gentleman's reading which is not void of Facts and of Doctrines, that he may not grow a Pedant in his morals or conversation."[17] Critics of the system argued that the commercialization of authorship gave too much authority to booksellers—tradesmen who placed profit motive above virtue and literary merit. At the time Goldsmith was "enthralled" in his "literary vassalage," as followers of the Washington Irving "poor Goldsmith" school describe his entry into the profession, the system was under constant attack, even by those such as Brown who were handsomely rewarded by it.[18]

Perhaps the most impressive direct challenge to *An Estimate,* and a second important influence on Goldsmith's views of authorship, was James Ralph's *The Case of Authors by Profession or Trade* (1758), printed by Goldsmith's employer, Ralph Griffiths. Robert Kenny calls *The Case of Authors* "the earliest comprehensive defense of the class" of professional writers.[19] Like Brown, Ralph recognized the gradual displacement of the "Voluntier, or Gentleman-Writer" by the "Writer by Profession."[20] But unlike Brown he offered what Philip Stevick calls "a sharply reasoned recognition of the fact that the paternalistic days of the Tory nostalgia are gone forever, that a mass audience and a class of professional writers is here to stay."[21] Enjoying critical acclaim but relative public neglect—the inverse fate of *An Estimate*—Ralph's book argued that "the Writer who serves himself and the Public together, has as good a Right to the Product in Money of his Abilities, as the Landholder to his Rent, or the Money-Jobber to his Interest."[22]

On which side did Goldsmith stand in this controversy? Readers of Goldsmith's prose can hardly avoid his frequent assaults on the press and the notion of professional authorship. His essays satirized booksellers, the periodical press, the reviews and magazines for which he worked, and the deplorable lot of the "labourers in the magazine trade" (I, 353). In some measure, his *Polite Learning* was a response to Brown. While Goldsmith's stated purpose in his introduction was to counter the rhetorical "invective" and "devious declamation" in works such as Brown's with the "calmness of deliberate enquiry" (I, 258), his view of contemporary authorship and the periodical press was in essential agreement with *An Estimate*. Critics have rightly acknowledged Goldsmith's debt to Brown's jeremiad and his orthodox rejection of professional authorship.[23] They have not fully recognized, however, a more subtle and contradictory strain in Goldsmith's attitude toward the profession. By 1760, when he was publishing his Chinese Letters in the *Public Ledger* (later collected as *The Citizen of the World,* May 1762), his attitude had shifted noticeably. Eschewing the posture of gentlemanly disdain he had adopted so frequently, he remarked sympathetically in the voice of his character, the Chinese Philosopher, "For while the nobleman triumphs in unmerited applause, the author by profession steals off with—*Nothing*" (II, 238). Nor have scholars noted the paraphrase of Ralph's argument that Goldsmith used in Letter XCIII (7 January 1761). The following passage suggests that Goldsmith had not only read *The Case of Authors,* but had been strongly influenced by its arguments:[24]

A man here who should write, and honestly confess that he wrote for bread, might as well send his manuscript to fire the baker's oven; not one creature will read him, all must be court bred poets, or pretend at least to be court bred, who can expect to please. . . .

And yet this silly prepossession the more amazes me, when I consider, that almost all the excellent productions in wit that have appeared here, were purely the offspring of necessity; the Drydens, Butlers, Otways, and Farquhars, were all writers for bread. Believe me, my friend, hunger has a most amazing faculty of sharpening the genius; and he who with a full belly can think like a hero, after a course of fasting, shall rise to the sublimity of a demi-god.

But what will most amaze, is, that this very set of men, who are now so much depreciated by fools, are however the very best writers they have among them at present. (II, 376–77)

Here, Goldsmith, himself no stranger to material want, rose to the defense of the profession from which he had launched his literary career. He had himself assumed a courtly mantle in much of his early work and disassociated himself from his colleagues in the press.[25] In *Polite Learning* he remarked: "To rank in the same despicable class with the dissertations, aenigma's, problems, and other periodical compilations with which even idleness is cloyed at present, is by no means my ambition" (I, 259). In Letter XCIII, however, he both identified with and celebrated the professional author. This passage offers insight into Goldsmith's early authorial stance and into his ambivalent and shifting views of the profession through which, to a degree, he sought to define himself as an author and to articulate his own aspirations for fame and fear of obscurity.

Scholars who use the "professional journalist" label to describe periodical writers in the Seven Years' War period acknowledge, implicitly, the growing power of an organized and vital press, struggling for a political voice and social legitimacy. Writing about the popular and financial success of the London dailies, triweeklies, and weeklies of this period, Lance Bertelsen concludes: "Supported by advertising revenues and sales, these newspapers represented not only viable economic concerns, but a material expression of the interaction of the values of politics, commerce, and wit."[26] The political journals, essay periodicals, and monthly reviews contributed, as well, to the growing conception of journalism as a profession. Together they formed what John Brewer calls "a press infrastructure, an interlocking, overlapping complex of publications" which provided careers for a growing number of novice and well-known authors.[27] As narrators of national events, as purveyors of foreign trends, as organs for political and religious debate, the journals of the High Georgian era began to assume "modern" shape; and their writers, many of them well-paid and influential, were indeed professionals.

The Shape of a Career

Several historical and literary events helped to shape Goldsmith's journalistic career, which began in 1757 and was largely completed by June 1762.[28] In May 1756, Britain had formally declared war on France; Admiral John Byng, whose failure to support the British garrison at the Island of

Minorca helped precipitate the Newcastle ministerial crisis, was executed one month before Goldsmith first appeared in the pages of the *Monthly*. On 6 July 1757, "an act for granting to his Majesty several rates and duties" doubled taxes on all periodicals and advertisements. This legislation had the unintended effect of increasing periodical size, without inhibiting the development of new magazines and newspapers.[29] The same year saw the publication of Smollett's *A Compleat History of England*, Edmund Burke's *A Philosophical Enquiry into the Origin of Our Ideas of the Sublime and Beautiful*, John Home's tragedy *Douglas*, and Thomas Gray's *Odes*—all of which Goldsmith reviewed for the *Monthly*. Another work published in 1757, Soame Jenyns' *A Free Inquiry into the Nature and Origin of Evil*, rivaled Brown's book in its influence on the authors of the period.

Against a background of war and ministerial crisis, Jenyns issued a deeply pessimistic assessment of human nature and of government, "the Offspring of Violence and Corruption," the wars of which were "in fact nothing else but robbery and murder."[30] His imprecations against luxury and the amorality of commerce profoundly influenced Goldsmith; and his paradoxical analysis of charity was one that Goldsmith reformulated frequently in *The Citizen of the World*: "All national provisions for the poor must not only be encouragements to idleness, but productive of contests, and oftentimes of cruelty, yet without such many honest but unfortunate people must inevitably perish."[31] Less hysterical and more intellectually measured than Brown's book, *A Free Inquiry* was an articulation of a strong national current: the perception of England's moral decline and of the inefficacy of government.

The end of Goldsmith's periodical career was marked by the dominance of political debate in the press. After George III acceded to the throne in 1760, John Stuart, 3d earl of Bute, gradually replaced the popular wartime minister William Pitt. Attempting to capitalize on the propaganda potential of the press, Bute was opposed in his efforts by John Wilkes, who began his notorious *North Briton* in June 1762 and was arrested for his "most infamous and seditious libel" in April 1763.[32] In literature, Voltaire, whose enormous influence on Goldsmith's career dates from its beginning, had completed *Candide*, and Laurence Sterne had published the first six volumes of *Tristram Shandy* (1760–61), a work Goldsmith described in *The Citizen of the World* as obscene, witless, and contemptuous of its readers (II, 224–25).

Events such as these demonstrably influenced Goldsmith's development as a journalist and author; yet the external circumstances surrounding his career, especially political and journalistic developments, have not been much investigated. What is needed, then, is a contextual analysis sensitive to these changes: an examination of the details of Goldsmith's journalism that conceives of his early writing not only as "the first rude germ"—to use Prior's phrase—of more celebrated work such as *The Vicar of Wakefield* (1766) and *The Deserted Village* (1770), but also as a separate phase in Goldsmith's life as a writer.[33] A number of basic questions about the first phase of Goldsmith's journalistic career have not been satisfactorily answered. On what basis did Ralph Griffiths, editor of the successful, established *Monthly Review,* hire an inexperienced and unknown "vagabond" as his live-in assistant? Did Goldsmith, in his work as a *"Monthly* drudge," develop critical principles consistent with his later authorial practice? What factors help clarify his break with Griffiths and his emergence as a writer for the rival *Critical Review?*

In 1759 Goldsmith emerged suddenly as a leading essayist in London newspapers and magazines. How did a writer, with only one coolly received treatise and a short-lived weekly periodical to his credit, find himself actively employed by several of London's leading periodical publishers? How might his affiliation with John Newbery have affected the ideological content of his journalistic writing? What factors explain his withdrawal from a profession that had sustained him financially and had contributed to his public recognition?

The general outline of Goldsmith's journalistic career can be divided into two major phases: his relatively brief career as a reviewer and his later emergence as a productive essayist and compiler for a variety of periodicals. The first phase began with his apprenticeship with Griffiths, for whom he worked principally as a "foreign correspondent" (April to September, 1757). Quitting his arrangement with the *Monthly,* he resumed this "correspondent" persona on his own and published *Polite Learning* in 1758. Wavering between his aspirations as an author and unrealized hopes for a successful medical career, he returned to reviewing. His second stint was for Griffiths' rival Tobias Smollett of the *Critical Review* (January 1759 to March 1760).

While still working for Smollett, Goldsmith began the second major phase of his career: as magazine compiler, social satirist, and moralist. In these capacities he developed a "chearful" satirical voice, an ideal first enunciated in his *Monthly* review of the *Connoisseur* (I, 14). Toward the end of 1759, Goldsmith was employed by John Newbery, at the time best known for publishing highly successful children's books. Accommodating Newbery's insistence on didacticism and adding his own satirical skill and developing political awareness, Goldsmith produced his finest journalistic writing for two Newbery-sponsored periodicals, the *Public Ledger* and the *British Magazine.* Shortly thereafter, Goldsmith was engaged primarily with longer works: translations, compilations, histories, prefaces, and so on. Retreating from full-time work as a journalist, Goldsmith wrote his "Indigent Philosopher" series for *Lloyd's Evening Post* (1762); these essays signaled what seemed to be a waning enthusiasm for periodical publication and marked the end of his active participation in London journalism.

Fame and Anonymity

Goldsmith's Preface to *Essays by Mr. Goldsmith* (1765), a partly humorous and partly bitter retrospective on his journalistic career, serves as a valuable introduction both to the problems he encountered as a London journalist from 1757 to 1763 and to some of the difficulties scholars have faced in studying his contributions to periodicals. Introducing his first collected edition of essays, Goldsmith commented on the perils of the profession: a paradoxical "success" without adequate remuneration, a public preoccupied with the sensational and the transient, the wholesale plagiarism of his essays, and the inherent limitations and "superficiality" of the form. With mocking and self-deprecating humor, he complained: "The public was too strenuously employed with their own follies, to be assiduous in estimating mine" (III, 1).

The journals featuring his work were "generally unsuccessful" and brought neither adequate income nor fame to a man who, by most accounts, compulsively sought to "shine" before his contemporaries. Yet he observed proudly of his essays, "I can by no means complain of their circulation. . . . Most of these essays have been regularly reprinted twice or thrice a year, and conveyed to the public through the kennel of some engaging compilation" (III, 1). With satiric disparagement, Goldsmith attacked the quality of the popular journals that proliferated during this period. He pointed out the common failure of their editors to acknowledge contributors, together with their tendency to misattribute essays and criticism. The author observed:

> If there be a pride in multiplied editions, I have seen some of my labours sixteen times reprinted, and claimed by different parents as their own. I have seen them flourished at the beginning with praise, and signed at the end with the names of Philautos, Philalethes, Philalutheros, and Philanthropos. These gentlemen have kindly stood sponsors to my productions, and to flatter me more, have always past them as their own. (III, 1)

Because of the anonymity of contributors, attribution remains a problem, despite the work of Seitz, Crane, Friedman, and others to establish the Goldsmith canon.

Finally, some mention must be made of the disruptive and exciting prospects of integrating Basker's newly attributed—or, in some cases, re-attributed—essays into the established Goldsmith corpus. If scholars ultimately accept the additional twenty-nine *British Magazine* pieces as Goldsmith's, they will probably arrive at some of the following conclusions. First, Goldsmith's association with Smollett and John Newbery, founders of the *British Magazine,* was decidedly more extensive than we had imagined. Certainly, Goldsmith was much more productive in 1760 than the relatively meager output of accepted essays had suggested.

Secondly, he had more experience as a fiction writer than scholars have supposed. Several of the tales newly ascribed to him exhibit characteristic roughness, poignancy, and moral concern; others display such a shocking degree of vulgarity as to call into question Goldsmith's authorship of them. The ideological stances these tales take are mostly compatible with those he takes elsewhere: for example, the importance of paternal authority, applied wisely, and of young people's acquiescence to that authority, especially in the choice of a spouse. Other tales, though, such as "The History of Omrah," obviously indebted to *Rasselas* (1759), contain graphic descriptions—for example, of poison dripping from the nipples of an old woman—that in light of his other writings seem obscene. And the portrayal of premarital sex in "Igluka and Sibbersik, a Greenland Tale" seems astonishingly unlike the work of the magazine moralist and author of *The Vicar* Goldsmith's readers know.

Several of the pieces are political essays that even further complicate an attempt to understand Goldsmith's politics. An essay on the approaching coronation of George III restates his distaste for the "luxuriousness" of the ceremonies. Another piece called "The Greatest Man of the Present Age" is unabashed puffery for William Pitt and stands in astonishing contrast to his frequent and thinly disguised attacks on the prime minister. In spite of the obvious problems inclusion of these new pieces presents, the weight of the external evidence Basker supplies demands their consideration. They will probably add little to Goldsmith's literary reputation; for example, the literary and rhetorical criticism in the long *Belles Lettres* series is mostly pedantic and commonplace. But they do reinforce the image of Goldsmith as one of the most active journalists of the period, one whose writings reveal an elusive contradictoriness and an ambiguous sense of "authorial self" in search of fame in a venue that discouraged public recognition.

Justifying his own collected edition, Goldsmith compared himself to a fat man in a shipwreck, threatened by his starving shipmates with cannibalism. Saying his mates were "taking slices from his posteriors," he "insisted with great justice, on having the first cut for himself" (III, 2). To some extent with his book *The Citizen of the World* (1762), and certainly with his poem *The Traveller* (1764), Goldsmith had tasted some of the acclaim he would later enjoy with *The Vicar, The Deserted Village,* and *She Stoops to Conquer* (first performed 15 March 1773 at Covent Garden). Yet, looking back on his career as a journalist, he seemed to feel uneasy about the public's reception of his "dull Essays." Departing from the modest tone of the Preface, the author addresses "Mr. Posterity": "Sir, Nine hundred and ninety-nine years after sight hereof, pay the bearer, on order, a thousand pound's worth of praise, free from all deductions whatsoever, it being a commodity that will then be very serviceable to him, and place it to the accompt of, &c." (III, 3).

While such payment may never be forthcoming, Goldsmith's career as a journalist, considered in its professional, social, and political contexts, promises ample reward to scholars of the High Georgian period. Many have used Goldsmith's work as a reviewer, editor, essayist, literary critic, and social commentator to illuminate his later writing as a novelist, poet, and playwright. This approach too often ignores or misrepresents the changing nature of journalism in the 1750s and 1760s. Periodical work no longer served primarily as a training ground for poets, fiction writers, dramatists, historians, and philosophers—as it may have done for the immediate heirs of Defoe, Addison, and Steele. With increased popular demand for newspapers and magazines, and with the sudden political instability that marked the accession of George III in 1760, journalism as a profession developed a new degree of autonomy, social status, and political importance. Though Goldsmith, like many of his contemporaries, complained about the oppressive nature of periodical writing and editing, and often referred to his contributions as "catch pennies" or "hack work," he nevertheless contributed significantly to a profession pursued by Johnson, Hawkesworth, Smollett, Ralph, Burke, and others who helped shape the literature and politics of this period.

This study will present new evidence clarifying the circumstances of Goldsmith's hiring by Griffiths. It will trace the development of Goldsmith's "foreign correspondent" persona that served him as reviewer, essayist, and "Citizen of the World." It will describe the professional factors—competition and cooperation among journals, the work of fellow journalists, the changing demands of periodical readers—that helped shape his early career. Finally, it will challenge the view of Goldsmith as apolitical and show that, in spite of his protestations to the contrary, his journalistic work was unavoidably political—a product and reflection of a nation at war, adjusting to a new king, ministerial crises, and the potential benefits and hazards of empire.

2

Goldsmith's Hiring and Its Periodical Contexts

> There are, at present, in the world of Authors, Doctors of Physic, who,
> (to use the phrase of one of them) have no great fatigue from the business
> of their profession: many Clergymen, whose sermons are not the most
> inconsiderable part of their compositions: and several Gentlemen of the
> Inns of Court, who, instead of driving the quill over skins of parchment,
> lead it through all the mazes of modern novels, critiques, and pamphlets.
> —Bonnell Thornton and George Colman

Though an angry chorus of London writers joined Brown in railing against
the commercialization of authorship, the dominance of booksellers and their
employees in the publishing process was a *fait accompli* by 1757. The types to
whom Thornton and Colman refer—physicians without patients, barristers
without clients, and Irish "vagabonds" with doubtful futures—found employment as news reporters, book reviewers, and essay writers in London's
booming periodical trade.[1] Any would-be journalist who applied for mem-
bership in an emerging class of patronless and anonymous "authors for hire"
faced two daunting tasks: he had to ingratiate himself with a bookseller or
editor willing to help initiate and sustain his career; and he had to develop
personae designed to appeal to his readership and to establish his credibility
as a reliable social observer, scholar, or critic.

These two requirements shaped Goldsmith's career as a journalist, as he
worked in his various capacities as reviewer, editor, and essayist. Both in his
relationships with booksellers and in his development of journalistic personae, he followed a general pattern of failure, adaptation, and ultimate
success—though certainly never pecuniary success. He was fortunate to find
employment with two of London's most prominent publishers. His apprenticeship with the first, Ralph Griffiths, ended abruptly and disastrously; his
tenure with the second, John Newbery, was much more profitable. Similarly,
his first experience with periodical editing and essay writing in the *Bee* failed
commercially. As Newbery's "Citizen of the World," however, he achieved a
measure of recognition and the opportunity to develop nonjournalistic projects: the poetry, plays, and novel for which he is best known.

The driving forces of his journalistic career were poverty, from which he would never fully escape, and lofty ambitions at which he had hinted well before he arrived in London. As early as 1754, in a letter written from Holland to his uncle Thomas Contarine, he gave a lively description of the Dutch people, such as he later provided in many of his essays, and he complained:

> Nothing surprizes me more than the books every day published, descriptive of the manners of this country. Any young man who takes it into his head to publish his traveles visits the countries he intends to describe passes thro them with as much inattention as his valet de chambre and consequently not having a fund himself to fill a vollume he applies to those who wrote before him.[2]

Thus while ostensibly preparing himself to become a physician, he was already showing signs of a second vocational interest, one that would lead him to the London periodical trade and provide him a "fund" for much of his early writing. Three years later, writing to his brother-in-law Daniel Hodson, he admitted: "Nothing [is] more apt to introduce us to the gates of the muses than Poverty."[3] But his turning to professional authorship may have been motivated by inclination as well as by hunger.

His initiation into journalism was, in part, a matter of good fortune (though he did not consider it so, in retrospect). He was hired as a reviewer by one of the most prominent editors and booksellers in London, Ralph Griffiths, whose other staff members were established professionals. Like many of his peers, Goldsmith expressed contempt for the state of English publishing—for the dominance of the bookseller and the vassalage of journeymen authors. The pseudonymous author "John Triplet," writing to the *British Magazine* on "the distresses of an hired writer," deplored that "fatal revolution whereby writing is converted to a mechanic trade; and booksellers, instead of the great, become the patrons and paymasters of men of genius. . . . Can any thing more cramp and depress true genius, than to write under the direction of one whose learning does not extend beyond the multiplication-table and the London Evening-post?"[4] Much as Goldsmith may have resented such an arrangement and argued for a return to a system of literary patronage, this unknown, unconnected Irishman's first assignment with Griffiths enabled him to establish a literary career.

A Reviewer's Credentials

Fourteen months before writing his first two critical notices for Ralph Griffiths' *Monthly Review* (April 1757), Goldsmith arrived in Dover after a two-year tour of Europe. Boswell suggested that he had financed this "Grand Tour" by selling himself as a paid debater at various European universities;

but more important, he had assembled a stock of firsthand observations about the French, Dutch, and Swiss upon which he would draw heavily in his authorial career. Having *"disputed* his passage through Europe," as Boswell related, he came to London in 1756 to establish a medical practice.[5] Unable to support himself as a physician, he took a position as temporary headmaster at the Reverend John Milner's Presbyterian school for boys at Peckham, in Surrey. Perhaps reflecting ironically on his experiences there, he observed in the *Bee* (November 1759): "Is any man unfit for any of the professions? he finds his last resource in setting up a school" (I, 456). And his Chinese Philosopher in *The Citizen of the World* provides a sample of an English newspaper advertisement: "England. Wanted an usher to an academy. *N.B.* He must be able to read, dress hair, and must have had the small pox" (II, 35). Either to promote the career of his temporary headmaster or, perhaps, to remove him gently from a position for which he was unfit, Milner arranged an interview for him with Griffiths toward the end of 1756 or early in 1757. The publisher was sufficiently impressed to offer Goldsmith a one-year agreement to review for the *Monthly*. For his efforts he would receive room and board as well as "some pecuniary stipend."[6]

If those arguing for 1730 as Goldsmith's birthdate are correct, he and Johnson were the same age, twenty-seven, when they began their authorial careers. Both writers received their first employment from a leading London periodical editor whose journal was engaged in a rivalry with another journal for readership. Johnson first approached Edward Cave, publisher of the *Gentleman's Magazine,* in 1737, when the journal was engaged in a "magazine war" with the *London Magazine*.[7] Twenty years later Goldsmith was hired by Griffiths, whose *Monthly Review* was being challenged by its rival, the *Critical Review*. The writers' initial approaches to their first appointments, however, were vastly different: Johnson pursued his prospective employer aggressively—tactlessly, Thomas Kaminski suggests.[8] By contrast, Goldsmith's hiring was serendipitous; by all accounts, he stumbled upon his first journalistic position.

Why would Griffiths have hired a man with an inauspicious background as a "vagabond," failed physician, and temporary schoolmaster? Brown's depiction of critics as garret-dwelling vermin notwithstanding, most reviewers were, in fact, experienced and reasonably accomplished authors. Having little documentary evidence, critics have resorted to speculation.[9] Several contextual factors, however, help clarify the issue and make this event seem somewhat less extraordinary than it seemed in the past. One contributing factor must have been Milner's strong recommendation. More than a year after the editor and his reviewer terminated their agreement, Griffiths threatened Goldsmith with prison for failing to repay a loan. Though Griffiths' accusatory letter is no longer extant, Goldsmith's reply suggests that the editor had blamed Milner for misrepresenting Goldsmith's character:

"You seem to think Doctor Milner knew me not. Perhaps so; but he was a man I shall ever honour."[10]

At the initial meeting at Peckham, Goldsmith probably convinced his future employer that his political views would be compatible with those of the Whig journal. Nangle points out that most of Griffiths' staff members had been either personal friends when they were hired or were recruited through acquaintances, so that he could be assured of their political "reliability." With few exceptions, his reviewers shared—or at least adopted in their reviews—Griffiths' Whig and Dissenting viewpoints.[11] And in his few reviews Goldsmith wrote that were at least marginally political, he closely echoed established editorial opinion—a fact commentators on "Tory Goldsmith" have overlooked.

The timing of Goldsmith's hiring is another relevant consideration. He spent all of his first stint with the *Monthly* during the journalistic "off season," when Parliament was not in session and the amount of published ephemera declined. John Brewer remarks on this pattern as it continued into the 1760s: "December to March was the most popular time of year for reviewing (and, by inference) for publication, while precious few pamphlets at all were discussed between July and October."[12] A new *Monthly* employee hired to begin in April would presumably enjoy seven relatively "slow" months during which he could adjust. Goldsmith later remarked on this tendency in one of his many satires on bookselling for the *Public Ledger:* "Nothing in [a bookseller's] way goes off in summer, except very light goods indeed. A review, a magazine, or a sessions paper, may amuse a summer reader; but all our stock of value we reserve for a spring and winter trade" (II, 214).

A different approach to this problem might be to compare Goldsmith's credentials with those of one of his contemporaries on the *Monthly.* Goldsmith's background is remarkably similar to that of James Grainger, whom Griffiths hired in May 1756. Like Goldsmith, Grainger had attended medical classes at Edinburgh University; he was well-versed in Latin; he had made his tour of Europe (1748) and returned to England, where his medical practice failed to attract patients; and like Goldsmith, he turned to periodical writing to survive *(DNB).* Like other *Monthly* staff members, both Grainger and Goldsmith shared the profile of the professional reviewer: diversity of interest, facility with foreign languages, knowledge of European culture, and financial desperation.

A more complete explanation for Goldsmith's hiring, however, must include a detailed account of the contentious journalistic environment Goldsmith entered in 1757. He portrayed the publishing industry somewhat misleadingly in *Polite Learning* and *Citizen of the World* as dominated by "Two Reviews," the *Monthly* and the *Critical,* both of which hired reckless and unqualified hacks as exclusive arbiters of public taste. That he himself served as "hack" for both journals and styled himself a "true critic" exemplifies the essential contradictoriness of the author as participant in, and critic of, the periodical press. Still, as a reviewer, his career was shaped, at least in part, by the competition between the journals and by the contrasting management practices of their editors.

Editors and their Staffs

In an *Idler* column for *Payne's Universal Chronicle,* Samuel Johnson argued that "the compilation of News-papers is often committed to narrow and mercenary minds, not qualified for the task of delighting and instructing; who are content to fill their paper, with whatever matter, without industry to gather, or discernment to select" (27 May 1758). [13] Such was the stereotypical view of reviewers, as well. In the anonymous satire *The Battle of the Reviews* (1760), the cast of *Monthly* dunces includes "Jack o' the Lanthorn," a long-winded and egotistical parson; "Sir Imp Brazen," a fawning and deceitful political writer begging for ministerial patronage; "Tanaquil Limmonad," a German alchemist and failed poet; "Martin Problem," a mathematician trying to invent the sort of nonsensical military machinery of which Sterne's "Uncle Toby" would have approved; and "Teady Mac Laughlin," a virtually illiterate Irishman with pretensions of being a great scholar. If the satire's portrayal of the diversity of reviewers' backgrounds is just, its depiction of them as unaccomplished hacks is not.

Active contributors to the *Monthly* at the time Goldsmith joined as Griffiths' assistant included a variety of experienced and accomplished scholars: the well-known dissenting theologians William Rose, John Ward, Benjamin Dawson, and Andrew Kippis; the philologist and defender of the established church, Gregory Sharpe; the physicians James Grainger, James Kirkpatrick, and William Bewley; the dramatist, satirist, and political writer, James Ralph; the historians John Campbell and Sir Tanfield Leman; and the actor Theophilus Cibber. Despite the similarity of his background to Grainger's, Goldsmith in 1757 was less accomplished and experienced than his colleagues on the *Monthly.* The need for more copy and for greater coverage of foreign news apparently led Griffiths to take on this relative novice—a decision he later claimed to regret.

James Prior's list of Goldsmith's contemporaries on the *Monthly,* derived from Griffiths' marked copies, has misled scholars in a number of respects. For one thing, it has led them to assume that several contributors who worked for the journal before and after Goldsmith's tenure were actually his colleagues. [14] The poet John Langhorne did not begin working for Griffiths until November 1761; John Cleland contributed only sporadically, all but seven of his reviews appearing before 1751; and the historian Owen

Ruffhead, who had been editing the political journal *Con-Test* at the time of Goldsmith's arrival, appeared on the staff in September 1757 and was not working for the *Monthly* during most of Goldsmith's tenure.[15] While these names added to Prior's argument for the "weight and talent" of Goldsmith's "coadjutors," they should not properly be seen as influential colleagues in 1757.

Secondly, Prior's assignment of a field of specialization to each contributor is also somewhat misleading. Nangle, whose index of contributors to the *Monthly* is our most important source of information on the subject, categorizes a reviewer's work as "dealing with works in his own particular field."[16] Though each reviewer may have been hired for his area of specialization, most were expected to take on a wide variety of subjects. A brief survey of the reviews of Griffiths' busiest employees in April, May, and June 1757 demonstrates the diversity of their assignments; the value of physician-writers such as Grainger, Kirkpatrick, and Goldsmith; and the prominence of religious issues in the *Monthly*.

In addition to his reviews of poetry by Newcomb and Dyer and a review in June of a collection called *Oriental Eclogues*, Grainger was responsible for *Medical Observations and Enquiries*. Kirkpatrick reviews *A Dissertation on the Malignant Ulcerous Sore-throat* in April, *The Great Shepherd: A Sacred Pastoral* in May, and the Marquis of Torcy's *Memoirs* in June. Writing most of the April Monthly Catalogue entries, James Ralph (of *Dunciad* notoriety) commented on a variety of social concerns reflected in the pamphlets he reviewed. Most of the pamphlets were brief, sixpenny octavos; they included six different treatises on the Admiral Byng controversy (like Goldsmith, Ralph noted that he was tired of the ongoing debate), a pamphlet entitled *The Present Dearness of Corn*, and another called *Further Objections to the Establishment of a Constitutional Militia*. Clearly, the nature of the *Monthly* placed a premium on diverse experience and multiple areas of expertise—qualities Goldsmith must have demonstrated in his initial meeting with Griffiths.

In spite of notices such as Ralph's in the April Catalogue and Goldsmith's of the fiction and poetry to which he had been assigned, the full-length reviews during Goldsmith's tenure at the *Monthly* were primarily of serious, scholarly subjects; assignment of a book to the Catalogue, for the most part, implicitly derogated its seriousness or value. In his book *British Literary Magazines*, Alvin Sullivan provides a summary interpretation of the *Monthly's* purpose: "Griffiths aimed at variety and comprehensiveness for his review; and although there was the occasional review of a highly technical book that might appeal to the intelligent interested layman, the greatest attention was given to those books which he believed would appeal to the largest reading public."[17] In the absence of reliable sales records, such a conclusion is largely intuitive. For the period of Goldsmith's employment, it would imply that such matters as Celtic history, classical translation, American colonial policy, and contemporary prosody appealed more to the popular imagination than the popular broadsides and sentimental ballads given short shrift in the Catalogues.

An anonymous letter "To the Authors of the *Monthly Review*" in May 1757 suggests another persistent misconception about the journal during Goldsmith's tenure: "The plan of your Review has its use, and the execution of it seems, in the main, to have given general satisfaction. Might it not, however, be extended a little, so as to admit, besides a mere abstract of books, something in a more critical way, especially on subjects of controversy?"[18] The writer's implication is that the journal had not advanced from its 1749 position of publishing only abstracts of new books. Walter Graham cites another such letter, published 9 May 1783, advising the editor "that the public demanded something more from the *Monthly Review* than mere abstracts." Graham suggests that the *Monthly,* to some extent as a response to this letter, "rapidly improved its articles."[19] While these readers could justifiably complain about the extended use of quotations from works, as scholars have also complained about the reviewers' lack of originality, in fact the extent and sophistication of critical comment had grown since 1749.

By 1757, reviewers such as Rose, Grainger, Kirkpatrick, and Goldsmith were applying their own critical principles to the works they reviewed. Although they often relied on critical commonplaces, and did indeed extract long passages from some of the works, they frequently did "something in a more critical way." Goldsmith's careful response to Burke is an example, as is his statement of dramatic theory in the review of *Douglas*. Another vivid example is Grainger's populist formula for prosodies in his review of *The Fleece*. He praises what he calls "Didactyc Poetry" with its "glowing and picturesque epithets, daring and forcible metaphors, pomp of numbers, dignity of expression":

> For the lower, or more familiar the object described is, the greater must be the power of language to preserve it from debasement. . . . The subject, in order to interest the Reader, should be of an universal, and especially of a national, nature; that such precepts ought only to be delivered, and such objects painted, as they can be represented to the imagination in agreeable colours.[20]

Grainger calls for a patriotic poetry which appeals to the common reader, a poetry treating the care of sheep and the labor of the loom. If his notion of poetry is unsophisticated, it is at least reflective of a popular mid-century movement—and is certainly more than a simple abstract of John Dyer's poetry.

Graham minimizes Goldsmith's role in the development of the *Monthly:* "He [Goldsmith] was an obscure hack writer, like most of his fellow-reviewers. His literary energy was turned into other channels after 1758, and the prestige of the later *Monthly Review* owes little or nothing to him."[21] Still, despite the brevity of his employment with Griffiths, Goldsmith worked competently, and was the most prolific contributor to the journal from May through July. If, as Graham claims, reviews of Home's *Douglas,* Gray's *Odes,* and Burke's *Enquiry* helped establish the reputation of Smollett's journal,[22] Goldsmith's reviews of those same seminal works for the *Monthly* made him a central figure in the early history of Griffiths' journal and in the rivalry between the two reviews.

Direct comparison of the staffs and management practices of the two reviews is complicated by a paucity of information concerning the operation of the *Critical* and by the difference between Griffiths' notion of running a journal and Smollett's. In fact, the notion of a *Critical* "staff" is somewhat misleading. The reviewer of Grainger's letter to Smollett claimed that, unlike the *Monthly,* the *Critical* was unattached to any bookseller, and its reviewers were independent contributors, uncensored by an editor.[23] Some evidence suggests that this characterization is at least partly accurate: the management practices of the two reviews were as different as their formats were similar.

Because of his conflicts with Goldsmith and subsequent vilification by nineteenth-century biographers, more has been written about Griffiths as an editor than about Smollett. The best-documented account of Griffiths is Nangle's study in his *Monthly Review Index.*[24] According to Nangle, the *Monthly* was centrally controlled, without delegation of editorial responsibility. Griffiths himself hired staff members, made review assignments, read all copy, checked proofs, and took final responsibility for the contents of the journal. He strove for impartiality, accepting neither unsolicited contributions nor prearranged "puffs"—Goldsmith's review of Brookes' *Natural History* being a notable exception—and he forbade staff members to review their own publications. Whether, as Nangle claims, he "ensured complete anonymity" for his staff members is highly doubtful, but he clearly attempted to prevent disclosure.[25]

Smollett's career as editor has been little studied, but much about it can be inferred, especially from his correspondence. While Griffiths' name was printed on each volume of the *Monthly,* Smollett never publicly disclosed his editorship of the *Critical.* He did admit it, however, in a letter to John Moore of 3 August 1756, in which he wrote that the journal "is conducted by four Gentlemen of approved abilities."[26] While historians had been aware of independent contributions from writers such as Samuel Johnson, David Hume, and the Scottish historian William Robertson, the discovery of marked copies for the first two volumes, first reported in 1957, reveals that Smollett and four of his colleagues were responsible for the bulk of the reviews in 1756. The four colleagues were Thomas Francklin, Samuel Derrick, John Armstrong, and Patrick Murdoch.[27] Armstrong, a poet and physician known for his long, didactic poem *The Art of Preserving Health* (1744), shared responsibility with Smollett for medical and scientific works.[28] Samuel Derrick, who figures prominently in *Life of Johnson* as Boswell's "first tutor in the ways of London," reviewed a variety of minor works for the *Critical* before becoming—as Boswell writes—"King of Bath."[29] Derek Roper suggests that Derrick was the "little Irishman" to whom Smollett referred as his "Amanuensis" and "Trash reader."[30] The fourth "gentleman," Patrick Murdoch, was like Armstrong a friend of the poet James Thomson, and an infrequent contributor during the first months of the *Critical*.

Unlike Griffiths, Smollett was not always responsible for assignments and often failed to read copy before it reached print—a practice for which he was forced to apologize on a number of occasions. In a letter of 10 August 1756, written after a reviewer had ridiculed Richardson's verbosity in the April 1756 issue, Smollett says: "I was extremely concerned to find myself suspected of a silly, mean Insinuation against Mr. Richardson's Writings, which appeared some time ago in the Critical Review, and I desired my friend Mr. Millar to assure you in my name that it was inserted without my privity or Concurrence."[31] Not only did Smollett fail to approve in advance the contents of the *Critical,* but he apparently played a progressively diminishing role in the periodical throughout 1757. A friend of John Home and supporter of *Douglas,* Smollett was clearly distressed by attacks on the tragedy in the *Critical.* He wrote to John Moore on 4 June 1757: "You are right in your Conjecture with regard to the Criticism upon 'Douglas', which I assure you I did not see until it was in print. I did not write one article in that whole Number."[32] Nor, apparently, did he approve the negative review of William Wilkie's *The Epigoniad:* "As yet I have not raised one Line of the Epigoniad. I am told the work has merit, and am truly sorry that it should have been so roughly handled."[33] Apparently not the attentive editor Griffiths was, Smollett channeled his talents into a variety of projects. He observed to William Huggins: "I am so involved ~~with~~ in [*sic*] the History of England, and different Provinces of the Universal History that I shall not for some years be able to engage in any other work."[34]

One observation in Nangle's account of Griffiths' management of the *Monthly* needs to be corrected: "Above all, he devoted his entire time to this one enterprise, dropping his other activities as publisher and bookseller as soon as the early success of the *Review* enabled him to do so."[35] Evidence abounds in newspaper advertisements and the "This Day Is Published" columns that Griffiths continued work as a bookseller. And in January 1758 he helped launch *The Grand Magazine of Universal Intelligence, and Monthly Chronicle of Our Own Times,* a sort of eighteenth-century *National Geographic.* Still, Griffiths was certainly a more active manager than Smollett, who spent several years developing and innovating, and then gradually withdrew.

Goldsmith probably appreciated his position of relative autonomy at the *Critical,* as opposed to the tightly controlled operation of the *Monthly.* No known falling-out between Goldsmith and Smollett occurred, and the two continued as periodical colleagues through 1760.

Setting aside his ideological biases, Samuel Johnson acknowledged that the *Monthly* was "done with most care."[36] Even though he sided politically with Smollett's journal, Johnson's comments on the two reviews, as recorded by Boswell, were fairly balanced. Observing that both reviews were written impartially ("I think them very impartial: I do not know an instance of partiality"), he praised the *Critical* for its support of "the constitution, both in church and state," but doubted that its reviewers finished reading the books they were reviewing. "The Monthly Reviewers are duller men, and are glad to read the books through."[37] Though he himself was an important reviewer in the late 1750s, Johnson in his public writings disassociated himself from the profession—much as Goldsmith did vehemently in *Polite Learning* and *The Citizen.*

One of the "dull men" to whom Johnson referred was William Kenrick, who replaced Goldsmith on the *Monthly* staff and who made him one of the victims of the "Battle of the Reviews." Prior vilifies Kenrick for his "libelous" attack on Goldsmith's *Polite Learning* and the "desperate malignity" of his character.[38] Aubrey Hawkins calls him "Goldsmith's able but ferocious successor."[39] However unfair Kenrick's review of *Polite Learning* may have been, it pointed out the hypocrisy of Goldsmith's adopting a gentlemanly stance to attack the reviewing profession, when the author of *Polite Learning* was himself supported by the book trade:

> We cannot help thinking, that in more places than one he has betrayed, in himself, the man he so severely condemns for drawing his quill to take a purse. We are even so firmly convinced of this, that we dare put the question home to his conscience, whether he never experienced the unhappy situation he so feelingly describes, in that of a Literary Understrapper? His remarking him as coming down from his garret, to rummage the Bookseller's shop, for materials to work upon, and the knowledge he displays of his minutest labours, give great reason to suspect he may himself have had concerns in the *bad trade* of bookselling.

Kenrick almost certainly had more evidence than that supplied by the text of *Polite Learning* to demonstrate that Goldsmith worked as a "Literary Under-strapper." In this case, Griffiths had sufficient motivation to break his rule of preserving reviewers' anonymity. But this review served a more important function. As his fellow *Monthly* writer Ralph had done in *The Case of Authors,* Kenrick defended the reviewer's legitimacy: "But, supposing the decay of Science and Polite Learning to be as certain as our Author would insinuate . . . to what is it owing? Why, according to this Writer, it is chiefly owing to

Critics, Commentators, and Literary Journalists! Those very measures which
have been taken to correct and refine the productions of genius, have, it
seems, contributed only to its decay."[40] For better or worse, London's review
journals and reviewers had a profound impact on book publication, readership, and the periodical press, and they played an important part in the
period's reexamination of authorship and journalism.

Diversity and Specialization

Griffiths' advertisement for his first issue (May 1749) promises "to give a
compendious account of those productions of the press, as they come out,
that are worth notice," a goal that put his reviewers' diversity to the test.[41]
Most members of the *Monthly* staff, regardless of special area of expertise,
reviewed books on a variety of topics, and their contributions defy precise
categorization. Typically, Goldsmith's assignments ranged from a pamphlet
urging true Christians to abstain from theatergoing (I, 18) to an anthology
entitled *The History and Philosophy of Earthquakes* (I, 60). Griffiths' journal
did, indeed, provide a fair sampling of the diverse productions of the London
press, and probably proved "serviceable to such as would choose to have some
idea of a book before they lay out their money or time on it."[42] Goldsmith's
approaches to his assignments were almost as varied as the materials themselves. They range from a sharp, one-sentence dismissal of a novel included in
the Monthly Catalogue (I, 16), to a seven-page extract from a translation to
which he added only a three-sentence preface and a one-line conclusion (I,
40–44), to a thorough summary and critical response to a philosophical text
(I, 27–35). Some of his reviews justify William Black's complaint: "They are
somewhat laboured performances. They are almost devoid of the sly and
delicate humour that afterwards marked Goldsmith's best prose work."[43]
Others, such as his delightfully ironic response to a diatribe against theatergoing, could have merited inclusion in Hopkins' study of Goldsmith's
satiric techniques.[44] The humor he displayed, both genial and savage,
certainly provides an important exception to Quintana's claim that the
Monthly was "staid in tone."[45]

The dual and apparently contradictory requirements of diversity and
specialization actually served Goldsmith well. He could develop a principal
journalistic identity—that of "foreign correspondent"—while at the same
time exposing himself to the variety of successful genres offered by London
booksellers. He could try on the masks of philosopher, poet, historian, and
"true critic"—roles to which he would return throughout his journalistic
career and in his later writings.

Though he may, indeed, have been well-suited for his new position,
Goldsmith apparently despised his work for Griffiths. He seldom made

written reference to his reviewing career, but he did include a bitter summary in his autobiographical testimony to Bishop Percy. Percy records:

> In this Thraldom ["Thraldom" is excised and "situation" substituted] he lived 7 or 8 Months Griffith[s] and his wife continually objecting to everything he wrote & insisting on his implicitly submitting to their corrections [. . .] & since Dr. Goldsmith lived with Griffith[s] & his wife during this intercourse the Dr. and he thought it incumbt. to drudge for his Pay constantly from 9 o'clock till 2.[46]

In spite of his often-repeated misgivings about writing for pay and his apologies for the "catchpenny" nature of his work, Goldsmith began a productive journalistic career with a highly successful editor and a well-established, influential periodical. A survey of the types of tasks he performed as a reviewer suggests that his damning account of working for the *Monthly* may have been hyperbolic.

3

The "True Critic"

Each gentle reader loves the gentle Muse,
That little dares and little means;
Who humbly sips her learning from *Reviews*,
Or flutters in the *Magazines*.
—David Garrick, "To Mr. Gray upon His Odes"

Quartered above Griffiths' shop at the Sign of the Dunciad in Paternoster Row, Goldsmith began his journalistic career with an entry in the Monthly Catalogue for April 1757; he dismissed with satirical scorn an anonymous fable, *The Royal Politicians; or, The Fox Triumphant* (I, 5). The Catalogue, a regular feature of the *Monthly,* supplemented longer critical reviews in keeping with Griffiths' intention to provide his readers with a complete and concise account of new publications. Generally, works deemed inferior were relegated to the Catalogue; entries typically were little more than one-sentence summaries, but they occasionally provided reviewers a chance to display their epigrammatic wit.

John Ginger describes Catalogue writing as "a chore imposed on unsuspecting newcomers."[1] This characterization is partly true. In his second month with the review, Goldsmith was responsible for twenty-three entries, slightly more than one-third the total of seventy-one. After this "initiation" he produced progressively fewer entries until the August issue, when he was apparently excused from this duty. In the months before Goldsmith joined the staff, the dramatist and political writer James Ralph (hired September 1756) and James Grainger (hired May 1756) had handled the bulk of the Catalogue work. When Goldsmith left the staff after the September issue, the barrister Owen Ruffhead, newly appointed to the staff, became a principal contributor. The Catalogue, though, was primarily a team effort. William Rose, a mainstay on the staff since its inception in 1749, contributed steadily, as did James Kirkpatrick (hired July 1751) and Griffiths himself.

The *Monthly* reserved its main articles for "serious" endeavors such as sermons, dissertations, histories, poetry, scientific treatises, and—occasionally—published plays. Because the judgments of Griffiths and his contemporaries were not, of course, always those of posterity, the Catalogue furnishes scholars with their only glimpse at critical response to a variety of genres. Political treatises, for example, were typically considered of transient interest, so that the well-observed political differences between the "Whig" *Monthly* and the "Tory" *Critical* are almost invisible in the full-length features; they appear primarily in epigrammatic Catalogue entries. Also, works of fiction were almost never accorded full-length reviews. Even a novelist as prolific and well-known as Smollett received no full-length treatments of his fiction. The Catalogue provided a disappointingly meager but nonetheless revealing reaction to the novels or "romances" of the period.

The *Monthly* "Drudge" and His Attack on the Romance

If Goldsmith considered Catalogue writing relentless drudgery, he used the assignment purposefully. The highlight of his Catalogue work was a persistent attack—sometimes playful, sometimes malevolent—on female authors and "romantic" novels and plays. Scholars have underscored the several major works he reviewed during his tenure with Griffiths; but his assault on the romance, carried out in stern, ironic, and condescending notices in the Catalogue, was as significant a feature of Goldsmith's early development as his responses to Edmund Burke, Thomas Gray, John Home, and others. Of the twelve works Goldsmith reviewed that could be described as romances, he treated eleven with scorn.[2]

Attacking the "romance" had been a well-established pattern among both periodical writers and novelists throughout the decade. In his interpolated satire on journalism in *Amelia* (1751), Henry Fielding's "periodical author" comments:

> In truth, the romance writing is the only branch of our business now, that is worth following. Goods of that sort have had so much success lately in the market, that a bookseller scarce cares what he bids for them. And it is certainly the easiest work in the world; you may write it almost as fast as you can set pen to paper; and if you interlard it with a little scandal, a little abuse on some living characters of note, you cannot fail of success.[3]

Johnson's *Dictionary* does not recognize *romance* and *novel* as nearly synonymous, as typical mid-century usage did. A *romance* is a "military fable of the middle ages" or "a lie; a fiction." A *novel* is "a small tale, generally of love," exemplified by the phrases "trifling *novels*" and "coxcomb's *novel*." Johnson did elaborate on the modern sense of the word *romance,* as it was used to describe popular novels, in *Rambler* Number 4: "The works of fiction, with which the present generation seems more particularly delighted, are such as exhibit life in its true state, diversified only by accidents that daily happen in the world, and influenced by passions and qualities which are really to be found in conversing with mankind." While he preferred this type, in theory, to the romance of "imaginary castles" and "personages in desarts," he warned that many recent examples are "great corrupters" of youth, a dangerous influence on their primary readers: "the young, the ignorant, and the idle."[4]

Ioan Williams describes the "conservative reaction to the novel" among reviewers and essayists in the 1750s. He notes that the successes of Richardson and Fielding and the growing number of booksellers and readers encouraged an unprecedented boom in fiction writing. The phenomenal quantity and disparate quality of the novels churned out by London presses in the 1750s provoked in journalists, as Williams observes, fears of "the perversion of the female imagination and the disintegration of middle-class standards of behaviour."[5] In his role as apprentice to Griffiths and hence partly responsible for the Monthly Catalogue entries, Goldsmith became a minor part of the "reaction" against the fictional romance. Robert Mayo observes: "A favorite device [of reviewers] was to seize upon some signal ineptitude or silly affectation of the novelist and blast him with his own petard."[6] Goldsmith mastered this device and used it for both comic and serious purposes.

Griffiths' editorial policy since the founding of the review in 1749 was to suggest a diminution of the "novel" as a literary form rather than to exhibit an obvious hostility toward it. His own review of a *The Memoirs of Fanny Hill* (1750), an expurgated version of Cleland's novel, was mildly favorable; it also exemplified a typical ambiguity in defining the genre: "This is a work of the Novel kind, thrown into the form of letters."[7] He argued against any inherent immorality in the genre, and showed surprise and amusement in noting a newspaper report of the suppression of *Tom Jones* in France.[8]

A majority of the works of fiction published in 1757 were ostensibly memoirs or scandalous histories, edited anonymously and attributed to "persons of quality."[9] One particularly prominent dispenser of these works was the bookseller Francis Noble, at his "Circulating-Library" in Covent Garden. Many of these works explicitly declared war on the values Goldsmith upheld in his letters and essays. *The Bubbled Knights* promised in its subtitle to demonstrate "the Folly and Unreasonableness of Parents laying a Restraint upon the Childrens Inclinations, in the Affairs of Love and Marriage."[10] *The History of Miss Katty N—* offered a "faithful and particular Relation of her Amours, Adventures, and various Turns of Fortune."[11] The affairs of a "notorious libertine" were recounted in *Memoirs of B— Tracey*,[12] and those of "several Persons of the highest Quality" in *The Prostitutes of Quality; or, Adultery À-La-Mode*.[13]

Like many of his predecessors, Goldsmith, as self-described "director of taste" in his function as reviewer, urged his readers to avoid this dangerous and inferior genre (I, 10). A letter to his brother Henry (13 January 1759) confirms that this early opinion was genuine, and not merely a reflection of editorial policy. Regarding the education of this nephew, Goldsmith warned: "Above all things let him never touch a romance, or novel, those paint beauty in colours more charming than nature, and describe happiness that man never tastes."[14] For Goldsmith the romance, at least as it was being executed, was morally dangerous and aesthetically appalling.

In skewering novels and novelists, Goldsmith was at his satiric best, demonstrating a flair for ironic attack. In a review of a "happily-ever-after" memoir entitled *True Merit, True Happiness,* Goldsmith wrote: "Reader, if thou hast ever known such perfect happiness, as these romance-writers can so liberally dispense, thou hast enjoyed greater pleasure than has ever fallen to our lot" (I, 17).[15] In later reviews, in *The Citizen of the World,* and in his letters, he reiterated a complaint first expressed in his reviews: "The young and the ignorant lose their taste of present enjoyment, by opposing to it those delusive daubings of consummate bliss they meet with in novels; and, by expecting more happiness than life can give, feel but the more poignancy in all its disappointments" (I, 17).[16]

Robert Hopkins has noted Goldsmith's penchant for adopting the diction and tone of his subject while boring at it from within.[17] Goldsmith's review of *The History of Two Persons of Quality* is an early instance of the technique:[18]

> The hero, like most other heroes of romance, is wholy employed in making love; the heroine, in returning his addresses with equal ardour; the hero kills his man; the heroine, too, in her way, dispatches every swain that meets her eyes: the hero has a certain nobleness in his manner; the heroine, a peculiar delicacy in her's:— what pity so much excellence has not found a better historian! (I, 16)

Goldsmith used short, parallel structures to mimic the genre's predictability and exploded his recital of the work's clichés with a stinging punchline. He learned quickly to use the minimal space allotted him in the Catalogues for derisive one-liners; in his review of *Memoirs of Sir Thomas Hughson* he reprinted the "fair promises" of its long, bombastic title page and noted: "Like a Smithfield conjuror, who, to draw company, exhibits at the door his best shew for nothing, this Author exhausts all his scanty funds on the title-page" (I, 17).[19] The review also substantiates the claim that Goldsmith was not prohibited from criticizing works sold by his employer: Griffiths was one of many London booksellers advertising and selling the work, and Goldsmith's curt dismissal disproves the popular claim that reviewers were forced to "puff" all works published or sold by their editors.

Those who consider *The Vicar of Wakefield* (1766) a satiric parody of the romance would find support in Goldsmith's contemptuous attitude toward the genre in his reviews. They should take note, however, of Goldsmith's caution about the use of satire, expressed in his review of *A New Battledore for Miss in Her Teens:* "His satyr is too injudiciously applied to be useful; as the tender age and sex, to whom his piece is addressed, requires rather to be instructed, than ridiculed into a becoming conduct" (I, 19). This anonymous address "For the Use of Boarding Schools" is an odd mix of broad satire, crude admonition, and an appeal to young women to consider primarily their own pecuniary interests in courtship. It warns: "A Girl of Fifteen is not old enough to suppose it probable for a Wretch to go about to sacrifice her Innocence and Happiness to Frolic."[20] Men are comprised entirely of "Vanity, Falshood, and Impudence" and must be "avoided at all Times and in all Places as much as possible."[21] What may have rankled Goldsmith, here, is a mercenary approach and a faltering tone in the treatment of parental authority over matters of courtship, a subject he considered of dire consequence. *A Battledore* warns with apparent mock seriousness:

> With respect to clandestine Courtships, as prudent as certain Misses may fancy themselves in cheating their *Fathers* and *Mothers* by providing Husbands for themselves without their Knowledge or Consent, they cannot in my opinion give a stronger Proof of their want of Common Sense. For it is very evident from a Multitude of Instances, how liable they are to make wrong Computations with regard to the exact Quantity of thousands, which Husbands of their own *seeking* may bring along with them.[22]

At this stage in his career, Goldsmith found satire an improper method of instructing the young; like Johnson (who, as Robert DeMaria argues, "saw his position as a writer in society as an educational position"), Goldsmith had a concern for young people which was pervasive throughout his writings.[23] Like satire, the novel was usually unsuitable for such instruction; but his objection was based, primarily, on its improper execution, not necessarily on the genre itself. While he called the form a "leaky vehicle," he also suggested that it could be developed usefully by a "philosopher of the first rank" (II, 341). Perhaps Goldsmith later saw himself as such a philosopher, able to lend the form the combination of humor and didacticism he felt it required.

Female authors bore the brunt of Goldsmith's attack. He advised Charlotte Bellmour, author of *The Fair Citizen,* that since she was "now happily married," she should realize "that one good Pudding is worth fifty modern Romances" (I, 82).[24] He decided that "Miss Cassandra," author of *An Address to Old Batchelors,* must have been "*debauched* by Appollo" (I, 56).[25] He was likewise indelicate in his disdain for the author of *Cambridge: A Poem:* "Gentlemen or Ladies, we grant, may *write* for their own amusement; but we could wish they would think before they *published,* for ours. [As for] our Poetess, indeed, (for this is a Lady's performance) . . . *we* cannot pay her *our* compliments, on the present occasion" (I, 21). He is more slyly ironic, but no less disdainful, of the poetic performance of Elizabeth Highmore, a boarding school governess (I, 21–22).

In a July Monthly Catalogue entry Goldsmith wrote a contemptuous review of *Memoires for the History of Madame de Maintenon, and of the Last Age* (I, 80–82), one of the more prominent "scandalous memoirs" in vogue at the time.[26] The writer/translator of this work, identified only as "the Author of *The Female Quixote*," was Charlotte Lennox, a longtime friend and protégée of Johnson's and one of the more successful female authors of the period. Johnson had assisted her with her second novel, *The Female Quixote* (1752); he had written a dedication for *Madame de Maintenon;* and he may later have contributed to her journal, the *Lady's Museum.*[27] Goldsmith's satiric complaints about the excessive length of the book anticipated those he made later in his Epilogue to Lennox's comedy *The Sister,* which failed after one night (Covent Garden, 18 February 1769). In the "Epilogue" Goldsmith writes: *"What! five long acts—and all to make us wiser! / Our authoress sure has wanted an adviser"* (IV, 382).[28]

Throughout his writing Goldsmith assumed a paternalistic attitude toward women. He felt their upbringings should be prudently dictated by their fathers, and they should be wary of romantic passion and unrealistic expectations for love and marriage. Women who wrote romances, in his view, threatened the security and propriety of their own sex by filling young women with false hopes and leaving them susceptible to filial disobedience and ultimate ruin. To the extent that novels—especially the scandalous memoirs to which Goldsmith was inveterately hostile—began to be perceived as a women's genre, they represented an inherent challenge to patriarchal control. Felicity Nussbaum argues: "The scandalous memoirists function, in large part, outside the family. Excluded from it, they also pose a threat to it."[29]

It is tempting to find biographical motivations for Goldsmith's hostility toward women writers. In a letter to his cousin Robert Bryanton, he alluded to his mother's "indolence."[30] He never married, nor do we have record of any sustained romantic involvement. What family ties he maintained were through letters to siblings and cousins. His condescending attitude, though certainly a product of societal bias, may have been exacerbated by an unwillingness or inability to form relationships with women and by a documented coolness toward his mother. Such speculation aside, the attack on women and the novel afforded him the opportunity to establish one of his many journalistic personae: that of a guardian of family virtue, upholder of traditional authority, and defender of the morality of young people.

Two decades later, when the novel had become an inextricable part of the publishing industry and further disseminated by circulating libraries, conservative commentators maintained their assault. One notable example was Vicesimus Knox who, in his *Essays Moral and Literary* (1779) decried the degeneracy of the genre. But he made a noteworthy concession: "Novels, it is feared, will not be dispensed with. Those then of Richardson and Fielding are allowed, yet not without reluctance. Every thing indelicate will of course be excluded; but perhaps there is less danger in the sentimental work. It attacks the heart more successfully, because more cautiously."[31] Knox's comments, although not contemporaneous with Goldsmith's career, might help explain a paradox that has troubled scholars: how could Goldsmith, in his short fiction for the *British Magazine* and in *The Vicar,* take up a genre he had so thoroughly condemned? The obvious solution—that Goldsmith's fiction is a skillful parody of the romance—disregards two centuries of reader response. Surely one of the principal explanations for the enduring appeal of *The Vicar* is its innocent and, at times, awkward poignancy—its sentimentalism.

Juxtaposing Goldsmith's book reviews with his later writings, one notes a consistent pattern: the reviewer complains of the flaws in particular works of poetry, satire, or fiction and offers correctives, and the essayist, poet, and fiction writer "improves" on the genres he had studied. If Prior is correct, Goldsmith developed an intimate acquaintance with the French memoir as a translator for Griffiths.[32] Whether, as Prior suggests, he translated "scandalous romances" is questionable, but he certainly translated Jean Marteilhé's *The Memoirs of a Protestant* (1758) for Griffiths and Anthony Hamilton's *Select Tales of Count Hamilton* (1760) for the bookseller J. Burd, so he was more directly involved with the romance than his contemptuous posture might have implied.

The Vicar of Wakefield, Goldsmith's own romance, may have been intended as a corrective to a "debauched" genre by making it sentimentalized, and so less dangerous.[33] However, his disdain for the genre may have had a subversive effect on the work by emerging, inconsistently, in the form of satirical reflections on romance conventions. And his relative inexperience as a fiction writer and avowed disinclination as a reader of novels may have contributed to the puzzling inconsistency in tone.

A second prominent feature of Goldsmith's Catalogue writing has more obvious biographical implications. Disappointed in his attempts to establish himself as a physician, Goldsmith was unremittingly harsh in his treatment of medical studies. *A Treatise upon Dropsies* was "not a treatise, but a quack-bill, lengthened out into the shape of a pamphlet" (I, 23). He also attacked *A Dissertation on the Properties and Efficacy of the Lisbon Diet-Drink* by John Leake, noted in medical annals for his studies of midwifery (I, 25).[34] Leake's pamphlet was a sixty-seven page advertisement for his product, and Goldsmith rightly compared it to "the number of quack-advertisements and handbills" with which it had to compete. The author boasts that his potion "expels Venereal Poison, or Scorbutic Acrimony . . . by affording the Venereal Poison a free Passage out of the Body by the Intestines." He argues throughout the superiority of his treatment to mercury in "promoting a free perspiration."[35] Goldsmith remarked facetiously: "What is this Lisbon Diet-Drink? a secret known to the Author only" (I, 25). Treatises on reducing fever and on stopping hemorrhages fared no better (I, 22–23, 23–25).

In her discussion of book reviewing in the late 1750s, Antonia Forster describes the contempt that many reviewers had for their own profession. At the lowest level of this enterprise were the "wretches" responsible for the Monthly Catalogues.[36] John Ginger suggests that the rapidity with which Goldsmith escaped this assignment was "a tacit recognition of his talent."[37] A reviewer's distaste for picking through dozens of leftover books and pamphlets is certainly understandable; but Goldsmith took advantage of this duty to display his satiric cunning, to rail against romantic excesses in novels and poetry, and to touch on diverse subjects to which he would return in his later periodical writing.

A Reviewer's Masks

Most reviewers specialized in one or two fields (though they often also wrote on subjects outside their areas of expertise), and Goldsmith was hired by Griffiths primarily to be his "foreign" specialist. More than most of his colleagues, however, Goldsmith displayed remarkable diversity in his reviewing. His assignments included important works in philology, drama, poetry, periodical writing, philosophy, history, travel literature, satire, and natural history—most of the genres popular in the late 1750s. He was either fortunate enough or perspicacious enough to review several of the most controversial and influential works of 1757, works written by some of England's foremost authors. An anonymous "hack," with no known previous experience either as author or critic, found himself on the staff of London's best established review and assigned the task of judging the likes of Edmund Burke, John Home, Tobias Smollett, David Hume, Thomas Gray, and George Colman.

Among Goldsmith's first assignments—as the "Gentleman who signs, D,"—was a review of Paul Henry Mallet's *Remains of the Mythology and Poetry of the Celtes* (April 1757), which was mostly an unacknowledged translation from a French source. Friedman argues persuasively that Goldsmith shows no evidence of having read Mallet's book (I, 4n).[38] Still, he applied his skill as a translator at a time when uncredited borrowing was commonplace in newspapers and magazines. The original part of the review implored scholars to discover their ancient native traditions: "The learned on this side the Alps have long laboured at the Antiquities of Greece and Rome, but almost totally neglected their own; like Conquerors who, while they have made inroads into the territories of their neighbours, have left their own natural dominions to desolation" (I, 6).

Mallet's work rode the crest of popular and scholarly fascination with philology among Goldsmith's contemporaries. The fascination continued with the publication of James Macpherson's *Fragments of Ancient Poetry* (1760) and Thomas Percy's *Reliques of Ancient English Poetry* (1765). Several of Griffiths' own reviewers later capitalized on this vogue: for example, Gregory Sharpe with his *Origin and Structure of the Greek Tongue* (1767) and John Cleland with *The Way to Things by Words, Being a Sketch of an Attempt at the Retrieval of the Antient Celtic* (1766). Goldsmith noted the popularity of philological study and used its methods and subjects in much of his later work.[39]

Introducing Goldsmith's review of Mallet, Griffiths identified the author as his foreign correspondent and expressed the hope that the writer would "excuse [the] striking out [of] a few paragraphs, for the sake of brevity" (I, 5n). Complaints about editorial revision were commonplace. A writer for the *Court Magazine* expressed outrage that "these fellows sometimes carr[ied] their insolence so far, as to presume to alter words and expressions in what a gentleman [had] taken the utmost care to polish and bring to perfection."[40] That Griffiths should assume such a public, apologetic posture toward abridging the first full-length contribution of his apprentice suggests a greater sensitivity on Griffiths' part toward editorial intrusion than many Goldsmith biographers have allowed.

One of Goldsmith's functions as "foreign correspondent" was coverage of works pertaining to the war. The Seven Years' War, as Robert Spector has observed, was the "chief subject . . . for almost all the periodicals" from 1756 to 1760,[41] and Goldsmith wrote notices of two pamphlets concerning the Admiral Byng controversy. Byng had been ordered to Minorca in April 1756 to support Fort St. Philip against French attack. After brief fighting, the Admiral left Minorca apparently without providing needed reinforcements. He was found negligent under the Twelfth Article of War and was executed.[42] The ensuing controversy contributed to the downfall of the Newcastle administration and to Pitt's call for a national militia.

In the Byng debate, Goldsmith acted as mouthpiece for Griffiths' pro-Newcastle position; thus he opposed Johnson, an ardent supporter of the Admiral.[43] Reviewing a pamphlet attempting to vindicate Byng, Goldsmith observed only that the public must be tired of the controversy (I, 17), and he praised a second treatise in support of Byng's execution, *Observations on the Twelfth Article of War* (I, 26). This anonymous pamphlet was written by the poet and playwright David Mallet, whose collected *Works* (1759) received a glowing endorsement from the *Monthly:* "Mr. Mallet's literary character sets him above any encomium from the pen of a journalist."[44] Like James Ralph, Mallet was a paid propagandist for Newcastle, and Goldsmith followed the

Monthly party line in supporting Mallet's work.[45] While Goldsmith's political reviews may appear insignificant—and they do, indeed, comprise a tiny fraction of his work for Griffiths—such one-sentence entries in the Monthly Catalogues formed the basis for the identification of the journal's party affiliation.

Three of the five books Goldsmith reviewed at length in the June 1757 issue concerned the history and proper conduct of the war. He praised *A Letter to an Officer of the Army, on Travelling on Sundays* (I, 61), and he wrote of *A Poem, Occasioned by the Militia-Bill Now Depending:* "This female Writer seems possessed of the true spirit of an Amazon. Homer is in his element, when in a battle; Virgil, in a storm; but our Poetess, in a militia-cavalcade" (I, 61). In this issue Goldsmith also assumed the role of Griffiths' correspondent who signed "B". His review of an "absurd" travel account, François-Xavier de Charlevoix's *Histoire du Paraguay,* is the second instance of Goldsmith's assuming the "correspondent" role which served him so frequently throughout his career (I, 50–56).

After a short trial assignment in April, Goldsmiths' work load increased dramatically; Griffiths tested the limits of his new employee's capacity for toil. Noting Goldsmith's "surprisingly self-assured tone," Ralph Wardle argues that he did his best work as a reviewer in the May 1757 issue of the *Monthly.*[46] In fact, he did far more work for the May issue than for any other. Goldsmith was responsible for approximately one-third of the total copy for the May issue. Not only did he contribute four full-length reviews and at least twenty-three of the Monthly Catalogue entries, but he also made extracts from foreign journals to produce "A Catalogue of Foreign Publications" and a "Literary News" column. Actually, until the September issue, the evidence of the reviewer's productivity belies Prior's assertion, repeated by later biographers, that Griffiths had reason to question his employee's industriousness.[47]

One of Goldsmith's first major assignments was John Home's tragedy *Douglas* (I, 10–14), arguably the most controversial play of the late 1750s. In his review, Goldsmith anticipated his own dramatic criticism in *Polite Learning* and in his highly influential article "An Essay on the Theatre," written for the *Westminster Magazine* (January 1773). *Douglas* had premiered in Edinburgh on 14 December 1756 and had scandalized the Scottish ruling party, which was offended by the idea of a clergyman's writing for the stage. Goldsmith, who claimed to have seen the play's debut at Covent Garden on March 14, followed critics predisposed toward disliking Home's effort. He chided David Hume for that philosopher's well-publicized and hyperbolic praise of the tragedy in the dedication to his *Four Dissertations* (1757). In attacking Hume, he echoed a similar complaint made in the March issue of the *Critical:* "The author of *Douglas* is as far from *Shakespear* and *Otway,* as London is from Edinburgh."[48] Reviewing a pamphlet supporting Home, *The*

Tragedy of "Douglas" Analyzed, the *Critical* declared that the vocal supporters of *Douglas* were "certainly the worst friends in the world."[49] Still, Hume's "offenses" in support of Home and his "rhapsodies against the religion of [his] country" did not preclude his admission to Goldsmith's "fame machine" as a historian (*Bee;* I, 448–49).

In spite of the fact that many of Goldsmith's comments on *Douglas* were probably derived from other reviews, he clearly began the process of establishing a critical voice and his own dramatic theory. He defined his critical persona as an "epicure" directing the tastes of the gluttons who have supported a "tedious succession of indifferent performances" (I, 10). *Douglas,* he argued, succeeded only because it had been compared "not with our idea of excellence, but of the exploded trash it succeeds" (I, 10). The "true Critic" deplored the mediocrity and "prepostrous distress" of Home's play (I, 11), but still predicted future success for the playwright.[50] He also rejected strict conformity to the unities: "A mechanically exact adherence to all the rules of the Drama, is more the business of industry than of genius" (I, 11), an idea he repeated throughout his journalistic work. His formula for successful drama included sublimity, sentiment, and passion in support of a moral—elements he found lacking in Home's play. The tragedies of his age, he wrote later in his *Westminster Magazine* article, were rife with "the pompous Train, the swelling Phrase, and the unnatural Rant" (III, 209). At least in capturing "the native innocence of the shepherd Norval" (I, 12) Home had avoided bombast.

The *Monthly* seldom reviewed published plays and even less frequently mentioned periodical compilations, but the appearance of a collected edition of Thornton and Colman's *Connoisseur* gave Goldsmith the opportunity to issue his first comments on essay writing; and in his review he articulated principles that would further his own self-definition as an author and critic. The *Connoisseur,* an essay-journal that had ceased publication on 30 September 1756, had been more a critical than a popular success, but Goldsmith found in its essays the essential virtues of an essayist's persona.[51] The persona created by Colman and Thornton "converses with all the ease of a chearful companion," remains "perfectly satyrical, yet perfectly good-natured," separates "simple folly" from the "absolutely criminal," and avoids Latinate diction in favor of common language (I, 14–15).

Though Lance Bertelsen notes that Goldsmith "effusively praised" the periodical, critics have greatly underestimated the debt Goldsmith owes to Thornton, Colman, and their joint persona, Mr. Town, in the *Connoisseur.*[52] The critic as a "Censor-General" gently ridiculing folly was a mask Goldsmith frequently assumed, especially in his first independent periodical work in the *Bee.* In several of his subsequent essays, Goldsmith closely followed Thornton and Colman in choice and development of themes.[53] Like other journals of this period, the *Connoisseur* attempted to free itself from the intimidating shadow of the *Spectator;* it encouraged experimentation and less dogmatic approaches to periodical writing in the late 1750s and 1760s.[54]

Goldsmith's third full-length review in May represented what seems in retrospect his most important assignment: Edmund Burke's *A Philosophical Enquiry into the Origin of Our Ideas of the Sublime and Beautiful* (1757). In a detailed response that Stephen Gwynn calls "a masterly piece of fluent, easy exposition," he faulted his former schoolmate at Trinity College, Dublin, for being "only agreeable when he might have been instructive" (I, 28), summarized Burke's treatise at length, and conducted a dialectic with the author in lengthy footnotes to his abstract.[55] Reciting the flaws he found in the *Enquiry,* Goldsmith articulated principles of prose composition that defined his own writing. Authors, he said, should avoid "obscurity and conjecture" that lead to an uncertain conclusion; the aim of philosophical speculation should be instructive closure, not obscurity and "inextricable difficulties" (I, 27). Originality is a philosophical "conductor" inferior to moral purpose and rhetorical clarity.

Though his complaints about Burke's obscurity suggest that he failed to read the *Enquiry* closely or to understand it fully, Goldsmith does some justice to the treatise in his subsequent summary and analytical footnotes, including his detailed account of the physiology of sight in relation to Burke's discussion of darkness and sublimity. The review concludes with praise for Burke's ingenuity and learning. Though his own style and subject matter differed radically from that of his Trinity schoolmate, Goldsmith was influenced by the *Enquiry.* For example, the analysis of taste in *Polite Learning* relied heavily on Burke's distinction between the sublime and the beautiful (I, 295). And in responding to Burke, he worked out aesthetic principles evident in his later poetry and fiction:

> Distinctness of imagery has ever been held productive of the sublime. The more strongly the poet or orator impresses the picture he would describe upon his own mind, the more apt will he be to paint it on the imagination of the reader. . . . Therefore, not from the confusion or obscurity of the description, but from being able to place the object to be described in a greater variety of views, is poetry superior to all other descriptive arts. (I, 31–32)

Goldsmith extols those virtues frequently praised in his own works such as *The Deserted Village* and *The Vicar*—the vividness of their description and their plain appeal to the reader's imagination.

Perhaps the most remarkable feature of his review of Burke is Goldsmith's chameleon-like assumption of a persona appropriate to his subject—a technique that would, indeed, become one of the marks of his journalistic work. Here, Goldsmith, a novice writer, presents himself unabashedly as a philosopher praising and censuring a colleague; his remarks are motivated not by "a captious spirit of controversy" (I, 35), but by a dispassionate concern for truth: "There is, perhaps, no investigation more difficult than that of the passions, and other affections resulting from them. The difference of opinion among all who have treated on this subject, serves to convince us of its uncertainty" (I, 27). While the regular part of the review adheres to the *Monthly* critic's duty to summarize, the notes argue with Burke in tones of philosophic assuredness: "Thus with regard to his distinction between delight and pleasure, we may here observe, That most of the real pleasures we possess, proceed from a diminution of pain" (I, 29). Even in the voice of a philosopher, though, he appeals to the "common sense" of popular wisdom: "Our author by assigning terror for the only source of the sublime, excludes love, admiration, &c. But to make the sublime an idea incompatible with those affections, is what the general sense of mankind will be apt to contradict" (I, 29). As a reviewer—whether of philosophical treatises, poetry, drama, or fiction—he represented himself as spokesman for the public: those readers of "good taste and good humour" whose trust he had to earn.

The philosopher turns historian in the June issue of the *Monthly*. Goldsmith introduces his review of Smollett's *A Compleat History of England* with a lecture on the use of historical evidence. The historian, he argues, must "punctually [refer] to the spring-head from whence the stream of his narration flows" (I, 44). According to Goldsmith, the historian who attends more closely to narrative style than to documentary evidence risks becoming little more than a romance writer; throughout the review, he makes oblique allusions to Smollett's successful career as a novelist and rather cautiously implies that *A Compleat History* is a triumph of a "nervous, and flowing" style over accuracy (I, 46). Goldsmith, who partly supported himself in 1759 and 1760 through his work for Smollett's *Critical Review* and *British Magazine*, sets narrow standards for historical research. In his view, the *Compleat History* failed to conform to these standards: "Strictly speaking, the eye-witness alone should take upon him to transmit facts to posterity . . . for, in proportion as History removes from the first witnesses, it may recede also from truth" (I, 44). Wardle calls the review "unnecessarily captious," but since the *History* was the work of the Griffiths' rival editor, it is reviewed less severely than one might have expected.[56]

Though Goldsmith took a position opposite to that of Samuel Johnson in regard to Charlotte Lennox, he found himself on Johnson's side in another matter. At work on his dictionary, Johnson was writing occasional anonymous reviews for the *Literary Magazine*, a journal he had helped initiate the previous year. James Clifford calls Johnson's scathing review of Jonas Hanway's *A Journal of Eight Days Journey To Which is Added an Essay on Tea* (*Literary Magazine*, 15 May 1757) one of the wittiest and best-known of his contributions.[57] For his attack on Hanway, Johnson was almost sued, and political pressure on the publisher of the *Literary*, Joseph Richardson, may have forced the end of Johnson's association with the journal.[58] After two months of well-publicized wrangling in the press, Goldsmith's review of the same work appeared in the July issue of the *Monthly*. Though his tone was less vitriolic, Goldsmith agreed with Johnson and rose to the defense of tea drinking. He faulted the travel account for being too much a "mental excursion" at the expense of description (I, 76). Though somewhat more conciliatory, Goldsmith found—as Johnson had—that Hanway had "acquired some reputation by travelling abroad, but lost it all by travelling at home."[59]

The August issue displayed Goldsmith's attention to a mentor he would never meet. In an anonymous letter he praised a new seven-volume edition of Voltaire's works and proclaimed his admiration for the French author. In the *Bee* and elsewhere Voltaire would become for Goldsmith the apotheosis of the man of letters. Writing to his brother Henry in 1759, he mentioned his own *Memoirs of M. de Voltaire* (first published serially in the *Lady's Magazine*, 1761) as a mere "catchpenny"; but this review seems to indicate the sincerity of his appreciation for Voltaire.[60]

Goldsmith's comments on *Letters from an Armenian in Ireland* are especially valuable for providing his early perspective on the satirical "foreign traveller" genre. Ironically, two of his complaints about this satire were later turned repeatedly against his own Chinese Letters. He began: "The Writer who would inform, or improve, his countrymen, under the assumed character of an Eastern Traveller, should be careful to let nothing escape him which might betray the imposture" (I, 90); he concluded with the observation that the author "seldom shews the methods of remedying the evils he complains of" (I, 94). Whether or not these censures have been justly applied to Goldsmith's own collection, the review provides an example of the methodology that defines much of Goldsmith's work: the discovery and articulation of the weaknesses in a well-established genre, and the improvement of the form through stylistic simplicity, humor, and morality. As *Polite Learning* attempted to improve on the rhetorically ineffective jeremiads that preceded it, and as *The Vicar* attempted to improve on a "morally corrupt" genre, so *The Citizen* borrowed a well-worn model and improved it. His description of the ideal form of the "traveller satire" in this review might have served as a sort of preface for the Chinese Letters: "If his aim be satirical, his remarks should be collected from the more striking follies abounding in the country he describes, and from those prevailing absurdities which commonly usurp the softer name of fashions" (I, 90–91).

Goldsmith's review of Gottlieb Wilhelm Rabener's *Satirical Letters*, also in the August issue, served the same purpose: to suggest the faults in this example of the genre, as well as its strengths, and to move toward a more generally applicable theory of humor.[61] Rabener's stated purpose and method certainly accord with that chosen by Goldsmith for his Chinese Letters three years later: "Some observations I had made on the foibles and vices of mankind, I have here illustrated in letters."[62] First Secretary of the Treasury at Dresden, Rabener offered tongue-in-cheek advice for bribing judges, escaping bankruptcy, and—appropriate to Goldsmith's experience at Peckham—tutoring children: "Can a man of learning and judgment, of manners and virtue, easily prevail upon himself to undertake an office, where the labour and vexation is great and certain, the profit small, and the honour still less and always precarious?"[63] The letters in the first volume are loosely connected, their satirical approach scattershot; the second volume is a somewhat more structured epistolary romance, offering stratagems by which "a prude" might successfully "get a husband."

Goldsmith argued that the work suffered in its translation from German— that "Foreign Humour . . . frequently dies in transplanting"; still, Goldsmith believed that the work succeeded in revealing its author's "intimate acquaintance with human nature," and that "his fools so delicately expose their own foibles by endeavoring to hide them" (I, 85).[64] Whether or not these collections of letters directly inspired *The Citizen,* they represent an initial working out of principles that directed the author in his later satiric writing.

Goldsmith provided Griffiths two final reviews for the September issue of the *Monthly* before leaving Paternoster Row, apparently with his editor's approval. Again, he articulated principles by which he would later construct his own models. His reviews of William Wilkie's *The Epigoniad* and of Thomas Gray's *Odes* both urged poets to give pleasure to a broader audience. He demanded a sort of populist aesthetic, a poetry suited to the "national character" rather than the academy.

Wilkie blundered in attempting "in a peculiar manner to bespeak the patronage of the learned." The poem, he complained, "seems to be one of these *new old* performances; a work that would no more have pleased a peripatetic of the academic grove, than it will captivate the unlettered subscriber to one of our circulating libraries" (I, 110). Indeed, *The Epigoniad* is prefaced by a forty-eight page treatise on epic poetry that attacks poetic rules as set down by critics and dares to complain of Milton's irregularity.[65] Goldsmith's criticism of the work was mild compared with that of a pamphlet respondent, who called the work "absurd to the last degree" and a "grievous blunder": "'Milton's poem is irregular!' but where is our author's regularity, when all must stop till the long winded story of the death of Hercules be minutely told, which, with other such foreign circumstances, take up the whole seventh book?"[66] Wilkie had attempted to follow in Homer's footsteps in an effort "to extend our ideas of human perfection, or, as the Critics express it, to excite admiration" (Wilkie, vii). For Goldsmith, however, the artificiality of the piece and the author's "disregard of the traditions of the antients" leave the reader with the suspicion that "the Poet believes not a syllable of all he tells us" (I, 111).

Gray's slender volume included two odes, the first a pastoral with echoes of Milton's *L'Allegro,* the second "founded on a Tradition, current in Wales, that Edward the First, when he compleated the conquest of that country, ordered all the Bards, that fell into his hands, to be put to death."[67] Goldsmith argued that Gray's prosodic choices doomed the project from the start: "Several unsuccessful experiments seem to prove that the English cannot have Odes in blank Verse" (I, 113). Again, he complained that Gray would not appeal to "the generality of Readers," and he advised the poet to *"Study the People,"* rather than to "amuse only the few" (I, 112).[68] His own poetry, more colloquial and less obviously learned than Wilkie's or Gray's, may have been a conscious reaction against what Goldsmith saw as the elitism of many of the poets who were his contemporaries.[69] And his disdain for "academic taste" remained fairly consistent. His narrator in *The Citizen* notes wryly "that the doctors of colleges never wrote, and that some of them had actually forgot their reading" (II, 125).

These complaints by Goldsmith and others about the *Odes* were exaggerated by George Colman and Robert Lloyd in their brutal parody, *Two Odes* (1760). The hero of the first is a "shallow Fop in antick vest" who finds himself "now in the Palpable Obscure quite lost": "The Bard, who shrouds / His Lyric Glory in the Clouds, / Too fond to strike the stars with lofty head! / He topples headlong from the giddy height, / Deep in the Canbrian Gulph immerg'd in endless night."[70] The satire captures the disappointment Gray must have felt in the reception of his poems, his ambitions and pretensions, and his "obscurity." Still, the satire hints at the notice Gray's work attracted and the relative importance of this reviewing assignment. Goldsmith's response to Gray, coupled with his application of Burke's notion of the sublime to poetry, coalesced in the theory of poetry he asserts in *The Citizen:* "In a word the great faults of the modern professed English poets are, that they seem to want numbers which should vary with the passion, and are more employed in describing to the imagination than striking at the heart" (II, 173).

Goldsmith also urged Gray to be less of an "imitator" and "more an original" (I, 114). For Prior, Goldsmith's own "excessive emulation" of his contemporaries is a censurable fault.[71] However, Goldsmith's skill in imitating and then improving popular genres might just as easily be praised. Prior observes:

> On his first entering into literary life, he found the attention of the reading part of the people fixed upon the essays of Johnson, and thence he became an essayist; the novels of Smollett were universally read, and he aimed to be a novelist; Gray,

Mason, Akenside, Armstrong, and others claimed the honours of poetry, and he aspired to be a poet; Hume, Smollett and Robertson having acquired high reputation in history, he desired to be a historian; and dramatic writers were so numerous and many so fortunate, that believing his own powers not inferior to theirs, he became a successful dramatist.[72]

Prior's explanation of Goldsmith's authorial process is oversimplified, but it does suggest the importance of Goldsmith's early career—the books and authors to which he was exposed—as an influence on his later writings. As a live-in assistant to a bookseller, he read and reviewed the types of books and pamphlets that appealed to the London readership. Just as important as the relatively positive models of Burke and Gray were the negative examples. If the press was, indeed, laden with fatuous and immoral romances, he would improve on the genre; if, as he complained, much of contemporary poetry had become either obscure or inane, he would become a poet of clarity and cogency; if historians were too often guilty of partisanship, his own historical writing and social observation would be politically neutral; if the theatre had grown stale, he would revive it. His short career with Griffiths, in addition to giving him a first-hand look at the periodical publishing industry, allowed Goldsmith to develop rhetorical and ideological stances that would serve him throughout his career.

As John Witherspoon remarked in 1765, "The skill of an author, like that of a merchant, lies chiefly in judging with readiness and certainty, what kind of commodities, and in what quantity, any particular age or place is able and willing to receive."[73] Reviewing work provided an excellent introduction to the publishing marketplace—it allowed Goldsmith to witness and condemn its failures and to emulate and, perhaps, improve on its successes.

4

In the Rival Camp

For how can Authors write when they are starving? It must naturally
follow, under the present Circumstances, that if a Man in a deep Con-
sumption can walk but little, so an Author, in great Need of Food and
Books, can write but little.
—Thomas Medley, Esq. [pseud.], *The Shandymonian*

The character of Goldsmith's second reviewing stint, with the *Critical
Review,* was quite different from his experience with the *Monthly.* He was not,
in the same sense, a "garreted" staff member, but one of a number of more
independent and irregular contributors. He had published a full-length
book, *Enquiry into the Present State of Polite Learning* (1759), which capitalized
on many of the works he had noticed and reviewed in his first foray into the
London publishing world. His lingering hopes to resurrect a medical career
in India were dashed by military conflict there, and he returned to "Grub
Street" with plans to establish his own magazine.[1] He also established a
series of important contacts that would assure him steady employment as a
compiler, translator, reviewer, essayist, and fiction writer.

A discussion of Goldsmith's association with the *Critical* is complicated by
several factors. First, the exact cause of his abrupt departure from the *Monthly*
has remained obscure. If he found reviewing work abhorrent, and tried to
distance himself from it in *Polite Learning* with unequivocal attacks on
booksellers and critics, why did he return to reviewing little more than a year
after his first experience with it? Secondly, documentary evidence concerning
the management of the *Critical* and its contributors is scarce. In his study of
Smollett as critic and journalist, for example, James Basker confines his
treatment of Smollett's editorial policies to 1756, the only year during
Smollett's tenure for which we have a complete and reliable source for
attributing reviews: Archibald Hamilton's annotated copies.[2] The extent and
range of Goldsmith's contributions to the *Critical* are far less certain than are
his reviews for the *Monthly.* Those reviews that have been confidently attributed to him suggest that his *Critical* work was more identifiably focused
than his *Monthly* contributions. Goldsmith had become, almost exclusively, a
literary critic, confining himself primarily to belletristic writing.

The Break with Griffiths

Why Goldsmith and Griffiths terminated their agreement after the September issue is unknown. The only direct evidence, the record of Goldsmith's contributions to the *Monthly* for 1757, suggests that the break occurred abruptly. His review of *The Epigoniad,* the only one he provided for the September issue other than the review of Gray's *Odes,* was incomplete. Griffiths' marked copy indicates that the publisher himself finished the article—an occurrence so anomalous as to suggest that the reviewer may have abandoned his duties before completing them.[3] Did Griffiths personally dislike his apprentice or disapprove of his work? Had Goldsmith decided on a change in career? Had a "serious quarrel" arisen between the two, as Forster conjectures?[4] Precisely why Goldsmith's first journalistic assignment ended prematurely has been as difficult to determine as Griffiths' reasons for hiring him in the first place. Relying on Goldsmith's recollections to Percy in 1773, James Prior expands upon them and offers an explanation for the separation which has largely gone unchallenged:

> Goldsmith [was] tired of his employer or employment, and Griffiths of an inmate less industrious or submissive than probably he had been induced to expect. The drudgery of the occupation, not less irksome than that of the school, required in fact with almost as much restraint upon his time, more unremitting labour of body and mind. . . . To sit down daily to furnish the stated number of pages for a periodical journal . . . can be no easy or enviable employment.[5]

There are several problems with this explanation. First, Griffiths' reviewers apparently had no prescribed number of pages to write. The length and number of contributions varied widely for all staff members, with no readily discernible pattern. Secondly, after leaving the *Monthly,* Goldsmith's literary output did not significantly diminish. By 11 January 1758 he had translated Marteilhé's *Memoirs of a Protestant.* Despite being recalled, early in 1758, to Milner's school at Peckham, he found time to complete *Polite Learning* before August and may have begun work on his Chinese Letters.[6] Further, the breach was not so severe as to prevent Griffiths' joining Edward Dilly to publish Goldsmith's translation of *Memoirs of a Protestant* (9 March 1758) or Griffiths' publishing four more reviews by Goldsmith in December 1758. Finally, Goldsmith's distaste for criticism was not so severe as to prevent his returning to the profession in January 1759.

The supposed quarrel with Griffiths has obscured the two most compelling reasons for Goldsmith's leaving the *Monthly:* his intention to publish longer works of his own and his desire to escape the anonymity of reviewing. A letter of 14 August 1758 to his cousin Robert Bryanton reveals his considerable ambitions and a serious fear that his early anonymous writings would go unrecognized:

There will come a day, no doubt it will—I beg you may live a couple of hundred years longer only to see the day—when the Scaligers and Daciers will vindicate my character, give learned editions of my labours, and bless the times with copious comments on the text. You shall see how they fish up the heavy scoundrels who disregard me now, or will then offer to cavil at my productions. . . . This may be the subject of the lecture:—"Oliver Goldsmith flourished in the eighteenth and nineteenth centuries. He lived to be an hundred and three years old, [and in that] age may justly be styled the sun of [literature] and the Confucius of Europe. [Many of his earlier writings, to the regret of the] learned world, were anonymous, and have probably been lost, because united with those of others."[7]

In his four extant letters written in 1758, Goldsmith expresses confidence in his future fame. To cousin Jane Lawder he casts himself as a descendant of Butler and Otway, and tries to forget his desperate financial troubles by consoling himself with the assurance of literary immortality.[8]

While these letters reveal his great hopes for *Polite Learning*, they also indicate his plans to secure a position with the East India Company in December 1758. Scholars have suggested that Goldsmith had not yet fully committed himself to a career as an author. Seitz argues that "from 1757 until at least as late as January 1759, his mind was occupied with the prospect of going as a physician to the coast of Coromandel [southeasern coast of India]."[9] His two ambitions, however, were not mutually exclusive; though he largely abandoned periodical work from November 1757 until January 1759, he was still furthering his authorial career. Given his productivity during this period and his self-identification as an "author by profession," Goldsmith's plan to join the East India Company certainly did not preclude his literary ambition.

By the summer of 1758 he had returned to London to solicit subscriptions for *Polite Learning* and to apply for the East India Company position. Writing to his brother-in-law, Daniel Hodson, on 31 August 1758, Goldsmith defended professional authorship and contradicted the prevailing, stereotypical view of a writer's life:

> I know you have in Ireland a very indifferent Idea of a man who writes for bread. tho Swift and Steel did so in the earlier part of their lives. You Imagine, I suppose, that every author by profession lives in a garret, wears shabby cloaths, and converses with the meanest company; but I assure you such a character is entirely chimerical. . . . You can't conceive how I am sometimes divided, to leave all that is dear gives me pain.[10]

This uncharacteristic encomium on the literary profession paints an idealized and misleading portrait of his life during that period. But it suggests that financial inducements, rather than disenchantment with periodical work, may have motivated his contemplating a medical career in India.

To help prepare for an examination by the company on 21 December 1758, Goldsmith apparently convinced Griffiths to act as security for a new suit of clothes—further evidence that their initial "breach" was not irreparable. Wardle speculates that Goldsmith's four reviews for the December 1758 issue of the *Monthly* were "by way of repayment" for his editor's loan.[11] However, when Goldsmith's application to the East India Company was summarily rejected, he failed to return the clothes to the tailor from whom they were borrowed. He apparently sold them to a pawnbroker, to whom he also gave as security copies of books Griffiths had lent him.[12] Griffiths threatened suit, to which Goldsmith responded in a letter of January 1759, pleading poverty and imploring the publisher's forgiveness.[13] The debt may have been satisfied by Goldsmith's giving Griffiths rights to the Voltaire biography; curiously, the bookseller advertised the biography in February 1759, but never published it.[14] Later in 1759 the *Monthly* writer William Kenrick attacked the "know-nothing" author of *Polite Learning*—evidence, perhaps, that Goldsmith and Griffiths had not resolved their differences.[15]

The publication of *Polite Learning* represented an important transition for Goldsmith: a movement toward a greater freedom to select his own subjects, and toward the possibility of public recognition. Adapting to a book-length treatise the role of "true critic" he had developed as a *Monthly* scribe, he also prepared himself for an essay career in the magazines. The short, topical chapters in *Polite Learning* resembled the serial essays popular in London magazines, and Goldsmith displayed the kind of firsthand knowledge of European culture that would make him popular with periodical readers and valuable to publishers. Though the book was apparently not received enthusiastically, it was a well-calculated effort to advance his career—an effort that clearly demonstrated his commitment to success as an author.

In a letter to the *Monthly* in 1774, Griffiths grudgingly acknowledged the role Goldsmith played in his brief stay with the review. Correcting the assertion that the writer was hired to "superintend" the journal, Griffiths noted: "It is, however, true that he had, for awhile, a seat at our board; and that, so far as his knowledge of books extended, he was not an unuseful assistant."[16] It was a backhanded testimonial to Goldsmith's unique role as an in-house employee and assistant to the editor for one of the most influential London periodicals of its day.

The "Battle of the Reviews"

Though social critics in the late 1750s and even the reviewers themselves portrayed the London reviews as a new and pernicious threat to English belles lettres, periodical reviewing was hardly a recent phenomenon. Since at least 1710, review journals had been evolving, their innovations sparked by competition for readers. However, the fierce and public "battle" between the *Monthly* and the *Critical,* waged not only within their own pages but in newspapers, magazines, pamphlets, and long treatises, contributed to the illusion that two titanic journals had achieved an unprecedented control over the London publishing industry and dictated public response to new works. In fact, their control was hardly exclusive, and competition among rival reviews had been evident for most of the century.

Michael de la Roche is often credited with establishing the first English review with his monthly journal, the *Memoirs of Literature* (1710–17). Included in the *Memoirs* were short book reviews (mostly abstracts or translations of abstracts) along with news concerning the Royal Academy and other original material.[17] John Wilford followed La Roche's short-lived journal with his *Monthly Catalogue* (1724–32), from which regular columns in both the *Monthly* and the *Critical* most likely derived their names. Beginning the tradition of symbiosis between reviews and newspapers, Wilford drew from periodical advertisements to provide more complete lists of new works published, including complete title, author (when available), and printer. Often, a one-sentence description of contents was appended. In 1725 La Roche returned to periodical publication. His *New Memoirs of Literature* (1725–27) followed Wilford's *Monthly Catalogue* in providing more complete publication details, but he added to his entries original summaries as well as quotations.[18]

Isaac Kimber challenged the *Monthly Catalogue* with his own *Monthly Chronicle* (1728). Kimber's journal added accounts of foreign and domestic news to the *Catalogue* format. Faced with this challenge from Kimber, and also by the formidable appearance of Edward Cave's *Gentleman's Magazine* in 1731, Wilford consolidated his *Monthly Catalogue,* making it a section of his miscellany, the *London Magazine.* La Roche, too, expanded his format and created the quarterly *Literary Journal* (1730–31), which added some limited critical commentary to its extracts. When Ralph Griffiths founded the *Monthly* in 1749, his format and method were essentially those of Wilford and La Roche: more description and quotation than critical commentary.

The appearance of the *Critical* in Feburary 1756, one year before Goldsmith began his career, renewed an atmosphere of competition and change. Established by Smollett and the printer Archibald Hamilton, the *Critical* solicited contributions from Thomas Francklin, David Mallet, Griffith Jones, Joseph Robertson, David Hume, and at least one review from Samuel Johnson. An advertisement in the *London Evening Post* (15–18 January 1757), promoting the second collected volume, proclaimed the success of the *Critical* in its challenge to the *Monthly:*

In spite of open Assault and private Assassination; in spite of published Reproach and printed Letters of Abuse, distributed like poisoned Arrows in the Dark; the

Critical Review has not only maintained its Footing, but considerably extended its Progress. The Breath of secret Calumny excites a Spirit of Inquiry and Comparison, from which the Work hath derived singular Advantage; and the loud Blasts of Obloquy, instead of tearing it up, serve only to prove its Strength and fix its Roots the deeper. Encouraged by the Favour of the Public, which is the only Patron they will ever solicit, their chief Attention shall be devoted to the Execution of their original Plan: They will continue to exert that Spirit and Impartiality, by which they flatter themselves the Critical Review has been hitherto distinguished. [19]

The *Critical* set itself up as the adversary of private interest, to which by implication the *Monthly* had fallen prey. The frequent attacks on the *Critical*, published in the London dailies and weeklies, may actually have stimulated interest in Smollett's review and furthered its self-proclaimed identity as the enemy of dullness and presumption.

Quarrels among London journals were legion throughout this period and were frequent targets for ridicule. A correspondent to the *Court* suggested:

I cannot help observing upon the present literary dispute, that were these assassins (for I can call them no better) to employ their weapons on other subjects, than upon each other, the public would be infinitely more obliged to them: for it certainly is one of the severest taxes that can be imposed on them, to pay for paper and print that affords us no other intelligence, amusement, or instruction, than that this man keeps a woman, that cheats his Bookseller; another passed through college without taking any degrees. . . . For my own part, I confess I must either give over reading entirely, or petition the Gentlemen *Literati* to give me something more worthy my money, and at less price. [20]

Such disputes, though, seemed more to pique public interest than to hurt sales of journals. And before the conflict between the *Briton* and *North Briton*, no journalistic feud of the war years attracted more attention than the "Battle of the Reviews."

Open hostility between the two journals erupted with the publication of an anonymous pamphlet, *The Occasional Critic* (1757), which Smollett assumed to have been written by Griffiths. Responding to attacks on the character of *Critical* reviewers, Smollett published an unsigned letter in his review for November 1757. He addressed it to the "Old Gentlewoman Who Directs the *Monthly Review*," insinuating, as others had, that Mrs. Griffiths was actually in charge of the *Monthly*; and he maintained that before this personal attack, his review would be content to have his rival "utter [her] reveries for the entertainment of deistical barbers and crazy anabaptists." He also hinted that the contributors to the reviews were not fully anonymous:

It is diverting enough to hear the directress of the *Monthly Review* accuse any society, as *physicians without learning, and critics without judgment*. . . . Though we never visited your garrets, we know what sort of doctors and authors you employ as journeymen in your manufacture. You cannot, with all your obscurity, so effectually wrap your sons in clouds, but that they will sometimes expose their features to the public.[21]

The ensuing conflict was so sensational that it focused all attention on the personal and political nature of this rivalry to the exclusion of some of the functional innovations by which Hamilton and Smollett challenged the *Monthly.* The *Critical* promised easier accessibility to its issues: each monthly advertisement in the *London Evening Post* noted that "Gentlemen, &c. may be served with the Critical Review Monthly; at their own Houses, at 1s. by ordering it of their Booksellers or the News-Carriers."[22] Competition among the various periodicals had brought new systems of delivery and wider availability. The *Centinel,* for example, promised free delivery of its weekly issues;[23] and the *London Magazine* advertised that copies could be bought from "all other booksellers and news carriers."[24] Advertisements for the *Monthly,* however, made no such claim; Griffiths may not yet have taken advantage of this trend.

Two more innovations of this sort have a direct bearing on our understanding of Goldsmith's emergence into this competitive environment. Responding to its competitor, the *Monthly* expanded in August 1756 from an average of 80–96 pages to 112 pages, a change that brought about the need for more contributors.[25] Griffiths also saw that the *Critical* had accommodated London's interest in foreign news and publications by adding a foreign section to what was otherwise the same basic format the *Monthly* had established. In February 1757 he added his own foreign section, written by "the gentleman who signs D." The connection between this "editorial fiction," as Friedman calls it (I, 5n), and Goldsmith has been noted by Caroline F. Tupper.[26] However, neither Friedman nor Tupper mentions a note published in the *London Evening Post* (5 February 1757) that added another dimension to this "editorial fiction." To his advertisement for the February issue Griffiths attached the following:

Note, A Succinct Account of Foreign Publications, by a Set of learned and ingenious Correspondents, is now commenced in the Monthly Review, and will be continued every Month, unless interrupted by the Accidents to which a Foreign Correspondence is liable. No performance worthy of Attention shall be overlook'd; and all due Regard will be paid to the Most Important.[27]

The note implies that the editor has hired a cadre of brilliant men to travel to Europe, at great risk to themselves in that time of war, to provide firsthand foreign literary accounts for London readers. In fact it was the soon-to-be-hired Goldsmith, lodged safely within Griffiths' own quarters, who would serve as "foreign correspondent."

Introducing his expanded coverage of foreign literature, Griffiths provided in his February 1757 issue an "Advertisement" and a letter from correspondent "D," both of which he wrote himself. He promised his readers "a nosegay, culled from the garden of a Brother Journalist," whom the editor described as an expert on foreign literary journals. Almost apologetically, he asserted that his first selection was not made "for want of other materials," and he promised for future issues a host of "curious and interesting performances." The letter that followed further promoted Griffiths' projected expansion and urged that "the good People of England know something of what passes among the Sons of Learning in other parts of Europe."[28]

James Grainger was Griffiths' first "Gentleman who signs D" and wrote the foreign articles for February and March. Other than a one-sentence review of *The Rival Politicians* for the April Monthly Catalogue (I, 5), Goldsmith first contributed to the *Monthly* as a replacement for Grainger. The addition of Goldsmith allowed Grainger, who had been on the staff since May 1756, to concentrate on his two areas of specialization: poetry and medicine. Relieved of his "foreign correspondent" assignment in April, he reviewed James Hervey's poem in blank verse, *Contemplations on the Night*,[29] as well as John Dyer's poem *The Fleece*.[30] For the same issue, Goldsmith reviewed Paul Henry Mallet's *Remains of the Mythology* by translating from the French book *Bibliothèque des sciences et des beaux-arts* (I, 5n); thus Griffiths' new reviewer immediately demonstrated his usefulness in coverage of foreign works.

While he is better known as the reviewer of Gray's *Odes*, Burke's *Enquiry*, and Home's *Douglas*, Goldsmith's central responsibility, and most likely the reason he was hired, was to provide coverage of foreign works, and thus to help Griffiths compete more effectively with Smollett's *Critical*. Excluding his thirty-seven known entries for the Monthly Catalogues—mostly brief reviews of topical treatises, romances, and other miscellanies—we know of twenty-four full-length contributions. Of these, seven are on explicitly foreign subjects and three on the American colonies; six concern the classics or European antiquity. Two-thirds of his major reviewing assignments conform to the foreign correspondent's role. After Goldsmith's breach with Griffiths, the editor replaced him with William Kenrick,[31] known to Goldsmith scholars for his attack on *Polite Learning* in November 1759. Kenrick's primary responsibility was for reviewing foreign literature; the similarity of his role to Goldsmith's provides further evidence that Griffiths perceived Goldsmith as his "foreign correspondent."

Another attempt by the *Critical* to gain competitive advantage had a bearing on Goldsmith's work. Smollett's periodical generally reviewed works a month or more earlier than its rival. This practice had a number of consequences. It allowed the *Critical* to have the "first word" on most new books and to be the first attacked for its harsh reception of a work. It also gave reviewers for the *Monthly* the advantage of perusing at least one critical opinion before formulating their own. Two of Goldsmith's reviews illustrate this point. The *Critical* reviewed Home's *Douglas* in March 1757; Goldsmith reviewed it in May. Though he might, indeed, have seen the tragedy himself and come to a judgment independently, his view did closely parallel the assessment of the *Critical* that the play had "a great deal of merit" but was deficient in "characters, sentiment, and diction."[32] Goldsmith also repeated the observation, made in the March issue of the *Critical* and also in the 15 March issue of the *Literary Magazine,* that Home's play did not merit Hume's comparison of it to the works of Shakespeare and Otway. Goldsmith's May 1757 review also relied extensively on comments made in the April 1757 *Critical:*

> There was a time, and that we believe, within most of our readers remembrance, when the *Spectator* and *Guardian* were held in such high estimation that a periodical paper of the same nature and on the same plan would have been looked on as a vain and fruitless attempt, or rather as a kind of literary treason against the universally acknowledg'd sovereignty of *Steele* and *Addison,* whose extraordinary and deserved success had intimidated every writer from striking into *their* paths, and of course turn'd the tide of genius into another channel.[33]

Goldsmith here borrowed from the *Critical* review the theme of the prohibitive genius of Addison and Steele that Colman and Thornton themselves articulated throughout the pages of the *Connoisseur.* Moreover, in placing in the *Connoisseur* in the "great tradition" of English periodicals, Goldsmith was almost certainly borrowing from the *Critical* reviewer.

Goldsmith's situation was reversed when he first contributed to the *Critical* in January 1759. His gently ironic review of Thomas Marriott's *Female Conduct* preceded by a month William Kenrick's harsh attack on the book for the *Monthly.* Similarly, and perhaps more directly pertinent to this "battle of the reviews," notice in the *Critical* of James Grainger's *A Poetical Translation of the Elegies of Tibullus* anticipated the *Monthly* notice, written by Griffiths himself, by one month. Thereby, the *Critical,* in a review much less hostile than Grainger's outraged response would indicate, fired the first shot in the open and acrimonious war between the two review journals.

Grainger, who had been on Griffiths' staff until May 1758, immediately issued a personal attack on the editor of the *Critical* in *A Letter to Tobias Smollett, M.D., Occasioned by His Criticism on a Late Translation of Tibullus, by Dr. Grainger* (January 1759). This pamphlet publicly identified Smollett for the first time as the editor of the *Critical* and accused him of being a "hack for hire." The attack came at a time when Smollett was enjoying a reputation as a successful historian. Advertisements throughout 1759 in the *Gazetteer* and in the *London Evening Post* ludicrously boasted of weekly sales of 10,000 copies of Smollett's *Compleat History.* (*Lloyd's Evening Post,* 20–22 January 1762, made the more modest claim that since 1758, 15,000 copies had been sold, "a Circumstance unknown in any other Age or Country.")[34] Grainger's exposure of Smollett's editorship of the *Critical,* a carefully guarded secret, threatened not only Smollett's reputation but the continued success of a venture much more profitable than the *Critical.*

In February the *Critical* responded venomously to Grainger's attack. The reviewer, perhaps Smollett himself, asked how Granger could have presumed Smollett's connection with the *Critical,* let alone his authorship of the Tibullus review. He also defended the idea of professional authorship, while identifying Grainger himself as a pen for hire:

> But the most astonishing circumstance of this charge, is, that it should be advanced by Dr. James Grainger, who, for many years, has been endeavoring in the darkest shade of obscurity to earn a subsistence by the same occupation . . . he has laboured, as an obscure hireling, in the Monthly Review, under the inspection and correction of an illiterate bookseller; who has often declared, that he (Grainger) had some learning and taste, but could not write a sentence of English. . . . The Critical Review is not written by a parcel of obscure hirelings, under the restraint of a bookseller and his wife, who presume to revise, alter, and amend the articles occasionally.[35]

If Grainger's "discovery" of Smollett was, indeed, mysterious, how Smollett learned of Grainger's work for Griffiths was no less a mystery. With only a few exceptions, reviewers' anonymity was carefully protected. William Rose's connection with the *Monthly* was apparently an "open secret;"[36] and in a letter of 12 April 1759, David Hume expressed confidence that his friend Adam Smith might be able to discover the author of a letter to the *Critical* concerning *The Epigoniad.*[37] Generally, though, if not for the later decoding of Griffiths' marked copies, posterity would have as little knowledge of the *Monthly* staff as it does of that of the *Critical.*

Grainger could previously have disclosed to Smollett his connection with the *Monthly.* They may have had at least a passing acquaintance in 1758.[38] However, if Grainger had told Smollett of his *Monthly* work, he would have made himself an obvious target for ridicule by attacking "hack writers." He would surely have anticipated Smollett's revelation. Could Goldsmith have been involved in these discoveries? He apparently began work for the *Critical* the same month the controversy began, and there is no evidence that any other former *Monthly* writers jumped to the *Critical* around this time. He had been stung by Kenrick's malevolent review of *Polite Learning* and by Griffiths' threats to imprison him for debt. He was well-acquainted with Grainger, who had introduced him to Percy in 1758.[39] Certainly Goldsmith could have provided Smollett with the inside information on the *Monthly* that the *Critical* revealed in its response to Grainger. And the observation about

Griffiths and his wife revising reviews was Goldsmith's principal memory of his work for the *Monthly,* as related in Percy's *Memoir.* Whether or not Goldsmith was involved in this round of the conflict between the reviews, the pervasive atmosphere of conflict provides a context which clarifies the initial stage of his journalistic career. Even if he was a relatively insignificant soldier in this "war," the conflict may have colored his perception of the reviewing profession. Goldsmith apparently concurred with John Brown's low opinion of the "two notorious Gangs of *monthly* and *critical* Book-thieves."[40]

The Battle of the Reviews, a mock epic in prose indebted to Swift's *Battle of the Books* (1704), gave a satiric account of the quarrel between journals and journalists. It vividly expressed the degree to which the dispute captivated London readers: "Parties were so strongly formed, that there was no going into a Coffeehouse in the Spirit of Peace or Neutrality, without being asked abruptly: 'Pray Sir, who are you for? Don't you think the *Monthly Review* has been damnably used? Was ever so large a Stock of Impudence collected in so small a Compass as in the *Critical*'s Declaration of War?' "[41] In his epic boast the author promised to "[trace] out a Path, untrodden" in an attempt "to convince the Literary World, and those connected with it, that Criticism is a Matter of too great Importance to be made a Trade of, or to serve Views purely lucrative, in either Author or Bookseller."[42] His first chapter established the book's tone; an extended simile compared authors to mushrooms, multiplying in the darkness of the London literary world and mostly putrefying in the poisonous air of contemporary criticism.

The author of *The Battle* makes a number of commonplace observations. He writes that books sell well only when their covers are neatly decorated, their pages gilt-edged, their printing decorative, and their title pages pompous.[43] (Indeed, advertisements in the dailies for books and magazines prominently mentioned illustrations, paper quality, and typeface, and reviewers often commented on a book's print quality—sometimes as its only redeeming feature.) He accuses reviewers for both journals of being biased and ill-qualified; and *Monthly* staff members are condemned for lavishing praises on the books Griffiths himself printed.[44] These half-truths have been effectively refuted by Benjamin Nangle; both editors attempted to avoid favoritism and prejudice.[45] The book also perpetuates a misconception that has not yet been effectively challenged: "A Piece makes its Appearance; the *Monthly Review* says positively that *it is white;* the *Critical,* that *it is black,* and *vice versa.*"[46] In fact, though their political differences and quarrels accentuated the contrasts between them, the review journals more frequently agreed in their assessments of new publications than they differed.[47]

The most frustrating task for modern readers of *The Battle* is satisfactory identification of its characters. Many of the pseudonyms are virtually impenetrable. Some of them are most likely fictional blends of several men. Griffiths appears as the ignorant hack "Rehoboam Gruffy," leader of the

Monthly. His only competition for leadership of the journal comes from John Cleland, "Squire *Mundungus,* the Author, of chaste Memory, of 'the Memoirs of a Lady of Pleasure,' who for the secret Services he had rendered the above Patron in forwarding many secret Editions of these Memoirs, had like to have the Preference."[48] "Sawney Mac Smallhead," the pseudonym referred to in the *Critical* notice of Grainger's pamphlet, is Smollett. The leader of the *Critical* ultimately emerged victorious in this mock war, in spite of his arrest for libel.[49]

Beyond these identifications, the satire adds little certain evidence to our knowledge of Goldsmith's contemporaries on the reviews. Still, it provides some context for the anomalous split in Goldsmith's early career. In the "Battle of the Reviews" he worked for both camps. The terms and strategies of that conflict had a great deal to do with his initial hiring and the progress of his career as a reviewer. And in the greater conflict between critics and defenders of the press, he appeared, at various times, on both sides of the debate.

A *Critical* Reviewer

In the summer of 1758 Goldsmith took lodgings at Green Arbour Court, located in the vicinity of the London publishers on Fleet Street and near the Temple Exchange Coffee House that he frequented.[50] During this period Goldsmith's literary companions included Grainger, who introducd him to Thomas Percy, and the publishers Robert and James Dodsley, who brought out his *Polite Learning* in April.[51] Another of his friends, Archibald Hamilton, who printed the *Critical Review,* probably introduced him to the principal editor of the journal late in the year. Tobias Smollett had begun the *Critical* in January 1756 as a direct challenge to Griffiths' journal. During his tenure as editor, which lasted until 1763, he solicited contributions from Thomas Francklin, a professor of Greek at Cambridge and the author of a celebrated translation of Sophocles (1759); Patrick Murdoch, known for his biography of James Thomson; and the poet John Armstrong. Johnson, Hume, the Scottish historian William Robertson, and David Mallet also contributed.[52]

Wardle claims that Goldsmith returned to reviewing "to tide himself over until his departure for India."[53] However, a letter of 13 January 1759 to his brother Henry implies that Goldsmith knew almost immediately after his interview with the East India Company that he had been rejected. He writes that he "met with no disappointment" in being rejected, though he also says, "[I] confess it gives me some pain to think I am almost beginning the world at the age of thrty [*sic*] one."[54] His work, as Wardle justifiably argues, began at this point to show a "growing sense of vocation."[55]

Uncertain attribution of contributions to the *Critical* has created an incomplete picture of Goldsmith's second position as a reviewer. Those reviews confidently attributed to him do suggest at least one conclusion: compared to his work for Griffiths, Goldsmith's assignments for the *Critical* were less diverse and more directly appropriate to his literary aspirations.[56] In his fourteen months as a regular contributor he established himself as the principal poetry critic for Smollett's journal. Though he did review material outside this area, he played a more narrowly defined role than he had on the *Monthly* staff. Unless attributors have vastly underestimated his contributions, he was also far less productive than he had been for Griffiths. As a *Monthly* reviewer he had resented the volume of work expected of him; contributing to the *Critical,* he was provided the freedom to work steadily on independent projects, including the *Bee* (October 1759).

Though most of his *Critical* work concerned minor poets, Goldsmith's reviews are valuable for their expression of his early poetic theory; they also involved him in a number of minor quarrels. In fact, he became embroiled in a literary controversy in his first month with the *Critical* (January 1759). His remarks on Thomas Marriott's *Female Conduct* began by commending the author for the "morality of his undertaking" (I, 147). He followed, however, with a sly satire on Marriott's "particular knack at concealing his wit" (I, 149).

In heroic couplets, Marriott delivered "an Essay on the Art of Pleasing, to be practiced by the Fair Sex, Before, and After Marriage." Goldsmith may have found "morality" in the poem's patriarchal assertions ("Hence ev'ry Wife her Husband must obey, / She, by Compliance, can her Ruler sway")[57] and its treatment of the romance conforms to Goldsmith's views.

> If, your first Innocence, you would retain
> Ah! read no book, that can your Fancy Stain;
> Read no romantic Tales, which Vice, array'd
> With Virtue's Habit, sports in Masquerade; . . .
> With Love ideal, they her Heart delude,
> And often transform her, to Coquet, or Prude . . .
> Romance is, to the Mind, a noxious Feast,
> Prepared by Art, to please a vicious Taste;[58]

In his preface, Marriott claims to have delayed release of his work, "having a secret Fear of the Annoyance, and ill Treatment, it [would] very probably receive from those malignant Critics, who live, in a Kind of piratical War, and avowed Enmity, with Advent'rous Poets."[59] In fact, he quite accurately anticipated the scorn with which his poem was met, and he retaliated with a long defense of *Female Conduct* and an attack on his reviewers. In the Monthly

Catalogue for July, Goldsmith met the challenge with uncharacteristic vitriol:

> A few months ago a poem entitled *Female Conduct* came from the press, published in the usual manner, without one single mark of the author's importance, and we in our usual manner found something in it to praise, and something to reprove. At this time we knew very little of Mr. Mariot, and, in the sincerity of our hearts, wished his dull, well-meaning efforts success. (I, 186)

He continued with a bitingly ironic apology to the poet, quoted one of the offensive passages, and praised in mock-heroic tones the "champion" the evidence had to deal with: "What strength of thought and diction, and what a flow of poetry are here!" (I, 188). His second review for the January issue was of a translation of Ovid's *Epistles,* and was written in the same vein, attacking the translator's "absurdities" and general ineptitude (I, 152–62).

Goldsmith reviewed a third classical adaptation, John Langhorne's *The Death of Adonis,* in March. Langhorne, already a well-established poet, began a seventeen-year tenure on the *Monthly* staff two years later.[60] In his notice Goldsmith complained that his contemporaries were incapable of writing true elegies; he declared Langhorne's work passionless, but "very elegant, and tolerably correct" (I, 167). In April he reviewed the work of a former contributor to the *Monthly,* John Ward.[61] Dismissing Ward's *A System of Oratory* as tedious, Goldsmith demonstrated his objectivity as a reviewer (I, 167). Ward, professor of rhetoric at Gresham College and vice-president of the Royal Society, had recently died, and Robert Dodsley, the publisher of *Polite Learning,* advertised Ward's book extensively in the March 1759 issues of the *Gazetteer and London Daily Advertiser.* Dodsley also sold an auction catalogue for Ward's collection of books; nevertheless, Goldsmith was unsparing in his criticism of Ward's *Oratory,* even at Dodsley's expense.

The most prominent author Goldsmith reviewed for the *Critical* was Arthur Murphy, playwright and contributor to the *Literary Magazine* and the *London Chronicle.* Murphy's tragedy *The Orphan of China* had opened 21 April 1759 at Drury Lane, with Goldsmith apparently in attendance. Its nine performances, the last on May 12, earned Murphy public acclaim and £231 from the play's three benefit nights.[62] Goldsmith closely followed John Brown's complaints about the public's "perverse" fascination for the Oriental, and then, typically, enumerated the tragedy's "faults" and "beauties."[63] He described the obvious pleasure of its opening-night audience and praised the work's poetic virtues: its "nervous sentiment" and "glowing imagery"; but he also argued that "the pathos begins without a proper preparation of incident" (I, 170–79).

With this review Goldsmith again found himself on the periphery of a literary controversy. Thomas Francklin, a fellow contributor to the *Critical,* renewed a long-standing feud with Murphy by ridiculing the tragedy to its author's face. The ensuing quarrel produced Francklin's *Dissertation on Ancient Tragedy* (1760), which included a personal attack on Murphy, and Murphy's *A Poetical Epistle to Samuel Johnson* (1760), a satire partly directed at Francklin.[64] Ultimately, despite reservations about the tragedy, Goldsmith sided with Murphy, who later contributed prologues and epilogues to Goldsmith's comedies.

Goldsmith continued his predominantly hostile reviewing in the June and July issues of the *Critical*. He disapproved of a translation of Jean Henri Samuel Formey's *Philosophical Miscellanies* (I, 180–83) and a "dry" travel narrative (I, 183–85). For the July issue, in addition to his rejoinder to Marriott, he argued against the need for Thomas Coxeter's edition of *The Dramatic Works of Philip Massinger* and cited his preference for Dodsley's earlier selected edition (I, 190). Though in this instance catering to his bookseller, Goldsmith rejected another of Dodsley's publications, *The Works of Mr. William Hawkins* (I, 198–205). Once again the review drew a published defense: a pamphlet published by "an impartial Reader," who, as Goldsmith mockingly observed, was Hawkins himself. In March of the following year, Goldsmith responded to this self-congratulatory epistle with the same tone he had used initially in his review of *The Works:* "But we, alas! cannot speak of Mr. H. with the same unrestrained share of panegyric that he does of himself" (I, 225).

Goldsmith's first journalistic opportunity away from reviewing came in September 1759, when he arranged with the publisher John Wilkie to work as editor, compiler, and main contributor to a new weekly essay-periodical, the *Bee*. Turning attention to his new venture, he contributed little else to Smollett's review. He praised an edition of Samuel Butler's work in the September issue and further expounded on his own theory of wit and satire (I, 206–12). Concluding his regular contributions to the *Critical* in March 1760, he reviewed *An Epistle to the Right Hon. Philip Earl of Chesterfield. To which is added . . . An Eclogue* by Irishman William Dunkin, who had been a classmate of Goldsmith's at Trinity College (I, 231n).

This review of Dunkin's work deserves careful attention. It is notable for its reiteration of Goldsmith's disregard for "academic" poetry; for its response to Dunkin's satirical attack on Grub Street; for the fact that Griffiths published the London edition of the work; and, finally, for possible biographical implications in Goldsmith's treatment of "Irishness." Goldsmith correctly remarks that the book "appears at once excessively merry, and extremely sorrowful" (I, 228). Prompted by "the Prince of Printers, Archibibliopolist, Intelligencer General, and General Advertiser of the Kingdom of Ireland," the *Epistle* satirizes the publishing industry;[65] the *Eclogue* is a solemn tribute to Irish poetry. Dunkin's satirical treatment of the state of authorship anticipates comments Goldsmith would make throughout his journalistic career. Dunkin writes: "Ministers of State, and Masters of the Literary Mint should treat their Authors, as the grand Monarch doth his Noblesse, that is, puff them up with pompous Titles, but at the same Time keep them poor in order to render them dependent."[66] Critics are "Witlings and Word-Catchers, who from damned Poetry have turned their Heads to foul Criticism, as Folks convert their Cast Coach-Horses to Dung-Carts."[67] He concludes his attack with poignant understatement: "For, although Poets may take great Licences, yet alas! *Grub-Street* is no Place of Privilege."[68]

Here, Goldsmith faced two problems: reviewing a work published by Smollett's rival and commenting on the poetry of a fellow Irishman, one he admitted was "author of many pretty poetical pieces" (I, 230). His solution was to adapt a gentlemanly and somewhat pedantic persona, and to conclude with the sort of "foreign traveller" anecdote that became so pervasive a feature of his journalistic work. Chiding Dunkin for the "affectation" of his poetry and his "indifferent prose," Goldsmith reacted with possibly unwarranted coldness toward his fellow countryman and toward a Griffiths publication.

More startling, however, in light of his own circumstances, is Goldsmith's apparent presumption in preaching to an Irish "inferior":

> The man who is bred at a distance from the centre of learning and politeness, must have a great degree of modesty or understanding, who does not give a loose to some vanities which are apt to render him ridiculous every where but at home. Bred among men of talents inferior to himself, he is too apt to assume the lead, as well from the press as in conversation, and to over-rate his own abilities. His oddities among his friends are only regarded as the excrescences of a superior genius; among those who live beyond the sphere of his importance, they are considered as instances of folly or ignorance. (I, 231)

In light of later slights by Boswell, Thrale-Piozzi, Reynolds, and others of Goldsmith's contemporaries who remembered the author's "oddities" at the expense of his "genius," these comments might allude to the difficulty he himself faced as an outsider, suffering ridicule by his "superiors" in London, attempting with obvious awkwardness to "shine" in social situations, and underestimating the obstacles to fame.[69]

The review concludes with a dialogue between "a traveller" and a Spanish scholar, the latter extolling the virtues of two poets who are "the eye" and "the heart" of the university. The traveler, who for Goldsmith would become a recurring voice of objective distance and common sense, asks what *"the public, I mean those who are out of the university"* think of the poets. The scholar responds: "The public are a parcel of blockheads, and all blockheads are critics, and all critics are spiders, and spiders are a set of reptiles that all the world despises" (I, 232).[70] As he had in his reviews of Wilkie and Gray, Goldsmith mocks the elitist tendencies of the poetry approved of by the academy, and he calls for a poetry with popular appeal, disengaged from the formal strictures and intellectual obscurity that he felt damned the verse of many of his contemporaries. The simplicity and enduring popularity of his own verse seems to confirm the sincerity of his position.

With the exception of his review of Brookes's *Natural History* (1763), Goldsmith concluded his reviewing career with these remarks on Dunkin's *Epistle*. Ironically, the retort of the Spanish scholar echoed Goldsmith's statements in *Polite Learning* that critics are "reptiles" whose "trade is a bad one, and they are bad workmen in the trade" (I, 290). "Writing for bread," he had argued, dulls the imagination, prevents the spread of reputation, and "turns the ambition of every author at last into avarice" (*Polite Learning;* I, 316). Nevertheless, his public "gentlemanly" disdain for the profession was not entirely consistent, and reviewing had provided him with an entrée into London's literary world and some relief from his financial woes.

Further, it had helped him establish a base from which to launch a career as an essayist, novelist, and poet. Not only had he made important connections in "The Trade," but he had had the opportunity to form theoretical approaches—many of them still half-formed and often contradictory—toward fiction, poetry, and satire, the genres in which he would work. He had taken advantage of his self-professed expertise in European letters to begin constructing a "foreign correspondent" persona, one he would later adopt in his most successful essays. In preparation for his work as a "compiler," a defining element of journalistic work, he was exposed to the pageant of literary works before the public eye, much of which he adopted for his own purposes. While the quantity of his reviewing work was fairly slight and his comments those of an apprentice who naturally lacked the maturity and scope of a Johnson, for example, Goldsmith's reviewing career tells us a great deal about his early development as an author and about the publishing industry to which he trusted his hopes for fame.

5

The "Weekly Historian"

When a Man has engag'd to keep a Stage-Coach, he is oblig'd, whether he has Passengers or not, to set out: Thus it fares with us Weekly Historians; by indeed, for my Particular, I hope I shall soon have little more to do in this Work, than to Publish what is sent me from such as have Leisure and Capacity for giving Delight, and being pleas'd in an elegant Manner.

—*Tatler* No. 12, 7 May 1709

Having established himself as a "true critic" for both of London's leading review journals, and having convinced the Dodsleys—if not the public—of his expertise in the state of European learning, Goldsmith exuded confidence in his first attempt at editing and writing his own magazine. Behind his humble appeal to the "terrible tribunal" of public opinion with which he began the *Bee* was a resolve to make himself a worthy successor to the great periodical essayists who had preceded him (I, 353). Three weeks later, his resolve seemed shaken; his introductory essay to Number IV bitterly complained about the *Bee's* poor reception. Considering possible reasons for the failure of his enterprise, he dismissed the suggestion that his title was to blame (I, 419). In fact, the anachronistic title and Addisonian tone may have been responsible: the public, in 1759, was rejecting attempts to revive the spirit of the *Spectator.*

More to its liking were the sorts of timely, satiric pieces he wrote for several of London's magazines and newspapers. Maintaining his genial tone and relying on observations he had made in his European travels, Goldsmith modified the "foreign correspondent" voice that Griffiths had first conceived for him. As "Citizen of the World," he won his first measure of acclaim and found steady employment under the auspices of booksellers like John Newbery. He withdrew from periodical work as his fame spread, especially with the publication of *The Traveller* in 1764. Borrowing heavily from his essays, Goldsmith reformulated his correspondent persona in heroic couplets. In his fictional capacity as "Citizen of the World" and cultural outsider, he gave his "comparative view of races and nations," as he did for the *Royal Magazine* (III, 66–86).

A Journalist's "Literary Loneliness"

When he launched his career as essayist and columnist for London magazines and newspapers in 1759, Goldsmith faced two central problems:
designing an appealing journalistic persona and creating an audience appropriate to that persona. These tasks were complicated by the development of
the bookseller as the dominant force in English letters and by the changing
demands of the reading public. When Thornton and Colman created the
Connoisseur and Johnson his *Rambler,* their challenge was to emerge stylis-
tically and thematically from the shadow cast by Addison and Steele, who
had been figures as imposing for periodical writers as Milton and Pope had
been for poets. Three years after the outbreak of the Seven Years' War, the
journalist's challenge was to cater to a public uninterested in the "essay-
periodical," as Spector calls it, and hungry for foreign news and political
commentary. The periodical writer could no longer content himself with a
posture of philosophical distance and gentlemanly ease; he had to reconcile
himself to a changing readership, to the booksellers' constant demand for
copy, and to the gradual demise of the fiction that the author was an
independent gentleman.

In spite of the efforts of Ralph and others to legitimize authorship as a
profession, and in spite of the popularity and wide distribution of London
magazines and newspapers, the periodical writer was forced to live with the
anonymity of his undertaking. In the absence of bylines and mastheads, the
contributor's identity was almost always subsumed under the ubiquitous
phrase "By Several Hands." John Sitter identifies a phenomenological construct he calls "literary loneliness," the "particular consciousness mid-eighteenth-century authors had of themselves as solitary writers for solitary
readers."[1] He shows how this conception manifested itself in the "easy" style
of authors such as David Hume, which dramatized the "private relationship"
between author and reader.[2] Goldsmith brought this same authorial ideal to
his first periodical performance, the *Bee.* An anonymous, gentlemanly persona wrote for the private entertainment of a "fit audience though few." Alvin
Kernan is partly correct when he observes: "The old image of the gentleman-
poet died hard, and even Oliver Goldsmith, along with Johnson probably the
greatest of the Grub Street hacks, tried to live out this role, often with results
more comic than tragic."[3] At the beginning of his career Goldsmith relied on
this old image to achieve literary recognition. But he learned from the failure
of the *Bee,* which was in part a nostalgic protest against "labourers in the
Magazine trade" (I, 353) and their "vulgar" readers (I, 417). The disdain he
had shown for coffeehouse readers and Grub Street hacks in *Polite Learning*
and in the *Bee* gradually diminished in his later periodical writing. And he
discovered various authorial roles, especially that of the "foreign correspondent," which would more fully accommodate the interests of his public.

When Kernan refers to the "comic results" of Goldsmith's maintaining the gentleman-author fiction, he is indicating the awkward public image that resulted. Boswell defined it as that of a clown dressed in multicolored finery attempting *ad absurdum* to impress his peers with his gentlemanly breeding. For readers of Goldsmith's journalism, however, the more significant result is the omnipresent, self-conscious examination of the profession, the unavoidable tension created by the author's expressed contempt for a profession in which he hoped to achieve fame. Mimicking the conservative rhetoric of his age, he longed for a return to a moribund system of literary patronage and decried the mechanization and vulgarization of the "magazine trade." And yet as an ethnic "outsider" with no political connections, his only hopes for success as an author lay with booksellers and the public—for better or worse, the new patrons of literature.

Goldsmith himself suggests the reason for his adoption of the gentlemanly persona in two of his Chinese Letters. In Letter XCIII, he writes: "All seem convinced, that a book written by vulgar hands, can neither instruct nor improve; none but Kings, Chams, and Mandarins, can write with any probability of success" (II, 376). This perceived bias on the part of his readers may be responsible for a persistent tension in Goldsmith's journalism between his self-declaration as gentleman-scholar at leisure, independent and aloof from the mercenary concerns and limitations of the tribe of hacks defacing English letters, and a vox populi decrying academic snobbery, satirizing the "great," and advocating the common sense of the masses.

Letter LVII describes the undeserved literary sway of the rich, dazzling readers with their empty pretensions and "brow beating them by their authority" (II, 236). The narrator praises the "good sense" of the English people, but expresses disappointment at their willingness to be led mindlessly by the nobility, who validate a work simply by signing its title page. The system of commercial publication and anonymous authorship provides an opening for talented writers, regardless of their social status; and yet any hint of an author's "low" station proves disastrous: "As soon as a piece therefore is published, the first questions are, Who is the author? Does he keep a coach? Where lies his estate? What sort of a table does he keep? If he happens to be poor and unqualified for such a scrutiny, he and his works sink into irremediable obscurity" (II, 238). To the extent he is able, then, an author such as Goldsmith must conceal his poverty behind a mask of privilege, risking ridicule if his actual circumstances are revealed. Such a system, Goldsmith suggests, reinforces authorial obscurity and handicaps those with more talent and ambition than means.

Another related problem Goldsmith faced in beginning a journalistic career in the late 1750s was the public preoccupation with the Seven Years' War. Spector demonstrates the extent to which the war drastically changed the nature of journalism. Essay-journals such as the *World* and the *Connoisseur*, both important influences on Goldsmith's initial conception of periodical writing, failed to survive the first year of the war. Readers preferred political journals such as the *Test, Con-Test, Monitor, Briton,* and *North Briton* to the less ephemeral, wide-ranging social and philosophical commentaries of the early 1750s.[4] Spector claims rightly that "the chief subject . . . for almost all the periodicals was the war itself, which, in these early years from 1756–1760, provided incidents and issues that commanded public attention."[5] This analysis of a press dominated by foreign affairs provides an important frame through which to view the beginning of Goldsmith's career in London's magazines and newspapers.

How could Goldsmith, whose essays and columns satirized the politicization of the press and coffeehouse readers' obsession with foreign news, effectively compete with London's successful political journalists? His first abortive attempts, the *Bee* and the *Busy Body,* clearly failed to do so. Spector's claim that these two journals were the only nonpolitical essay-periodicals attempted during the war is exaggerated—the *British Magazine* is an obvious exception.[6] But the rarity of such attempts indicates the difficulty Goldsmith faced in trying to establish himself as an essayist. Responding to this trend, contemporaries such as Johnson, Hawkesworth, Murphy, and Smollett all became more blatantly political in their periodical writing.

Goldsmith, however, was either less interested or less knowledgeable about the inner workings of party politics, though he certainly recognized the public appeal of political topics. His initial response was to cast himself as the standard-bearer for the *Spectator,* writing for the ages rather than for the masses. Explaining the poor public reception of the *Bee* he wrote:

> From these considerations I was once determined to throw off all connexions with taste, and fairly address my countrymen in the same engaging style and manner with other periodical pamphlets, much more in vogue than probably mine shall ever be. To effect this, I had thought of changing the title into that of the ROYAL BEE, the ANTI-GALLICAN BEE, or the BEE's MAGAZINE. I had laid in a proper stock of popular topics, such as encomiums on the king of Prussia, invectives against the queen of Hungary and the French, the necessity of a militia, our undoubted sovereignty of the seas, reflections upon the present state of affairs, a dissertation upon liberty. . . . All this, together with four extraordinary pages of *letter press,* a beautiful map of England, and two prints curiously coloured from nature, I fancied might touch their very souls. (I, 418)

As this early example shows, one method he found for appealing to public taste was to satirize it. Such protests against a public fixation on politics and foreign affairs were themselves timely and much in vogue. An equally common satirical object was the ornamentation of magazines. A new printing style, attractive paper, and new maps and engravings were advertised prominently by the publishers of the *Literary, London,* and *Gentleman's,* for example, throughout this period. What better way to attract the notice of readers in private clubs and coffeehouses than to call attention to the periodicals that furnished them with entertainment?

But Goldsmith, in his later essays, dealt more directly with the topics he satirized in the *Bee*. Complete defiance of popular trends and topics would have meant sure failure, and he was forced to compromise. Throughout the remainder of his journalistic career he maintained satirical disdain for the "English passion for politics" (*Citizen*, II, 31) while simultaneously addressing the issues most concerning his readers. Goldsmith was certainly not the apolitical essayist some critics have believed him to be. Nor did he remain completely aloof from the ephemeral issues of his day. Instead, he successfully drew upon his own experiences as a European traveler and as "foreign correspondent" for the *Monthly*, to create an appealing persona that accommodated changing public tastes.

One of the by-products of the war was a national insecurity, inflamed politically by the defeat at Minorca and literarily by the jeremiads of Brown and others. These phenomena engendered the "reflections upon the present state of affairs" and "dissertations upon liberty" that Goldsmith satirized but nonetheless made staples of his journalism. This insecurity also created an appetite for national introspectiveness that Goldsmith fed with the method perhaps most dominant in his journalism: cultural and political comparisons between England and the other nations of the world. In the "foreign correspondent" Goldsmith created a characteristic voice: a learned and neutral observer elevating himself above partisan debate while still satisfying the penchant of his readers for foreign news, cross-cultural comparisons, and critiques of the "present state of affairs" in England.

In the Great Tradition

Before establishing his foreign correspondent persona in its varied incarnations, Goldsmith attempted to assume the weighty mantle of the "great tradition" of the English essayists. Like the authors of the *Connoisseur*, Goldsmith began his journalistic career paying homage to his famous predecessors in the art of periodical satire—and by implication placing himself in that tradition. He considered Isaac Bickerstaff, the fictional creation of Swift and Steele, to be the perfect blend of "solidity" and "good humour" (I, 14). Swift, "that lover yet derider of human nature," as Goldsmith called him (III, 36), and the author of the *Tatler* were honored with places in Goldsmith's "fame machine." First place in the "machine," however, was Addison's. Addison and his *Spectator* furnished an important source for essay ideas. Goldsmith's "A Description of Various Clubs" (III, 6–21), for example, was largely derived from "The Hum-Drum Club" in the *Spectator* (No. 9, 10

March 1711). And he freely alludes to the *Spectator* in other essays, in *The Vicar* (IV, 167), and in *She Stoops to Conquer* (V, 159). But equally important for Goldsmith and many of his contemporaries, Addison's periodical work loomed as an unreachable ideal, to which almost all subsequent attempts had to be compared unfavorably. The writer of a three-part biographical tribute in the *British Magazine,* "The Life of the Right Hon. Joseph Addison, Esq.," described him as the apotheosis of the virtuous Englishman: "His genius was immortal, his performances equally perfect; nothing puerile in the most early, nothing below his genius in the last. . . . He was a pattern for our imitation; in a word, a sincere Christian."[7]

When Goldsmith bemoaned the failure of the *Bee,* he compared its reception to that of the *Spectator:*

> The Spectator, and many succeeding essayists, frequently inform us of the numerous compliments paid them in the course of their lucubrations; of the frequent encouragements they met to inspire them with ardour, and increase their eagerness to please. I have received *my letters* as well as they; but alas! not congratulatory ones; not assuring me of success and favour; but pregnant with bodings that might shake even fortitude itself. (I, 419)

Addison's success presented a barrier to anyone attempting to follow in his path. Given the range of his subject matter and the gracefulness of his style, how could any of his successors hope to measure up? Goldsmith credited him, along with Dryden and Pope, with "improv[ing] and harmoniz[ing]" the English language to such a degree that the efforts of his successors have been obscured (III, 423). When Goldsmith, in his preface to Wiseman's *Grammar,* recommended works "to delight and rectify the growing mind," he mentioned the *Spectator* prominently (V, 311).

What made the *Spectator* worthy of recommendation was its harmony of plain style, good humor, and morality. This link between virtue and purity of language became an essential tenet in Goldsmith's philosophy of composition. In the *Spectator* he found examples of stylistic ease and genial satire, the most frequently identified characteristics of his own writing. In his first attempts at essay writing in the *Bee* and the *Busy Body,* Goldsmith emulated the style and content of the *Spectator.* These periodicals allowed him to practice the stylistic simplicity and light social satire he had found so appealing in the *Spectator.* But the quick demise of these journals forced him to experiment with new methods and voices that would appeal to a High Georgian readership.

A second and almost equally influential predecessor was Samuel Johnson. So much has been written about the social relationship between "Doctor Major" and "Doctor Minor" that critics have overlooked Goldsmith's awareness of Johnson's journalistic presence well before they actually met. If

Percy's remembrance of the initial meeting between Johnson and Goldsmith on 31 May 1761 is accurate, Goldsmith commented favorably on Johnson's periodical work eighteen months before first encountering his mentor.[8] In the *Bee* essay "A Resverie" [*sic*] (3 November 1759) Johnson is admitted to the coach of fame by virtue of his authorship of the *Rambler.* Goldsmith's first portrait of his later mentor is not entirely flattering: in the narrative, Johnson is enraged because his *Dictionary* will not be sufficient grounds for literary immortality, and he refers to his own periodical as "a mere trifle" (I, 447). The coachman, however, favorably compares the *Rambler* to the *Spectator,* even though Johnson's essays "by being refined, sometimes become minute" (I, 448).

In Goldsmith's opinion, Johnson's essays are not as amusing as those in the *Spectator* papers or in the *Connoisseur,* but they express as well or better than any other contemporary works the moral character of their author. In Chinese Letter XL for the *Public Ledger* (26 May 1760), Lien Chi Altangi witnesses the "decadent" state of English poetry, but acknowledges two "poets in disguise": Johnson and Smollett. Imbued with "strength of soul, sublimity of sentiment, and grandeur of expression," they channeled their talents into media other than poetry: "for aught I know they never made a single verse in their whole lives" (II, 171). For Goldsmith, like much of the English reading public, Johnson had become nearly synonymous with the *Rambler.* Clifford notes that "the title became firmly attached to Johnson, and many people referred to him as 'The Rambler,' or as 'Rambling Sam.' "[9] For this specific project, his future protégé accorded Johnson a first place among his contemporary authors. Goldsmith's "Fountain of Fine Sense" essay for the *British* (May 1760) placed Johnson, along with Gray and William Mason, with those writers capable of "conveying strong sense in the wildest sallies of poetical enthusiasm" (III, 117).

Goldsmith considered the Johnsonian persona, as developed in the *Rambler,* to be the epitome of morality and intellectual expansiveness.[10] As a worthy successor to the *Spectator,* the *Rambler* was among those works best suited to educate young people—a principal responsibility, Goldsmith insisted, for any author.[11] The problem, however, for any would-be follower of the *Spectator* and *Rambler* tradition was twofold: how to establish a reputation in the shadow of such giants as Addison and Johnson, and how to overcome the barriers to achievement erected by a corrupt "anarchy of letters."

The "Fame Machine" essay is, on one level, an allegorical account of Goldsmith's frustrated attempts to establish himself as a writer. Johnson is considered by him one of those few to have successfully overcome these impediments:

> Yet, notwithstanding the republic of letters hangs at present so feebly together; though those friendships which once promoted literary fame seem now to be

discontinued; though every writer who now draws the quill seems to aim at profit, as well as applause, many among them are probably laying in stores for immortality, and are provided with a sufficient stock of reputation to last the whole journey. (I, 444)

Lacking the advantages of some of his precursors, the author of the *Bee* could only ride "mounted behind, in order to hear the conversation on the way" (I, 450). The *Bee,* then, was in Goldsmith's view a worthy if yet-unrecognized successor to the *Spectator* and the *Rambler,* upholding the tradition of the moral, speculative gentleman-author in an age that rewarded mediocrity (*Bee,* "The Characteristics of Greatness," I, 428–30). The ultimate failure of his periodical was proof, in his view, of the decadent state of English letters.

The *Bee:* Goldsmith's "Pretensions to Lawful Inheritance"

Goldsmith the journalist is probably best known for his weekly periodical the *Bee,* first published by John Wilkie on Saturday, 6 October 1759. Critics have cited the essays, tales, poems, and reviews in the *Bee* as the first fruits of Goldsmith's maturation as an "original" writer. Equally important for a periodical editor, however, was his skill as a "compiler," translating and adapting from previous sources (usually unacknowledged), then synthesizing and framing his material coherently to suit the editor's purposes. Of the forty-two pieces appearing in the eight numbers of the weekly (6 October to 24 November 1759), at least twenty-two are more accurately described as compilations than as original essays. For this process Goldsmith found French sources especially useful, but he also borrowed heavily from his own *Polite Learning* and from his reviews. The image he presented of himself as an "unexperienced writer" in his introduction to the series is misleading (I, 353). He had, by this time, established the foundation for much of his subsequent work as a critic, essayist, and fiction writer, and his *Bee* should not be seen as an unanticipated expression of his talents.

The idea of originality as an inherent virtue among authors was not a commonplace for Goldsmith's contemporaries. Edward Young was certainly not reiterating a widely held notion when he linked originality and genius in his *Conjectures on Original Composition* (1759).[12] To condemn the *Bee,* as some critics have done, for its lack of originality is to apply a standard of achievement that is inappropriate to the function of a periodical "compiler."[13] James Kuist points out that the term *magazine* as originally conceived by Edward Cave, the founder of the *Gentleman's Magazine,* suggested a "storehouse of articles kept for the common good" and included "digests of well-received articles from other publications and an assortment of public information."[14] William Cooke, who was acquainted with many of the prominent journalists of the 1760s, reflected on an editor's responsibility to assemble "extracts from [the] best modern publications—sketches from history—theatrical criticisms—moral or humourous essays—poetry, &c. It was the first qualification of an Editor then to be able to execute this business in a creditable manner."[15]

Not recognizing that adaptation, acknowledged or not, was part of the normal "compiling" function of an editor, Wardle asks how he could have justified such practice and concludes that Goldsmith considered the *Bee* "pure hackwork."[16] Evidence from the *Bee* itself suggests otherwise: in his introduction to Number IV, the editor is stung by the relative failure of his work, and his tone is highly indignant (I, 415–20). Pleading entrance to the "Fame Machine" in his narrative "A Resverie" [*sic*], Goldsmith carries only a copy of the *Bee,* of which the driver has never heard. While the coachman does not allow him a seat beside Johnson, Hume, and Smollett, Goldsmith at least rides along behind. He retains the aspirations to literary fame he made manifest in his early letters; he fully expected to be honored by posterity. The *Bee,* at least initially, was intended as much more than hack work; it was perhaps designed to help its author earn a place behind Johnson and his *Rambler.*

Goldsmith's introduction to the first issue continued his satiric assault on the book trade, but also defined the author and his intended audience. The genteel reader that Goldsmith imagined was one who had been disappointed by the grandiose claims of other magazine writers and booksellers; Goldsmith promised him an elegant fund of wit to cheer his retirement. Assuring his readers that he was untainted by the arrogance of professional journalism, the author vowed unresting devotion to good taste and amusement.[17]

The *Bee* promised to follow no strict organizational plan, and indeed it did not. However, some sort of generic pattern, though inconsistent, can be discerned. The first three issues featured most of the genres with which magazine readers would have been familiar: light verse, literary and theatrical criticism, translations, analyses of foreign culture, didactic fiction, and short treatises on morals. The next three numbers were somewhat less generically diverse; the seventh contained little that was original; and the eighth, four pages shorter than the others, represented the greatest departure from his initial conception.

Perhaps the most frequently anthologized piece in the series is "A Resverie." Goldsmith prefaced this "Fame Machine" dream narrative with an attack on those critics who "blot reputations" (I, 444). The narrator of the dream first learns that Addison, Swift, Pope, Steele, Congreve, and Colley Cibber have already made their passage on the imaginary coach—Cibber, en route, giving Pope a black eye. The coachman, while denying Goldsmith a seat, lets him "ride a while for charity" (I, 445). John Hill, an actor and periodical writer, is denied entrance, and so apparently is Arthur Murphy.

Friedman acknowledges some doubt about identifying Murphy in the narrative; his character is described only as the author of "some farces, a tragedy, and other miscellany productions" (I, 447n). However, Goldsmith plants at least three verbal clues, echoes from his review of *The Orphan of China,* which make the attribution almost certain: Murphy's overuse of the word "virtue," a flaw noted in the review, is satirized in the narrative; the coachman's advice to "follow nature" is identical to Goldsmith's in the review; and the coachman "hope[s] in time he might aspire to one [a seat in the Fame Machine,]" a conclusion almost identical to the one the review had reached.

In the tale Samuel Johnson offers his *Dictionary* as proof of his deserved place, but is at first denied, until the coachman learns he is the author of the *Rambler.* David Hume, similarly, is rejected for *An Enquiry Concerning Human Understanding:* "Right or wrong (said the coachman) he who disturbs religion, is a blockhead" (I, 448). He is, however, accepted as a historian. Although still his employee at the *Critical,* Goldsmith did not shy from criticizing Smollett. In the dream he is rejected as a historian on grounds Goldsmith had enumerated in his *Monthly* article on Smollett's history; Smollett is accepted, however, as a romance writer. Here, Goldsmith offers one of his few conciliatory remarks on this genre: "a well-written romance is no such easy task as is generally imagined" (I, 449), and he cites his admiration for Cervantes, one of the few universally accepted pillars of respectability as a fiction writer.

While Goldsmith's reviewing assignments seldom included the theatre, his four theatrical reviews for the *Bee* provide theatre historians with vivid, concrete details on the nature of dramatic performances at Drury Lane, Covent Garden, and the King's Theatre in the Haymarket. For example, he deplored the common practice in tragedies of stagehands' laying down carpets immediately before a death scene to prevent the soiling of the performer's costume—a practice which made the imminent death obvious to the audience (I, 362). He berated stage extras and leading ladies such as Mrs. Cibber for dropping out of character by "ogling the boxes" or curtseying to acknowledge applause in the middle of a scene (I, 390). He also provided, in minute detail, patterns of gesture for actors in a number of contemporary performances, such as a Drury Lane production of Fielding's *Mock-Doctor* (I, 360–61). If he had one central dramatic thesis, it may be the following observation, consistent with his comments on other art forms: "From a conformity to critic[al] rules, which, perhaps, on the whole, have done more harm than good, our author has sacrificed all the vivacity of the dialogue to nature" (I, 450–51).

His "A City Night-Piece," a meditative prose poem, was highly uncharacteristic of his periodical work. It was as ambiguously and self-consciously poetic as Goldsmith ever appeared in his early writing. He adopted the tone of Young's *Night-Thoughts,* frequently ranked by Goldsmith's contemporaries as one of the best poems by a living author.[18] In "A City Night-Piece" a solitary night-wanderer reveals a heightened sensitivity to despair and gloomily rejects the hypocrisy of his age. The piece is, in part, an open-ended exercise in the poetic sublime and, in part, hazy social criticism. The author evidently thought enough of the work to include a later version in *The Citizen of the World* (II, 452–54).

The bitterness of Goldsmith's introduction to Number V foretold the quick demise of the *Bee,* and the last two numbers betrayed the editor's flagging hopes for his project. The fact that Goldsmith chose nothing from the last two numbers for his *Essays by Mr. Goldsmith* (1765) may be his own admission of their inferiority. Biographers speculate that the project had exhausted the author; however, we have very few letters and little reliable testimony during this period to support that claim. In addition to editing the *Bee,* he had also been contributing to the *Busy Body* in October and November, and he was probably continuing work on his Chinese Letters. However, his productivity by no mean diminished after the demise of his periodical. More likely, by the end of November, he decided that further production of the *Bee* would prove unprofitable, so he directed his talents toward producing light satire for a variety of essay-periodicals.

Perhaps the best explanation for the commercial failure of the *Bee* is suggested by Robert D. Spector in his article on the function of the persona in the *Connoisseur.* "At mid-century with the outbreak of the Seven Years' War," Spector says, "it proved fatal to have personae suggestive of frivolity or levity."[19] He lists "Mary Singleton" of the *Old Maid* (1756) and "Nicholas Babble, Esq." of the *Prater* (1756) as examples of personae that failed to attract an audience interested in politics and foreign affairs. Indeed, critics treated the *Prater* even more roughly than the *Bee.* The *Monthly* for May 1757 curtly dismissed the periodical, remarking: "We have one thing to say in behalf of Sir *Nicholas Babble* . . . that his assumed name and title page are truly expressive of the character and contents of all the rest of the performance."[20] In the first number of his *Idler,* Johnson alluded to the difficulty his fellow periodical writers faced in choosing an appropriate name:

> Those who attempt periodical essays seem to be often stopped in the beginning, by the difficulty of finding a proper title. Two writers, since the time of the Spectator, have assumed his name, without any pretensions to lawful inheritance; an effort was once made to revive the *Tatler;* and the strange appellations, by which other papers have been called, show that the authors were distressed, like the natives of America, who came to the Europeans to beg a name.[21]

Goldsmith's choice of a title was not unlike that of the *Tatler Revived* (1750), to which Johnson might be alluding; the "Bee" was a well-worn persona, used by Eustace Budgell in 1733 and repeated in the *Bee Revived* (1750).[22]

Attempting to follow in the footsteps of the *Rambler,* he found that the rules for success had changed: the single-author periodical with a fictitious persona that had served Johnson so well was moribund in 1759. George S. Marr might have added the *Bee* to "that class of paper which was really a light sermon"—a group that included the *Connoisseur,* the *World,* and the *Rambler.* As Marr says, "The tendency now was (in entire opposition to the *Rambler*) to drop papers of that nature entirely and write directly for amusement by describing new fashions and occupations without attempting any moral reflections."[23] With an old-fashioned, lightly didactic tone and a frivolously named persona, Goldsmith's periodical was probably doomed from its inception.

"Perfectly Satyrical, Yet Perfectly Good-Natured"

The review of the *Bee* in the *Critical* (December 1759), relegated to the Monthly Catalogue—as were reviews of most periodicals fortunate enough to receive mention—hinted at the journal's reception: "The Bee seems to have collected her sweets for the use of an ungrateful public." It added, however, that while the writing "doesn't compare with the honied lucubrations of an Addison or a Johnson," it was "preferable to many modern funds of entertainment."[24] If the public ignored him and critics received him unenthusiastically, London booksellers certainly took notice of his talents. In the year following the demise of the *Bee,* Goldsmith was one of London's most prolific contributors to the popular periodicals.

Having seen the fame of other newspapers and magazines "fly like unpinioned swans," while his *Bee* "move[d] as heavily as a new-plucked goose" (I, 415), Goldsmith turned to a style and subject matter better calculated to appeal to his readership. He turned away from the meditative, didactic tone and timeless material he had frequently employed in the *Bee* and adopted a more satirical and topical approach. In addition to exposing the follies of contemporary fashion and taste, he developed his "foreign correspondent" perspective—perhaps the role that best distinguishes his journalistic career from the work of his contemporary essayists.

Encouraging his participation in the widening field of London periodicals, the bookseller and playwright Israel Pottinger invited him to contribute to the short-lived weekly, the *Busy Body,* edited by Edward Purdon, in October 1759. For the 13 October issue Goldsmith wrote "A Description of Various Clubs" (III, 6–16). While the clubs survey had been a popular vehicle for essayists since Addison, Goldsmith's satire successfully employed his unique combination of stinging irony and genial wit. In the piece the author is presented as an outsider, drawn to the various London social establishments by their promises of culture and society. He becomes astonished at the pretense and puerility of all the various classes frequenting the clubs. A second contribution, "On Public Rejoicings for Victory," (20 October) is remarkable in its context (III, 16–21). Writing for a blatantly nationalistic periodical, Goldsmith reports ironically on England's excessive celebrations following the victory at Quebec. Again, the reporter is an outsider observer, one determined to "peep in at every frequented place of resort" (III, 18). He thereby distances himself from the ecstatic jubilation of the masses, and quietly expresses misgivings about the prospects for peace.

In December 1759, Goldsmith wrote the first of eight known contributions to a second Pottinger venture, the *Weekly Magazine*. He adopts a familiar voice, that of an English gentleman, in a letter entitled "A Description of the Manners and Customs of the Native Irish" (III, 24–30). His tone is condescending and his generalizations about the rural Irish poor are simplistic; his narrator merely rehearses the Irish stereotypes by which Goldsmith himself had been victimized. A second contribution (29 December), called "Some Thoughts Preliminary to a General Peace" (III, 30–4), warned England of the dangers of colonialism, and, as Wardle claims, "expressed principles which were to underlie his political thinking for years to come."[25] For the same issue he wrote an amusing biographical tribute to George Berkeley, which included the anecdote about the latter's experimental "mock hanging" (III, 34–40).

Goldsmith's last known contributions to the *Weekly* were published in January 1760. For the issue of 5 January, he contributed a long satiric poem, "The Double Transformation: A Tale" (IV, 367–71); a brief biography of fellow Irishman Robert Boyle (III, 40–45); and a satirical epitaph, "Serious Reflections on the Life and Death of the Late Mr. T—— C——, by the Ordinary of Newgate" (III, 46–48). Goldsmith's "Ordinary" expresses mock astonishment that Theophilus Cibber, son of Colley Cibber, should perish by drowning rather than at the end of a rope. Recalling Theophilus' troubled lifetime, the Ordinary delivers a comic treatise on the three ways of getting into debt, all of which Cibber (and the author of the essay, incidentally) had thoroughly mastered.[26]

One of Goldsmith's contributions for 12 January was "A Sublime Passage in a French Sermon"; as he had in his review of Ward's *System of Oratory*, in it Goldsmith demands oratorical passion rather than a "phlegmatic" adherence to rhetorical rules (III, 49–51). His indictment of the English manner of delivering sermons is irreverent, even contemptuous. In another contribution, "The Futility of Criticism," he reiterates his insistence on a criticism emphasizing beauty rather than rules (III, 51–3); and in an essay "On the Present State of Our Theatres," he laments the lack of a third London theatre, a condition which had lessened competition and resulted in the production of few new plays. He also deplores his contemporaries' taste for pantomime and "monstrous farce" (III, 54–56).

Goldsmith's editorship of the *Bee* produced at least one direct benefit for the journalist that Goldsmith scholars have overlooked. John Wilkie, publisher of Goldsmith's first essay work, was a member of what Donald Eddy calls the "syndicate," a group of editors, publishers, and printers affiliated with John Newbery. Together they produced several of London's leading periodicals.[27] Members of this group included William Faden, who printed the *Rambler,* the *Literary Magazine,* the *Public Ledger,* and the *Universal Chronicle;* Robert Dodsley, with Newbery one of the sponsors of the *London Chronicle;* Griffith Jones, editor of the *Public Ledger* and *London Chronicle,* and a contributor to the *Critical;* and Wilkie, one of the publishers of the *Public Ledger* and the *London Chronicle.*[28] Newbery helped finance several of these periodicals, including the *Universal Chronicle,* the *London Chronicle,* the *Public Ledger,* and the *British.* Though the *Bee* was not enthusiastically received, Goldsmith's affiliation with Wilkie brought him into the "syndicate." In 1760 and 1761, he became, along with Smollett, one of its most important writers.

One of the peripheral members of this group was the publisher John Coote, who invited Goldsmith to contribute to his *Royal Magazine, or Gentleman's Monthly Companion.* Coote was closely associated with Newbery; their names appeared together, for instance, on the title pages of the *Lady's Museum* and the *Christian's Magazine* between 1760 and 1762.[29] He also printed Smollett's *Briton* (1762–63), a journal supporting the Bute ministry. In the *Royal* for December 1759, Goldsmith published his first piece for Coote, an Eastern tale entitled "The Proceedings of Providence Vindicated" (III, 58–66). Goldsmith continued his association with the *Royal* in 1760 with his four-part series "A Comparative View of Races and Nations" (June–September, 1760), in which he drew on his extensive experience as a European traveler and his lifelong interest in comparing different cultures with his own. His narrative persona—an English world traveler returning home to extol the virtues of English laws, customs, and climate—bears witness to the barbarous customs and inhospitable climate of foreign lands. The traveler's vision of England as the best of all possible worlds is hyperbolic but not discernibly ironic: in these essays Goldsmith displays an ardent nationalism absent from most of his other periodical work.

Goldsmith reunited with Wilkie on another project in September 1760; he wrote for the *Lady's Magazine* and may have acted as editor. Percy notes only, "He conducted for Wilkie the bookseller, a Lady's Magazine."[30] His contributions for September and October were light essays geared toward his female readership. "Of the Assemblies of Russia" lists the prudishly restrictive rules governing Russian soirées (III, 145–47), and "A Lady of Fashion in the Times of Anna Bullen Compared with One of Modern Times" (October) provides a lighthearted account of a woman's daily life "before the time of Elizabeth" (III, 147–49). His essay "Some Remarks on the Modern Manner of Preaching" (III, 150–55) repeats criticisms of English preaching he had made in the *Bee* ("Of Eloquence") and in the *Weekly Magazine* ("A Sublime Passage in a French Sermon"). Though little is known about Goldsmith's possible editorship of the *Lady's*, the journal served as a vehicle for serial publication of his *Memoirs of M. de Voltaire*, a short, anecdotal biography. Installments of it ran each month from February through November 1761. The *Memoirs*, never completed, appear to have been an albatross for two booksellers. Griffiths first advertised the work in the *Public Advertiser* for 7 February 1759, but the work was not published at that time, and Griffiths may have sold the rights to Wilkie, who promised speedy publication in the *Advertiser* for 23 May 1760. Apparently, Goldsmith still had failed to complete the work, and Wilkie may have seen serial publication of the completed part as a last resort.

While Goldsmith enjoyed productive relationships with Wilkie, Coote, and Pottinger, the most important professional contact he made after terminating the *Bee* was with Newbery himself, the most prominent member of the "syndicate." Like Griffiths, Newbery was a well-established publisher. Arthur Murphy described him as "a man of a projecting head, good taste, and great industry."[31] The ensuing relationship between publisher and author led to lasting recognition for both men: Goldsmith as novelist and "Citizen of the World," Newbery as the bookseller honored in *The Vicar* (IV, 94–95).

6

"The Philanthropic Bookseller": Goldsmith's Work
for Newbery

To All Young Gentleman and Ladies, Who are good, or intend to be good, This Book Is inscribed by Their old Friend In St. Paul's Church-Yard.

         —Dedication, *The History of Little Goody Two-Shoes*

The task of assessing Goldsmith's journalistic career and of identifying some sort of consistent "self" in his periodical contributions has been complicated by the proposed reinclusion of twenty-nine *British Magazine* pieces into the accepted canon. The external evidence for accepting the "Reed-Wright" attributions is certainly reasonable, if not absolutely definitive. As James Basker points out, D. F. McKenzie's record of stationers' company apprentices establishes the fact that Thomas Wright served as apprentice—and perhaps as a manager or record keeper—to Archibald Hamilton, printer of the *British Magazine*.[1] Therefore, Wright may well have had records, no longer extant, of Goldsmith's contributions to the *British* when he assembled the 1798 collection of *Essays and Criticism.*

Acceptance of these essays suggests several profound, exciting, and disturbing consequences. First, it would extend Goldsmith's active periodical career to the beginning of 1763. It would also, as Basker claims, make Goldsmith the most prolific contributor to a journal that attracted the talents of Johnson, Smollett, and Garrick.[2] It would enhance our record of Goldsmith's early experimentation with fiction—almost all of it epistolary and written from a great variety of points of view such as he developed throughout his periodical career. It would add a substantial body of criticism to his known corpus, although much of the *Belles-Lettres* series disappointingly seems somewhat commonplace and pedantic.

With some of the pieces, however, any attempt to reconcile the authorial voices and attitudes with the previously established canon is maddeningly difficult. The opinions expressed in some of the political essays directly contradict those Goldsmith articulates elsewhere. And the newly reattributed tales, although they frequently display the rough quaintness and patriarchal morality exhibited in his other fiction, are at times shockingly vulgar and distinctly uncharacteristic. Certainly one of the marks of Goldsmith's journalism is its diversity of tone and its adaptability to the venue for which he was writing and to its perceived community of readers. Indeed, his career was a perplexing mixture of self-contradiction and dissonant voices. To insist that the new essays conform to identifiable patterns in the established canon, therefore, is probably unreasonable. Nonetheless, they certainly complicate the already elusive aim of presenting a unified picture of Goldsmith as journalist.

Newbery and His Moral Concerns

John Newbery, along with Smollett, planned *The British Magazine, or The Monthly Repository for Ladies and Gentlemen* in December 1759. Walter Graham justifiably observes that this journal was one of the most ambitious of its time; it included more pages (fifty-five per issue) and more fiction than any previous periodical.[3] The publisher may have wanted to fill the void created by the demise of Newbery's *Literary Magazine* the previous year. Concurrently, he planned the *Public Ledger* to compete with other dailies such as the *Gazetteer*. For his new daily he brought together many of the men who had worked on the *Literary:* Faden as printer, Jones as editor, and Wilkie as copublisher. For his monthly journal he enlisted Smollett, editor of the *Critical* and successful novelist and historian. And he hired Goldsmith, who had worked with Wilkie and Smollett, to be a primary contributor to both journals. Thus, in January of 1760 began Goldsmith's fruitful association with Newbery.

In addition to the *Literary,* Newbery had founded the *Universal Chronicle, or Weekly Gazette* (April 1758) in which Johnson first published his *Idler* papers; he may also have provided financial backing to John Payne, publisher of the *Rambler.*[4] From 1751 to 1760 Newbery had published fourteen books by his son-in-law, the poet Christopher Smart.[5] But his chief stock-in-trade was children's books: basic grammars and spelling books, children's magazines such as *A Museum for Young Gentlemen and Ladies* (1750), and didactic collections of stories such as *Fables in Verse for the Improvement of the Young and Old,* by "Abraham Aesop" (1757). During his lifetime, he was probably better known for introducing *Jack-the-Giant-Killer* (1744) and the immortal *Goody Two Shoes* (1765) than he was for promoting the careers of Smart and Johnson.[6] Almost half of the books published under his imprint in 1760 concerned the proper moral instruction of young people; several others were conduct books for polite "ladies" and "gentlemen."[7] His address "To the

Parents, Guardians, and Governesses of Great Britain and Ireland" exemplified Newbery's often-repeated solution to the "depravity" of the times:

> It has been said, and said wisely, that the only way to remedy these Evils is to begin with the rising Generation, and to take the Mind in its infant State, when it is uncorrupted and susceptible of any Impression; To represent their Duties and future Interest in a Manner that shall seem rather intended to amuse than instruct, to excite their Attention with Images and Pictures that are familiar and pleasing; To warm their Affections with such little Histories as are capable of giving them Delight, and of impressing on their tender Minds proper Sentiments of Religion, Justice, Honour, and Virtue.[8]

Goldsmith's recommendation of Newbery's books for children in his preface to Charles Wiseman's *A Complete English Grammar* (1764) might be seen as a puff for his bookseller. But his remarks are consistent with the views he expressed on education throughout his career:

> Were I to advise beginners, especially children, they should read only such Books as are easily understood, and written in the most plain and natural style, upon subjects capable of interesting the virtuous part of their passions, or subduing those which lead to Vice. Nor can I here avoid recommending several of this nature, published by Mr. *Newbery,* which seem happily adapted to delight and rectify the growing mind, and lead it up to truth, through the flowery paths of pleasure. (V, 311)

Seeing virtue and simplicity of style as necessary ingredients in didactic tales, he articulated a theory of fiction he had developed as a reviewer and described an important facet of much of his own work.

In a sharp break from tradition, Smollett's editorship of the journal was revealed in its first month of publication; the *London Chronicle* advertised this particular in its 29 January 1760 issue. In fact, the *British* was initiated, in part, as a vehicle for the serial publication of Smollett's *Sir Lancelot Greaves,* a poorly received romance of eighteenth-century knight-errantry. In *The English Novel in the Magazines,* Robert Mayo provides an excellent discussion of the *British* and its pioneering work in serial publication.[9] While he notes that *Sir Launcelot Greaves* was clearly not the first fiction serialized in a magazine, as some have maintained, the work "broke new ground in being a long piece of original fiction written expressly for publication in a British magazine."[10] Of course, Goldsmith was simultaneously publishing his Chinese Letters, not a "romance" but a work of fiction that capitalized on this developing trend in magazine serializing. The growing popularity of various types of magazine serials profoundly influenced his career. From the beginning of 1760, when Smollett began publishing his novel and Goldsmith began his association with the *British,* until the end of Goldsmith's journalistic career, most of his writing was published in serial form: his Voltaire biography for the *Lady's Magazine,* his "Series of Literary Essays" for the *Public Ledger,* his "Indigent Philosopher" series for *Lloyd's,* and his "Comparative View of Races and Nations" series for the *Royal.*

Like the other miscellanies, the *British* published a hodgepodge of Oriental tales, informal histories, reflections on current events, brief reviews of new publications—even mathematical puzzles. Other than Smollett's novel, however, the most conspicuous feature throughout the issues was a series of *exempla.* These "moral tales" were designed to edify parents and their children on the hazards of romantic love and the need for matrimonial prudence. Apparently as concerned as Goldsmith over the dangers of romance fiction, Newbery and Smollett published tales that dramatized the didactic in fiction. For this reason Spector labels the *British* dogmatically conservative.[11]

The *British Magazine* and Goldsmith's Early Fiction

Responding to this characteristic of the *British,* Goldsmith experimented with some fiction writing of his own. One such attempt, both exemplifying and satirizing the romance genre, was "The History of Miss Stanton," a narrative Prior calls the "first rude germ" of *The Vicar of Wakefield.*[12] Although one of Goldsmith's nineteenth-century biographers, Austin Dobson, refers to "Miss Stanton" as a "farrago of foolery and anticlimax,"[13] the story has been largely overlooked by scholars commenting on *The Vicar.* This tale, with its "artfully artless" narrator and its apparently absurd conclusion, clearly anticipates *The Vicar.* In a letter entitled "To the Authors of the British Magazine," the narrator identifies himself as one who is "unused to correspond with Magazines," but who believes that his "true though artless tale" offers a sensible alternative to the "fictitious stories of distress" that crowd the journals (III, 128). He then introduces Mr. Stanton, "a clergyman with a small fortune . . . esteemed by the rich, and beloved by the poor," who lives in bucolic bliss with his beloved daughter Fanny (III, 128). Shattering their tranquillity, the rake Mr. Dawson, a dissimulating "man of the world," wins the trust of father and daughter and elopes with the "deluded" Fanny. The grief-stricken Stanton vows revenge, pursues and discovers Dawson, and challenges him to a duel. After the first volley Stanton falls, apparently dead. Seeing Fanny collapse upon the "lifeless" figure of her father, Dawson repents of his infamous ways and immediately offers marriage to Fanny. Upon hearing the offer, Stanton rises up and admits to having "pretended to be dead." The narrator says the two were "immediately conducted to the church, where they were married, and now live exemplary instances of conjugal love and felicity" (III, 132).

This tale, though contrived, calls to mind many of the ambiguities and narrative complexities which have puzzled readers of *The Vicar*. Its narrator is contemptuous of romance fiction and its implausibilities, yet he tells a romantic tale which stretches credulity. He insists on didactic responsibility in fiction, yet the tale's obviously simplistic message and comic closure ironically undercut its apparent didactic function. Prior accounts for these difficulties by suggesting that the story was "obviously hurried to a conclusion and written probably when the press required an immediate supply of matter."[14] Yet with its rural charm, its simple but effective characterization, its experimentation with personae, and its elusive levels of irony, "Miss Stanton" is an important predecessor of *The Vicar* and deserves serious consideration by critics of Goldsmith's novel.

Goldsmith contributed another piece similar in function, "A True History for the Ladies." This exemplum on parental responsibility and filial duty warns of the corrupting nature of romance fiction (III, 120–23). His introduction repeats a warning he had issued in his review of *True Merit, True Happiness:* "In the flowery paths of novel and romance, we are taught to consider love as a blessing that will last for life: it is exalted above its merits; and by teaching the young and unexperienced to expect more from it than it can give, by being disappointed of their expectations, they do not receive from it even those advantages it has to bestow" (III, 120). The purpose of the tale then, is to illustrate this point. Goldsmith uses the genre to reform it, to neutralize its dangers and delusiveness, and to mock its implausibilities. As Friedman observes, the tale is an adaptation from *Tatler,* Number 192, ascribed to Addison (III, 123n). Again, Addison serves as a sort of moral beacon; Goldsmith's unacknowledged debt functions, here, to underscore the moral seriousness underlying an apparently trivial tale.

The story shares much in common with "Miss Stanton" and, indeed, with *The Vicar.* There is the same combination of paternal foolishness—in this case a father's preventing a marriage from purely "mercenary motives"—and filial disobedience that produces disastrous consequences. An older brother, Thomas, disobeys his father's wishes and marries for love; his brother, James, accepts an "extremely sensible" choice of a mate. (Goldsmith comments slyly that the marriage of the younger brother "would by no means have served as the subject of romance" [III, 122].) A typically absurd central event exemplifies the differences between the two relationships. With their ship on the verge of sinking, both couples face death at sea, confronted with the choice of saving himself or dying with his bride—for some unexplained reason, rescuing the brides was not an option—Thomas vows to die with his wife, while the younger brother chooses the more sensible course of saving himself. Miraculously, the ship does not sink after all. Defying expectations,

Goldsmith relates that the passionate couple came to lose their affection for each other in a few short weeks; the younger brother and his wife, though, "rubbed thro' life with much content, and now and then some sparring" (III, 122)—presumably the most one should expect from marriage.

This short narrative presents many of the problems that have engaged critics for much of the twentieth century. How can Goldsmith combine serious didactic intention with ironic undercutting and obvious implausibility? Part of the answer might lie in Goldsmith's ambivalence toward the romance genre. He views the form, at least as it was normally practiced, as trivial at best and, at worst, as a genuine threat to the happiness and morality of its readers. Some of the contempt he feels for the genre, then, interferes with his attempt to reform it with genuine feeling and realistic outcomes. To this extent, all of his fiction is experimental, an attempt to subvert reader expectations and to moralize the genre. His apparent confusion of purpose and tone and the ambivalent responses of his readers suggest that he was only partially successful.

The pieces newly ascribed to Goldsmith generally conform to the same pattern. The didactic purpose of "The History of Alcanor and Eudosia" (May 1760) is presented in the introduction by its "letter-writer": "Give me leave, through the canal of your magazine, to communicate a story, which is not more romantic than true; and may serve as a lesson of prudence and morality to those parents, who think there is nothing but affluence necessary or essential to the happiness of their children" (*British,* 305). Before his arranged marriage is consummated, Alcanor loses his money, and Eudosia's father calls off the wedding. As a result, the two lovers part. He dedicates his life to restoring his fortune; she dedicates hers to charity. The story ends with an *Evangeline*-like deathbed reunion. In this short romance, Goldsmith achieves a degree of sweetness and simple poignancy. His didacticism and plot contrivances seem forgivable here, in the context of unabashed sentiment and consistency of purpose.

Another piece, "On the Imprudent Fondness of Parents" (August 1760), is written from the point of view of a father who has failed to exercise proper parental authority. Using the same narrative device found in "Miss Stanton" and in *The Vicar,* his narrator confesses to his limitations: "I am conscious of my own incapacity to write what may deserve public attention" (*British,* 532). The author hopes that the morality of the tale will overcome the inexperience or simplicity of its teller. The narrator admits to being "old, oppressed with the infirmities of declining age, and doomed to end the miserable remains of life, in an obscure country-seat" (*British,* 532). He has been the victim of filial ingratitude and his own failure as a parent.

"On the Proper Enjoyment of Life" (August 1760) presents the reader once again with a tale of marriage without parental consent, this time written from the point of view of a younger brother. The narrator tells of his elopement with a woman and his hopes of achieving domestic bliss on a small farm. Again, an unlikely event intercedes: through a series of accidents, he inherits wealth and is "rushed into the pageantry of high-life." "Thus irresistibly sucked within the vortex of dissipation," he says, "we grew giddy in a rapid whirl of unnatural diversion: we became enamoured of tinsel liveries, equipage, and all the frippery of fashion" (*British*, 474). The tale becomes an exemplum on the dangers of luxury, to which this couple had become especially vulnerable by their initial act of disobedience.

In what may be an unintentionally hilarious conclusion, the letter writer asks the magazine editor for advice. The editor, presumably Goldsmith, assumes the persona of a stern physician in his response: "Retire from London, and engage in the avocations of husbandry; use the cold bath every morning, ride twenty miles every day before dinner, eat moderately of plain English food, go to bed by eleven, rise before eight, and fast one day in the week" (*British*, 474). Even in its apparent silliness, the piece fits one of the magazine's central mandates: to provide lessons in conduct for young people.

A more frank instance of this approach—and one that seems in several respects uncharacteristic of Goldsmith's work—is "Igluka and Sibbersik, a Greenland Tale" (April 1760), an exemplum on the dangers of premarital sex. That such a subject should be broached in a forum such as the *British Magazine*, even though placed in such a remote setting, seems anomalous, if not a bit shocking. The "foreignness" of the piece, though, and its occasional comic absurdity somewhat mitigate its force. The narrator admonishes his readers: "Such an intimacy between the two sexes is often productive of the most fatal consequences, which even the purest sentiments, and the most determined virtue cannot always prevent" (*British*, 239). Two otherwise wholesome and virtuous lovers, engaged to be married, share an "unguarded moment" and a bearskin rug, after which "the amiable, the virtuous, the sentimental Igluka was undone" (*British*, 239).

Curiously, at the "climactic moment," the narrator disrupts his high-minded tone with comic deflation: "in an evil hour she surrendered up her virgin treasure, while the sea-mews and carlieus screamed, the bears growled, and seals grunted in concert, as if to celebrate these portentous rites" (*British*, 240). Surely the author must have intended for his reader to smile at this ludicrous image of bears growling and seals grunting in time with illicit igloo passion. The author further dilutes the moral force of his tale in his conclusion. After a near-disaster—the young man's "love was succeeded by a species of disgust"—the couple is joyfully reconciled: Igluka was not, after all, undone. While this tale contains elements consistent with his known works of fiction, its playful attitude toward a subject he treats elsewhere with seriousness and delicacy will likely leave Goldsmith scholars skeptical of its ascription to him.

Another newly reattributed piece that presents similar problems is "The

History of Omrah," a long Oriental tale serialized in the first three issues of the magazine (January–March, 1760). Although it adopts a popular form and borrows loosely from *Rasselas,* published the previous year, "The History of Omrah" is burdened by a slow-moving plot and florid descriptions. To some extent it conforms to the generic description provided by "an author" who attacks Lien Chi Altangi in Chinese Letter XXXIII: "Eastern tales should always be sonorous, lofty, musical and unmeaning" (II, 145). Its hero is "resolved to improve his mind by travelling into foreign countries" (*British,* January 1760, 3), where he becomes disllusioned by the treachery and violence he witnesses. Many of the themes presented here are consistent with Goldsmith's interests and also with the conventions of the genre: Omrah must overcome diversity, develop a "sensibility of heart," and survive the "waters of despair." He must also decide between a life at court and one of retreat. Ultimately, he becomes a proper "man of sentiment."

The most startling feature of the work is the author's gratuituous description of two "old hags" in the first and third parts of the tale. The graphic language he uses is unmatched elsewhere in Goldsmith's known canon. Of the first he says, "There was hardly any vestige of her nose remaining: her teeth, her palate, and her throat, were half-consumed with putrefying sores" (*British,* January 1760, 3). The second "old hoary hag" is described in even more shocking terms: "Her bloated dugs, that hung down to her waist, were sore and cankered; yielding, instead of milk, a constant distillation of poison, which tortured her so severely, that she shrieked aloud at every drop that fell from the nipple" (*British,* March 1760, 120–22). If this work was, indeed, written by Goldsmith, it contradicts the prevalent image of the author as a gentle, moral humorist, and at least partially subverts the didactic claims of the journal.

Those like Robert Hopkins who see Goldsmith as a satirist in the tradition of Swift might find support for their argument in another "new essay," "A Letter to the Authors of the British Magazine, Containing an humble Proposal for augmenting the Forces of Great-Britain" (January 1762),. This "modest proposal," in its crudity and bluntness, further subverts the expectations of readers familiar with Goldsmith's work. Because of mounting military losses, the letter declares, women ought to be included in the armed forces: "All those who are fit to bear children are likewise fit to bear arms" (*British,* 33). Relating the pitched battles he has witnessed between "athletic" women, he argues that the "female drudges of Ireland, Wales, and Scotland" ought to be conscripted. He concludes that while the Amazonian women warriors cut off their right breasts "so that [they] might not impede them in bending the bow," there is "no occasion for this cruel excision in the present discipline, as we have seen instances of women who handle the musquet, without finding any inconvenience from that protuberance" (*British,* 35).

While these pieces do not fully conform to the profile of typical *British*

Magazine contributions or fit with the Goldsmith persona as developed in his Chinese Letters or in *The Vicar,* they are examples of an author experimenting, not always successfully, with tone, irony, theme, and, most prominently, with point of view. In his other short fictional pieces for the *British,* Goldsmith indeed developed an impressive variety of narrative voices. In "A Reverie at the Boar's-head tavern in Eastcheap," he assumes the voice of "the only living representative" of the "character of old Falstaff," who must be taught that life in merry old England was as "degenerate" as that of the present day (III, 97–112). Goldsmith takes on the character of an impoverished actor, wandering in St. James Park and telling the tale of his downfall in "The Adventures of a Strolling Player" (III, 133–42). He assumes the role of opera critic in "On the Different Schools of Music" (February), and that of a scientist in his letter entitled "The Effect which Climates Have upon Men, and Other Animals" (May). And Goldsmith twice returns to the dream narrative first attempted in the *Bee.* The first "dreamer" visits the "fountain of fine sense" (III, 115–18) and the second journeys to the "mansions of Poetry and Taste" (III, 124–27). The ancients, who were treated as superior to moderns throughout the *British,* are the exclusive residents of Goldsmith's "mansion."

The evidence Basker presents also urges reinclusion of the series "On the Belles Lettres" (July 1761 to January 1763) in Goldsmith's canon. Much of the work is simple scholastic disquisition, a rhetoric primer for young readers. The first few essays, however, elucidate principles of authorship that Goldsmith had first articulated as a book reviewer. Again assuming the mantle of "true critic," he rails against those with misguided pretensions and consequent "false taste": "The spruce prentice sets up for a critic, and the puny beau piques himself upon being a connoisseur" (*British,* July 1761, 353). Of course, four years earlier he had, as a spruce prentice and puny beau, set himself up as critic and connoisseur.

At the heart of his criticism is an author's self-definition and self-justification. He holds that the greatest stylistic virtue is simplicity: "beautiful nature, without affectation or extraneous ornament" (*British,* August 1761, 434). The foundation of taste is morality—specifically, the shared sensibility and mutual responsiveness developed between author and reader: "The heart, cultivated by precept, and warmed by example, improves in sensibility . . . [and] by distinguishing the influence and scope of morality, and cherishing the ideas of benevolence, it acquires a habit of sympathy which tenderly feels responsive, like the vibrations of unisons, every touch of moral beauty" (*British,* September 1761, 493). Through simplicity and a cultivated sensibility, the moral author achieves something like the "sublime" as Goldsmith had defined the term in his notes to Burke's *Enquiry.* He considered the genre of poetry "superior to all other arts" (I, 32), and in his own poems he attempted to apply this theory. His "distinctness of imagery," stylistic simplicity, and the benevolence of his narrators coalesce in his best poetry, and in much of his fiction, to create a sympathetic, responsive reader.

The Chinese Philosopher

While writing for the *British,* Goldsmith was publishing an average of ten Chinese Letters each month for Newbery's *Public Ledger* (24 January 1760 to 14 August 1761). These letters, similar in format to Johnson's *Idler* essays in the *Universal Chronicle,* appeared as the lead articles in the sixteen-column format the *Ledger* had introduced. Goldsmith probably took the idea for the letters from a popular pamphlet written by Horace Walpole and favorably reviewed in Griffiths' Monthly Catalogue in May 1757. Though the review of *A Letter from Xo Ho, a Chinese Philosopher at London, to His Friend Lien Chi at Pekin* was written by William Rose, Goldsmith almost certainly read the work when he was the principal Catalogue contributor for the *Monthly.* Rose's notice called it "an imaginative satire on our late political revolutions; and particularly in the inconstant disposition of the English nation."[15] Walpole's pamphlet went through five editions in its first year of publication.

Adopting a character name and the essential format from Walpole's pamphlet, Goldsmith achieved his first popular success. His epistolary satire spawned imitators and forced format changes in competing journals. Robert L. Haig argues that with the appearance of the Chinese Letters, "A threat to the circulation of long-established dailies must have been felt almost at once."[16] Contracted "to furnish papers of an amusing character twice a week," Goldsmith earned £100 per annum for his *Public Ledger* work.[17] The 119 letters he wrote, ranging in subject matter from mad dogs to English gardening, were published as *The Citizen of the World* on 1 May 1762. The collection received lukewarm notices from both the *Critical* and the *Monthly.* Smollett's journal praised Goldsmith's humor and good sense, but commented on his being frequently unoriginal.[18] The *Monthly* noticed that Goldsmith's Chinese philosopher, Lien Chi Altangi, had "nothing Asiatic about him"—a complaint Goldsmith himself had made about works of this type.[19] At least one contemporary critic, though, thought that *The Citizen* elevated Goldsmith to the first rank of British authors. In *An Historical and Critical Account of the Lives and Writings of the Living Authors of Great-Britain* (1762), William Rider compared *The Citizen* to Montesquieu's *Lettres persanes* (1721). He set the tone for much subsequent commentary, on Goldsmith's "having found out the Secret to unite Elevation with Ease, a Perfection in Language, which few Writers of our Nation have attained to."[20]

The search for unifying elements in *The Citizen* has produced a wide variety of critical approaches, the most successful of them allowing for the difficulty of such a task, given the work's periodical nature. Many of the letters were

evidently prepared well in advance of their publication; others were composed in response to public events occurring only days earlier. They represent, as Wayne Booth describes, a "Self-Portraiture of Genius,"[21]—an
attempt "to show my own erudition," as Goldsmith wrote in a letter to
Edward Mills.[22] Many of these essays Goldsmith selected for inclusion in his
Essays by Mr. Goldsmith seem timeless; others are as temporal as the daily
news with which they were surrounded in the *Ledger*. Biographers and critics
since Percy have recognized the autobiographical nature of Goldsmith's
Chinese visitor and the "Man in Black." As observers of the occasionally
inexplicable and absurd elements of English society, the two characters
generally seemed to represent the author's politics, his difficulties with
women, his self-perception as a man of sentiment, and his preoccupation
with the double-edged sword of luxury.

Critics have not said much, however, about the title given to the collection
in 1762. The term "citizen of the world" conveys Goldsmith's idealized sense
of himself as a journalist: as worldly, untainted by parochial concerns,
experienced as a traveler and observer of the world's diverse customs and
achievements, and as disdainful of the pettiness of local faction. John Langhorne's use of the term in *The Effusions of Friendship and Fancy* (1766) is
instructive: "Are we not citizens of the world? Are we not all fellow subjects
of the universal monarch? Is not the universe our home? And is not every
man a brother? Poor and illiberal is that charity which is confined to any
particular nation or society."[23] The title "citizen of the world" bestows on its
central character, and by implication on Goldsmith, the broadness of vision
and liberality needed to evaluate English society fairly and accurately.

An important unifying element in the letters is the author's analysis of the
"republic of letters" and the examination of his own place in the world of
reviewers, essayists, and booksellers. References to the London publishing
industry are legion, and they reflect the ambivalence and frustration of one
for whom the profession of journalism was not only a livelihood but a
principal topic of discourse. They reflect an author reluctantly shifting from
the nostalgic longing he expressed in *Polite Learning* for the moribund
patronage system to bitter disdain for a commercial press and its "vulgar"
clients who silence genius and reward dullness—and, finally, to partial
acceptance of a system justified by the essential right-mindedness of the
public response. Even though the specific genre in which he wrote was well-
established, journalism as an industry was highly unstable, being subject to
rapid political shifts, changing reader expectations, and internal competition
and contention. This instability, along with Goldsmith's frustration with his
continued anonymity in a "mechanic" trade, probably accounts for the
recurrent and occasionally contradictory discussions of the press in his letters.

Goldsmith's account of book reviewing is relentlessly harsh: book "answerers" are cannibalistic, dull, and envious—failed authors who have sold

themselves to booksellers concerned only with profit. In the "anarchy of letters" they are the lowest form of life, "mercenary wretches" paid to execute their employers' vicious bidding. The tenor of his remarks is consistent with the early ubiquitous defensiveness with which authors prefaced their books. Because of the apparent power of the reviews and critical response in general, writers universally began their works expressing, as Charlotte Lennox puts it, "The Dread which a Writer feels of the public Censure."[24] Goldsmith complains:

> There are a set of men called answerers of books, who take upon them to watch the republic of letters, and distribute reputation by the sheet; they somewhat resemble the eunuchs in a seraglio, who are incapable of giving pleasure themselves, and hinder those that would. . . . Such wretches are kept in pay by some mercenary bookseller, or more frequently, the bookseller himself takes this dirty work off their hands, as all that is required is to be very abusive and very dull. (II, 60)

This picture badly represents the reviews and their staffs as managed by Griffiths and Smollett. It perpetuates a public misconception that Goldsmith must have known to be inaccurate. Both periodicals employed some of England's most eminent talent; and Griffiths, though he set the tone and editorial policy of the *Monthly,* and indeed was one of its most prolific contributors, was hardly the hatchet man Goldsmith describes.[25] Nor are the reviews as frequently "abusive" as Goldsmith implies. Perhaps his vitriol is a product of his abrupt, unpleasant separation from the *Monthly* and of disappointment with the progress of his own career. Little evidence suggests that poets could, as Goldsmith claims, "buy reputation from [the] book answerers" (II, 60). Certainly reviewers and authors quarreled vehemently, and the "Battle of the Reviews" elicited a great deal of name-calling. Still, Goldsmith presents us with a distorted and hyperbolic picture of a developing profession:

> Here you may see the compilers, and the book answerers of every month, when they have to cut up some respectable name, most frequently reproaching each other with stupidity and dullness: resembling wolves of the Russian forest, who prey upon venison, or horse-flesh when they can get it; but in cases of necessity lying in wait to devour each other. While they have new books to cut up, they make a hearty meal; but if this resource should unhappily fail, then it is that critics eat up critics, and compilers rob from compilations. (II, 86)

Like many of his fellow authors, he seems to be anticipating critical condemnation of his own work and to be issuing a preemptive defense.

Another anecdote reinforces this view. Lien Chi Altangi learns of a critic who writes "best and bitterest when drunk" (II, 216) and says: "There is no work whatsoever but he can criticise, replied the bookseller; even though you write in Chinese he would have a pluck at you. Suppose you should take it into your head to publish a book, let it be a volume of Chinese letters for instance; write how you will, he shall shew the world you could have written better" (II, 216). This letter, published in the *Public Ledger* of 23 June 1760, hints at the author's plans to publish a collected volume; the collection appeared almost two years later (May 1762). The letter provides another instance of Goldsmith's only partially disguised concern for his career and the reception of his work.

Through his "Chinese" persona, Goldsmith expresses alarm at the anarchical state of English publishing: "I have reckoned not less than twenty-three new books published in one day; which, upon computation, makes eight thousand three hundred and ninety-five in one year" (II, 124). He looks askance at the openness of a system that permitted an unknown Irish "vagabond" with dubious credentials to gain admittance: "In England, every man may be an author that can write; for they have by law a liberty not only of saying what they please, but of being as dull as they please" (II, 124).

Letters XXIX and XXX present a portrait of an authors' club; in effect the portrait is a satirical compilation of the types he had encountered in his journalistic career. His tone, though, is good-humored rather than malicious. His description of "doctor Nonentity" vaguely suggests Edmund Burke: "He makes essays on the origin of evil, philosophical enquiries upon any subject, and draws up an answer to any book upon twenty-four hours warning" (II, 125). Another of the characters demonstrates the necessary journalistic versatility: "I have actually written last week sixteen prayers, twelve bawdy jests, and three sermons, all at the rate of sixpence a-piece" (II, 131). He is eagerly awaiting the next ministerial blunder, which will ensure a regular income for him and his companions. A third character, "Mr. Tibs," may be partly autobiographical. Tibs is "a very *useful hand*" who "throws off an eastern tale to perfection" and who "understands the *business* of an author as well as any man" (II, 126). Tibs' physical appearance roughly matches that of Goldsmith as presented by Reynolds, Boswell, and Thrale-Piozzi (though it is hard to conceive of Goldsmith's admitting to the accuracy of such a portrayal): "You may distinguish [Tibs] by the peculiar clumsiness of his figure and the coarseness of his coat: however, though it be coarse, (as he frequently tells the company) he has paid for it" (II, 126). If Goldsmith is, indeed, admitting himself into the club of authors, he may be acknowledging the obvious fact of his own participation in this "anarchy of letters."

Perhaps the most discernible shift in Goldsmith's attitude toward his profession occurs in his references to English readership. Recognizing that his hopes for fame rest on public acceptance, he attemps a sort of reconciliation with his audience: the "vulgar" tasteless masses, led like sheep, become the "public," a "good and a generous master." In an essay of 23 June 1760, Goldsmith has Lien Chi Altangi encounter the cynical "Mr. Fudge, the bookseller." The bookseller says, "Others may pretend to direct the vulgar, but that is not my way; I always let the vulgar direct me; wherever popular clamour arises, I always echo the million" (II, 214). People buy books, he observes, not to learn, but to see their own prejudices reinforced. A best-selling book is one without moral or satirical purpose, and "no book sold better," he says, "except the criticisms upon it, which came out soon after. Of all kinds of writing that goes off best at present, and I generally fasten a criticism upon every selling book that is published" (II, 215–16).

By September 1760, Goldsmith's attitude toward the public and toward the profession in general become much more conciliatory: "In a polite age, almost every person becomes a reader, and receives more instruction from the press than the pulpit." (II, 311). The "anarchy of letters" he had found so abhorrent he now finds tolerable: "The only danger that attends a multiplicity of publications, is that some of them may be calculated to injure, rather than benefit society. But where writers are numerous, they also serve as a check upon each other, and perhaps a literary inquisition is the most terrible punishment that can be conceived, to a literary transgressor" (II, 313). He seems to accept—and even applaud—the end of patronage and the possibility of literary success and financial reward: "At present the few poets of England no longer depend on the Great for subsistence, they have no other patrons but the public, and the public collectively considered, is a good and a generous master" (II, 344). His letter of 17 October 1760 provides even clearer evidence of his reconciling himself to the commercial press for which he toiled, and it hints at his own hopes for success with the new rules for authorial accomplishment: "The ridicule therefore of living in a garret, might have been wit in the last age, but continues such no longer, because no longer true. A writer of real merit now may easily be rich if his heart be set only on fortune: and as for those who have no merit, it is but fit that such should remain in merited obscurity" (II, 344). As one who had emerged from Griffiths' garret with genuine hopes for fame, his remarks reflect a newly found optimism about the profession and "writing for pay." He even gives some grudging homage to his fellow magazine compilers: "The dullest writer . . . dresses up his little useful magazine of knowledge and entertainment, at least with a good intention" (II, 313).

At one level, then, the letters can be seen as a veiled autobiographical narrative, tracing the author's hopes and fears for his work and its reception. Lien Chi Altangi attempts to fend off a criticism almost universally made of "Eastern" writing: "I could not avoid smiling to hear a native of England attempt to instruct me in the true Eastern idiom. . . . What is palm'd upon you daily for an imitation of eastern writing, no way resembles their manner, either in sentiment or diction" (II, 145). In other words, his own writing, critical attack notwithstanding, is genuine. The author necessarily writes with a defensiveness born of the literary climate of predatory malice: "We should find every great attempt suppressed by prudence, and the rapturous sublimity in writing cooled by a cautious fear of offense" (II, 265). He clearly hopes to survive as an outsider, one with a lofty perspective, one who has "become a perfect Epicure in reading" (II, 387)—though with hilarious self-mockery, he adds that "esays upon divers subjects can't allure me, though never so interesting" (II, 388). But at the end of the work, when he finds himself inadvertently embroiled in controversy, he observes: "Yet by being thus a spectator of others dangers, I must own I begin to tremble in this literary contest for my own" (439). In the end, taste, prudence, versatility, and good humor are no guarantees of success.

On 14 August 1761, the *Public Ledger* published its final Chinese Letter, and in the following issue (19 August), Goldsmith introduced a new series of "Literary Essays" designed to redress the lack of literary news, especially from foreign sources, in the London periodicals. Essays in this series were printed as letters entitled "To the Compiler." In his "New Fashions of Learning" Goldsmith faulted writers for appealing "to the multitude"—a factor responsible for the proliferastion of "letters, reviews, magazines, and criticising news-papers" (III, 161). While essay writing "may justly give a scholar disgust," it may also be considered "the art of bringing learning from the cell into society" (III, 161–62). Further softening his stance on the profession, Goldsmith took a more conciliatory tone toward the business of periodical writing than he had displayed in *Polite Learning* and in his earliest journalistic efforts.

Goldsmith's work for his "philanthropic bookseller" helped establish him as a competent journalist, well-known at least among the booksellers. He certainly owed much to Newbery, as he did to Griffiths, for promoting his career. Scholars have noted, however, that there was a side to Goldsmith's relationship with Newbery that has not received the attention that the Goldsmith-Griffiths feud has attracted. Clara Kirk comments:

> Since Goldsmith was incapable of living within any budget, Newbery subtracted the amount Goldsmith needed for room and board, gave him advances on forthcoming books, kept careful records of all his transactions with his wayward and gifted writer, and passed the accounts on to his nephew Francis Newbery at his death some ten years later. Thus Goldsmith remained, in a sense, permanently enslaved to the Newberys and to other less generous publishers for the remainder of his comparatively short career.[26]

Goldsmith entered into a second "thraldom," this one apparently more agreeable to him. Like his first situation with Griffiths, it failed to free him completely from poverty; it did, however, present him with steady employment and the potential means of achieving celebrity as an author. And it provided him outlets for his best work as a journalist.

7

Defining a Self: The Essayist and His Readers

News paper writers, and coffee-house politicians, may indeed alarm us
with the account of some important affairs which never existed but in
their own imaginations, and set half the fools in the kingdom gaping at
the wonderful intelligence; but men of any understanding are not so
easily taken in.

—"The Politician," *Court Magazine* (December 1761)

For Goldsmith, constructing an authorial self and conceiving of a readership
was a complex process, driven by personal failure and ambition, the percep-
tions of the booksellers and editors for whom he worked, the generic
instability of journalistic forms, and his own conflicting views of "the
people." Vincent Carretta cites "one widely acceptable political definition of
the people" that appears in *The Vicar:* "that order of men which subsists
between the very rich and the very rabble. . . . In this middle order of
mankind are generally to be found all the arts, wisdom, and virtues of
society" (IV, 101–2).[1] One problem with accepting this view as Goldsmith's,
however, is that it is espoused in the novel by a demonstrably flawed narrator.
In the scene in which it occurs, Primrose debates with a radical exponent of
"liberty," one whose credibility is destroyed by his claim: " 'Now, I read all
the politics that come out. The Daily, the Public, the Ledger, the Chronicle,
the London Evening, the Whitehall Evening, the seventeen magazines, and
the two reviews; and though they hate each other, I love them all' " (IV, 98).
Such an avid reader of periodicals is suspect indeed, and Primrose's espousal
of middle-class integrity appears reasonable in this context. However, it is
not the virtuous "middle order" but the mindless radical, one "discontented
with the present government" and disrespectful toward royal authority, who
reads newspapers and magazines. "The people" are not his readers. Such a
perception creates an ultimately unresolvable conflict between an author
attempting to accommodate his readers and a readership sharply at odds with
his values.

To an extent, Goldsmith cast himself in the role of reformer, both of his
readers and of his "trade." Wolfgang Iser argues that "the eighteenth-century
novel reader was cast by the author in a specific role, so that he could be

guided—directly, or indirectly, through affirmation or negation—toward a conception of human nature and of reality."[2] Perhaps the relationship between Goldsmith and his readers should be seen as a synthesis of the three models Iser creates to differentiate among the strategies of Fielding, Richardson, and Smollett. According to Iser, Fielding provides his reader "a lens by means of which he will learn to see the world clearly and be able to adapt himself to it"; Richardson's characters are a vehicle for "self-analysis" and "self-revelation"; and Smollett offers a "medium for an intensified observation of the outside world."[3] Lien Chi Altangi and Goldsmith's other "foreign correspondent" personae offer such a lens through which the reader must construct an "objective" view of the social order, and through which the author provides his "intensified observations." And the entire journalistic canon can be seen as a sort of metafiction of self-discovery and professional identification.

Such a model, though, presumes authorial control over the relationship between writer and reader. To a great extent, the voices and strategies Goldsmith employs were prescribed by editorial policy and politics, by the roles assigned him by booksellers and editors, and by established or newly formed journalistic conventions. Michael McKeon begins his book *The Origins of the English Novel, 1600–1740* with a recognition of "the destabilization of generic categories" in the seventeenth and eighteenth centuries, especially the changing "status of 'romance' as a general epistemological category."[4] Similarly, the categories of journalistic work underwent rapid change in the Seven Years' War period. Book reviewing, to the extent that it involved fairly sophisticated theoretical responses to texts and authors rather than simple paraphrase, was less than a decade old, and the idea of competing review journals was utterly novel. The newspaper as a forum for public debate, as well as a medium for advertising and disseminating court and foreign news, was still in its infancy. On the one hand, the magazine miscellany, after three decades, was rapidly evolving; it was becoming more specialized and involving itself more fully in political affairs and literary controversy. On the other hand, the single-author, single-essay periodical, one of the mainstays of early eighteenth-century journalism, was nearly defunct. Perhaps most significantly, the relationship between books and periodicals and between authors and the public was to an unprecedented degree mediated by booksellers and a "press infrastructure."

In the midst of these intimidating and often baffling changes, Goldsmith constructed a career. Quintana may be overstating the case in his praise of Goldsmith's achievement, but his concern about excessive attention to the author's personal idiosyncracies is well-taken: "It is his triumph to have expressed in imaginative art better perhaps than any of his notable contemporaries that fine equipoise of civilized thought and feeling which marked the period we think of as High Georgian. It is time that we concerned ourselves less with his ugly face, his awkward social presence, and more with the actual nature of his achievement as a writer."[5] His aesthetic achievements are the more remarkable, though, not for being a product of High Georgian civility but of the commercial and political constraints inherent in a developing profession and a transformed "state of letters."

By the time he began to establish himself with his booksellers as a competent essayist and compiler, the Seven Years' War was three years old, and the periodicals he had considered exemplary, the *Rambler* and the *Connoisseur,* had passed into journalistic history. How did he first conceive of himself as a periodical writer? What social influences forced a reexamination of that first conception? How, too, did his imagined reader change from his initial essays to his later work? In his collected edition *Essays by Mr. Goldsmith* (1765) he attempted a final self-definition as an essayist. How well does that definition mesh with earlier ones? These questions and problems suggest a fresh perspective for analyzing the development of Goldsmith's journalistic career.

Booksellers and Coffeehouse Readers

The phenomena that coalesced to produce this "decadent state" of English letters did not originate entirely in the Seven Years' War period. Foreign news, though particularly salient in the periodicals of Goldsmith's day, had been a prominent feature of newspapers throughout the century. Similarly, the economic interconnectedness of booksellers and coffeehouses was a feature of the eighteenth-century press observable in the early decades of the century. Nor was the involvement of booksellers in periodical production unique to the High Georgian period. Borrowing a rhetoric of alarm from John Brown, Goldsmith wrote about the commercialization of literature, the low taste of coffeehouse readers, and the politicization of the press as if they were menacing new forces threatening English letters. In fact, by the time Goldsmith entered the profession, the link between booksellers, the periodical press, and London's clubs and coffeehouses was a *fait accompli.*

George Rudé describes the symbiotic development of coffeehouses and periodicals as a response to the economic and political interests of a growing mercantile-class readership: "As the coffee-house arose in response to the City's commercial and political needs, so the coffee-house, in turn, engendered the newspaper."[6] He argues that the press was "a powerful factor in forming and expressing the opinions of a politically literate middle class."[7] If Goldsmith objected to pandering to commercial or political interests, whether from personal conviction or as a function of his gentlemanly persona, he was forced to accommodate such interests in his work for the *Public Ledger* and *Lloyd's,* both catering partly to a readership of people in trade. The clubs and coffeehouses represented a broad cross section of potential readers, a diversity that Goldsmith both celebrated and satirized in "A Description of Various Clubs." Mentioning some of the very clubs he himself frequented, he acknowledged the dominance of the coffeehouses in English social life— though his persona, as an outsider, failed to fit into any of their societies. As centers for partisan debate, literary discussion, and dissemination of news, the coffeehouses were a feature of London's social landscape that journalists ignored at their peril. As Bryant Lillywhite concludes in his catalogue of London coffeehouses, "Almost every phase of public interest and activity . . . found expression or outlet in the life of a coffee-house."[8] Appealing to such a readership, essayists like Goldsmith wrote short, lively satires on manners and morals and provided newsworthy accounts of the war and foreign affairs.

Robert Spector traces the demise, in the early years of the war, of those journals in the *Spectator* tradition, like the *World,* the *Connoisseur,* and the *Bee,* that failed to "appeal to the public's hunger for political and military news."[9] The bookseller John Rivington's advertisement in the *London Evening Post* (19 March 1757) for the short-lived *Humanist* tested the waters for interest in religion by addressing it "to all those Few frugal and temperate Ladies and Gentlemen, who can afford to sequester ten Minutes in a Week from pleasurable Pursuits and important Amusements."[10] Rivington and his family had been one of the century's most successful publishers of religious matter, but his efforts in 1759 to appeal to a "polite" audience with religious themes was unsuccessful. Goldsmith, too, had made a distinction, in the first number of the *Bee,* between the "readers of a more refined appetite" he hoped to attract and the "devourers of compilations," who were objects of contempt (I, 356). In fact, the "devourers," rather than the "temperate ladies and gentlemen," seemed to comprise the better part of the periodical readership.

Complaints about the glut of newspapers and "compilations" were not a new phenomenon. Jeremy Black describes the quarrel which took place in the late 1720s between coffeehouses and periodical publishers, "the former claiming saturation and complaining of the cost."[11] Johnson complained about the excessively voracious appetite of coffeehouse readers and the super-fluity of London's periodicals in *Idler* No. 7 (27 May 1758): "Whatever is found to gratify the publick, will be multiplied by the emulation of venders beyond necessity or use. This plenty indeed produces cheapness, but cheap-ness always ends in negligence and depravation."[12] Whether or not these papers were trivial or redundant in their reporting, public demand supported this proliferation.

London booksellers and printers had realized, as early as the 1730s, the potential profitability of periodical publication. Michael Harris observes: "To the London printer a periodical, in particular a newspaper, remained the potential basis of successful business. For a low initial investment a paper could provide regular work with a continuous and easily monitored re-turn."[13] The periodical provided some of London's approximately seventy-two booksellers (estimate for 1763) a fairly low-risk opportunity to stabilize their businesses.[14] Though copies of a periodical were read in the cof-feehouses and elsewhere by a number of different readers, approximately 9.4 million of the required newspaper stamps were issued in 1760, as opposed to 7.3 million in 1750.[15] Public demand and the proliferation of periodicals generated a high demand for copy; hence, Goldsmith's active participation in the profession was facilitated.

Another important feature of the period was the establishment of what Harris calls a "classic management structure" dominating the book and periodical trade: "The term 'book trade' . . . is itself ambiguous, embracing a vast range of interlocking activity: from type-founders and paper-makers to hack authors, from prosperous business men to destitute entrepreneurs, and from complicated commercial structures to low-key personal operations."[16] Robert and James Dodsley, for example, were involved in selling writing paper, as well as publishing books and periodicals; and Newbery sold patent medicine, in addition to his work as "printer-bookseller." Robert Haig, in his study of the *Gazetteer,* notices the gradual blurring of the distinction between the functions of printers and booksellers.[17] Both the "printer" and the "bookseller" sometimes took on the functions of what are now referred to as the editor or publisher. Often, as in the case of Griffiths, oversight of printing operations, book sales, and periodical publication was in the hands of the same manager. Consequently, the terms "printer" and "bookseller" were applied ambiguously, given the diverse management structures of the various businesses. At least in the cases of Griffiths and Newbery, the terms were often used synonymously, and generally as equivalent to "publisher."

These men, at least in the distribution of periodicals, formed a cooperative network. The bookseller R. Baldwin's advertisement in the *London Evening Post* that his *London Magazine* would be "sold by all other booksellers and news carriers," was a fairly standard announcement. In developing new delivery systems, the booksellers were both competitive, as in the case of the *Monthly* and *Critical,* and cooperative. For the most part, though, they banded together to form what Kernan calls "the interlinking chain that extended from the print shop, to the publishers—or booksellers, as they were then known—to the marketplace and the Grub Street writers."[18] One reason the coffeehouses were such a vital link in this chain is that they were both an outlet and a source for foreign news, that "first Demand made by the Reader of a Journal," as the *London Chronicle* put it.[19]

On 11 January 1759 the *Gazetteer* issued a plea for foreign intelligence from ship captains or officers visiting London's coffeehouses. Fresh, accurate, and entertaining foreign news was the explicit *raison d'être* for many of London's journals. The introductory essay for the first issue of the *Universal*

Chronicle (8 April 1758) acknowledged: "The number of News-Papers already published is so great, that there appears, at the first view, very little need of another." But the authors justified their undertaking by promising greater accuracy and earlier intelligence. The *Public Ledger* also promoted itself as a source for the "speedy Circulation of Intelligence" (12 January 1760) and hired Goldsmith as a sort of "foreign correspondent" to help fulfill this duty. The *Gazetteer* followed suit; on 29 October 1760 it promised: "The Readers of the Gazetteer may depend not only upon having the usual foreign Advices communicated as early as possible, but they will sometimes, by means of a Correspondence, very lately established, have the advantage of Articles not easily to be acquired."

The exact nature of the "foreign correspondent" and even of "foreign news" was ambiguous. Black observes: "Not only was foreign news poorly differentiated from domestic items; in addition the differing types of foreign news were mingled without distinction or apparent organisation, other than by place of origin of news items."[20] The correspondent could be an actual observer of military affairs or foreign relations, or he could be a fictional creation. He could relate the progress of the Byng trial or describe events occurring throughout Europe to readers in England. One recurring function was to give an account of the foreign book trade; interest and exchange in foreign books peaked between the years 1759 and 1762—perhaps as a result of the urge, stimulated by the war, to measure English progress against developments in foreign nations.[21]

The "Foreign Correspondent"

In establishing a role for himself as a contributor to a variety of London periodicals, Goldsmith frequently assumed a fictional role first created for him by Griffiths: the "foreign correspondent." Like most other reviewers, he had been assigned a diverse assortment of newly published works—from medical treatises to poetry collections—but the number of foreign works he was assigned clearly distinguished Goldsmith's work from that of his peers. He brought this same diversity to his essay career; like his predecessors, he tried his hand at a variety of types of essay: light social satire in the manner of Addison, moral and literary criticism reminiscent of Johnson and Hawkesworth's contributions to the *Adventurer,* and dramatic theory similar to Murphy's for the *Gray's Inn Journal.* But the most prominent and distinguishing type of essay which Goldsmith wrote was the "foreign correspondent" type. By continuing his "foreign correspondent" persona, Goldsmith could apply what he had learned in his earlier European travels, he could maintain the illusion of distance from the periodical trade and its political infighting, and he could appeal to a clearly established public appetite for foreign news and cultural comparison. The frequency with which he assumed this role and his attendant success best differentiate Goldsmith's journalistic work from that of his contemporaries.

Goldsmith used the "traveler" or "correspondent" persona to generalize about foreign cultures and to evaluate his own. This type of periodical contribution, a natural offshoot of his nearly contemporaneous work on *Polite Learning* and his plans for *The Citizen* and *Memoirs of M. de Voltaire* (probably begun late in 1758), was by far his most frequently used approach and, as such, the single most dominant feature of his journalistic career. While this method was certainly neither exclusive nor original—in fact, many of his contributions were translations and adaptations—the prevalence of this approach at least demonstrates in part how Goldsmith the journalist perceived himself and his authorial voice. In some of his essays for the *Bee* and even more frequently in his later essays, Goldsmith created the illusion of distance and objectivity by using the epistolary form. More and more frequently he wrote letters "To the Authors" which identify the correspondent as a nonpartisan "citizen of the world," whose expertise ranged from Russia to Africa to South America; the persona was that of a man eminently qualified to serve as self-appointed counselor to a declining England. His purpose seems twofold: to amuse his readers with often condescending, anecdotal summaries of the barbarous customs of the uncivilized; and to evaluate the strengths and weaknesses of foreign nations as an indirect means of attacking aspects of English customs.

Development of this persona can also be seen as a product of Goldsmith's acute sense of himself as a cultural outsider in London. His "Irishness" may have doomed his medical practice and contributed to his exclusion from full recognition by the London "salon"; at best, he was its charming fool, pressing too hard for social acceptance. As a "foreign correspondent," however, he could please the public while tweaking the sensibilities of those who had rejected him. Behind a mask of erudition and impartiality, Goldsmith could escape cultural isolation and style himself a "philosopher of the first rank," without national bias, party affiliation, or indebtedness to the affluent.

In *Polite Learning* Goldsmith had developed a collection of synoptic cultural observations that would form the basis of many of his later "correspondent" essays. Nations of the world and their peoples were rated in terms of their social, political, and literary progress. The result was a sort of cumulative "scale of cultures." Ironically, Goldsmith satirized this type of journalism in Lien Chi Altangi's Letter V (*Public Ledger,* 7 February 1760); "An Englishman not satisfied with finding by his own prosperity the contending powers of Europe properly balanced, desires also to know the precise value of every weight in either scale. To gratify this curiosity, a leaf of political instruction is served up every morning with tea" (II, 31). The letter satirized the stereotypes such journals perpetuated: "The superstition and erroneous delicacy of Italy, the formality of Spain, the cruelty of Portugal, the fears of Austria, the confidence of Prussia, the levity of France, the avarice of Holland, the pride of England, the absurdity of Ireland, and the national partiality of Scotland, are all conspicuous in every page" (II, 32). In fact this sort of "instruction" and observation is one of the distinguishing characteristics of Goldsmith's early work and a vehicle for a great deal of veiled political commentary. Presumably the "foreign correspondent," while satisfying the appetites of his readers, provided a corrective to these simplistic stereotypes with a set of his own.

Near the bottom of Goldsmith's scale is Spain, "long fallen from amazing Europe with her wit" (*Polite Learning,* I, 282). His single exception to the "barbarity" of this nation is Padre Feijóo, who exposed the "monkish stupidity of the times" (I, 283). The same theme is repeated in the third issue of the *Bee:* Father "Freijo" is the lone civilizing force in a nation which "has, for many centuries past, been remarkable for the grossest ignorance in polite literature" (I, 413). With his enormous range—encompassing literature, science, history, theology, philosophy, and politics—and his productivity, Fray Benito Jerónimo Feijóo y Montenegro (1676–1764) serves as a sort of spiritual mentor for Goldsmith: a voice of reason, morality, and learning from the darkness of ignorance. One of the *British Magazine* essays newly reattributed to Goldsmith, "An Essay on Fascination" (December 1760), is "Translated from the Spanish of the celebrated Padre Feijóo"; this study of the "evil eye" attacks a "species of superstition" that Goldsmith apparently found endemic in Spanish culture.

Italy, "a warm country ever producing an effeminacy of manners among the inhabitants" (*British Magazine;* III, 112), fares little better than Spain: with the sort of short, dismissive paradox he frequently employs, Goldsmith concludes: "In Italy, then, we shall no where find a stronger passion for art or science, yet no country making more feeble efforts to promote either" (*Polite Learning;* I, 276). The same claim and same rhetorical structure form the center of his *Bee* essay "Some Account of the Academies of Italy": "There is not, perhaps, a country in Europe, in which learning is so fast upon the decline as in Italy; yet not one in which there are such a number of academies instituted for its support" (I, 473). Two suggestive lines from *The Traveller* epitomize his view of this country: "Could Nature's bounty satisfy the breast, / The sons of Italy were surely blest" (IV, 253; ll. 111–12). Only for its opera and music is Italy praised, and even then primarily for the purpose of criticizing English opera, as is evident in his *Bee* essay "Of the Opera in England" and his *British Magazine* piece "On the Different Schools of Music."

Germans, too, are presented as objects for contempt. They are treated in *Polite Learning* and in his essays as militaristic and unproductive. Again, Goldsmith's judgment takes the form of a scornful, satiric antithesis: "But let the Germans have their due; if they are often a little dull, no nation alive assumes a more laudable solemnity, or better understands all the little decorums of stupidity" (I, 279). For the first issue of the *Bee,* he translates a letter from Voltaire which presents the stereotype of the Prussians: "It is an easy matter to conceive how regular machines must behave, who have long been used to war" (I, 369)—an observation consistent with Goldsmith's conclusions in *Polite Learning* and with the antiwar posture he assumes in many of his essays.

Goldsmith remained fairly reticent on the subject of Germany from 1760 to 1762, when Pitt's war policies, particularly his German subsidies, came under harsh attack from the Earl of Bute and his supporters in the press.[22] The Prussian alliance had been one of the most contentious issues of the war since its beginning—rooted, in part, in the old "Tory" attacks on the king's Hanoverian connections.[23] While Goldsmith steered clear of the controversy, which was raging in journals such as the *Test, Con-Test,* and *Monitor,* his serial installments on Voltaire for the *Lady's Magazine* frequently paint an unflattering picture of the Prussians and hint at his opposition to the German alliance.

Other "backward" nations, too, are held up for comparisons favorable to England. The Polish are "directed by a low sordid interest," a "wretchedness" which, by contrast, should make the Englishman take enthusiastic pride in his own liberty (*Bee;* I, 371). In "On the Assemblies of Russia" for the *Lady's Magazine* Goldsmith ridicules the etiquette of Russian social gatherings with an implicit comparison to England's more progressive rules of decorum. The Russians are a savage people who are "now at that period between refinement and barbarity, which seems most adapted to military atchievement" (II, 354). Most barbarous of all are the peoples of South America: his "South American Giants" article for the *Public Ledger* half-seriously considers travellers' accounts of a race of giants dwelling there (III, 167–69).

Goldsmith describes his own Irish people in an essay for the *Weekly,* "A Description of the Manners and Customs of the Native Irish" (III, 24–30). Presented as a letter from an "English Gentleman"—and so perhaps deliberately reflective of the prejudices of that class—the essay praises Irish Protestants, who are "almost all originally from England" (III, 24) and display a typically English roughness and generosity. In contrast to the English, however, they are "foolishly prodigal" and frequently unreliable (III, 25). The "Papists" or "original Irish" are "fawning, insincere, and fond of pleasure"— traits that have dangerously infected their Protestant counterparts (III, 25). This comparative view, however, may be facetious; its tone is even more hyperbolic than others of this type, and its narrator may well be unreliable.

Still, Goldsmith's journalistic voice consistently distances him from his Irish roots—symptomatic, perhaps, of the author's perception that his being Irish is a barrier to literary recognition. His treatment of Ireland in the *Weekly* essay is consistent with the comments he makes to his brother-in-law Daniel Hodson in a letter of December 1757. There he expresses his contempt for a country from which he received only his "brogue [an]d his blunders," but claims affection for the place based solely on his affection for Hodson and other of his friends.[24]

R. W. Seitz argues that Irish tradition and political thought provided the foundation for Goldsmith's ideology—his "conservative Tory liberalism," as Seitz calls it. He sees Goldsmith as a champion of a middle class threatened by "the encroachments of commerce and the new imperialism." Such an "admiration for the English middle class," which Seitz sees as the essence of Goldsmith's philosophy, is not always evident in his journalism; and if his Irish roots were vital to his ideological development—as they must, indeed, have been—he deliberately tried to suppress this influence.[25] Like many of his fellow countrymen working anonymously for English periodicals, he recognized the danger of being identified as Irish. A writer of a mid-nineteenth-century history of the Irish periodical recites the "defects" in the Irish character, giving stereotypes that obviously lingered more than a century after Goldsmith left the profession: "But the greatest defect of all, in the Irish character, is want of toleration in matters of opinion, and an exorbitant vanity that influences conduct in grave circumstances affecting the greatest interests, and that leads men to keep back all others from promoting them, rather than not occupy the most prominent position themselves."[26] For English readers and their hardened prejudices, an Irish correspondent would be unreliable, and Goldsmith's correspondent persona is, foremost, an English gentleman. Even when Goldsmith satirizes the English prejudice against the Irish, as he seems to in his *Weekly* essay, he is careful not to reveal himself.

Another of Goldsmith's national characterizations played a vital role in his developing ideological stance. His portrayal of Sweden was multidimensional and changing; the nation's place in Goldsmith's scale declined as the author's metaphoric use of this culture changed. *Polite Learning* depicts it as a land of literary promise with "a language rude, but energetic" (I, 283). Borrowing, as he did frequently, from the travel accounts of Justus Van Effen,[27] Goldsmith writes in the *Bee* that though the Swedes "languish under oppression," they are honest and courageous—a legacy of their late monarch Charles XII (I, 379). Another *Bee* essay, chastising the English for their lack of "political frugality" cites Sweden as "the only country where the science of economy seems to have fixed its empire" (I, 442).

Goldsmith also uses Sweden to focus his observations on England's participation in the war. In an essay for the *Weekly*, Sweden becomes a "wretched" nation, impoverished in spite of its former military glory. Again, Goldsmith's analysis is more self-serving than genuinely analytical: it provides an allegorical warning about the dangers of further English military conflict and extensive colonization. In his "On Public Rejoicings for Victory," written four days after news of the taking of Quebec reached London on 16 October 1759, Goldsmith represents Sweden as a political symbol of the hollowness of military victory: "It is very possible for a country to be very victorious and very wretched. The victories of Sweden have oppressed that people so much, as to render them quite insignificant in the political scale of Europe ever since" (III, 21).

In Chinese Letter LVI "on the present situation of affairs, in the different countries of Europe" (8 July 1760), Goldsmith again uses Sweden allegorically to create one of the clearest manifestations of his own political views. Despite the fact that he frequently professes himself to be opposed to party politics, he betrays his royalist sensibilities:

> Sweden . . . though now seemingly a strenuous assertor of its liberties, is probably only hastening on to despotism. Their senators, while they pretend to vindicate the freedom of the people, are only establishing their own independence. The deluded people will however at last perceive the miseries of an aristocratical government; they will perceive, that the administration of a society of men is ever more painful than that of one only. They will fly from this most oppressive of all forms, where one single member is capable of controlling the whole, to take refuge under the throne which will ever be attentive to their complaints. (II, 235)

Readers of the *Public Ledger* could hardly fail to read this analysis as an endorsement of royal prerogative and a challenge to the "Old Corps" Whig aristocracy facing its imminent demise in 1760.[28]

Goldsmith's analysis of the Ottoman Empire serves a similar political end. In an essay for the *Weekly* (29 December 1759) Goldsmith warns that the Ottoman Empire is "one of the most extensive, yet perhaps one of the most feeble empires in the world; is it not possible for England to have colonies too large for her natural power to manage?" (III, 32). His comparison here is consistent with his disapproval of the war with France and his often-cited fears of colonial overextension. He repeats this admonition with the same analogy in a Chinese Letter for the *Public Ledger* (Letter XVII, 13 March 1760): "The colonies should always bear an exact proportion to the mother country; when they grow populous, they grow powerful, and by becoming powerful, they become independent also; thus subordination is destroyed, and a country swallowed up in the extent of its own dominions. The Turkish empire would be more formidable, were it less extensive" (II, 74–75). The "best English politicians," he argues, are cognizant of this danger; by implication, the present ministry is not.

Switzerland heads Goldsmith's "scale of cultures." In his role as correspondent promising literary news from abroad, Goldsmith writes to the "Compiler" of the *Public Ledger:* "Among the kingdoms of Europe which best deserve the wise men's attention, I think Switzerland may be at present placed in the foremost rank" (III, 164). A translated letter from Voltaire published in the *Bee* praises the nation's tranquility and its cultivation of learning (I, 391–93). In another *Bee* article Goldsmith praises the Swiss legal system—"government by custom"—again for the purpose of criticizing England, "burdened with a multiplicity of written laws" (I, 484). His admiration for the Swiss in his essays anticipates *The Traveller* and its idealized view of the Swiss accepting their poverty and their barren soil with grace and patriotism.

As one might expect, the most frequent and complex cultural comparisons in Goldsmith's journalism are between England and France. The patriotic clamor in Goldsmith's series "A Comparative View of Races and Nations" for the *Royal* is typical of this journal's chauvinistic tone: "Examine every [other] state in Europe and you will find the people either enjoying a precarious freedom under monarchical government, or what is worse, actually slaves in a republic, to laws of their own contriving" (III, 68). But the "Hail, Britain!" exclamatory tone of this series is anomalous in the context of Goldsmith's other comparisons of the two rival nations. More frequently, Goldsmith uses France's literary and cultural accomplishments to wag an accusatory finger at England. In *Polite Learning* Goldsmith contrasts the "agreeable enthusiasm" of the French in learning and taste with the failure of the English to recognize and reward their deserving authors: "While we with a despondence characteristic of our nation, are for removing back British excellence to the reign of Queen Elizabeth, our more happy rivals of the continent, cry up the writers of the present times with rapture, and regard the age of Lewis XV. as the true Augustan age of France" (I, 298). Lien Chi Altangi reports on the prejudice of an "English journalist" who complained that the "French are the most contemptible reasoners (we had almost said writers) that can be imagined" (II, 87). Such criticism comes most frequently, he observes, from "indifferent writers." Goldsmith praises the French system of patronage and implicitly argues that the decline of the English system has resulted in the neglect of talent and the undeserved affluence of those writers who acquiesce to popular taste. In addition, he admires the taste and learning of French women to the detriment of the women of England (I, 299–300); their deplorable dress and manner are also frequent targets in later essays.

Late in 1758, while he was arranging for the publication of *Polite Learning,* Goldsmith worked on his *Memoirs of M. de Voltaire,* unpublished until its serial appearance in the *Lady's Magazine* (February–November 1761). To some extent Goldsmith created, from a loose account of Voltaire's life prior to 1750, an alter ego through which to compare French and English accomplishments. Highlighting Book II, an account of Voltaire's stay in England, is a critique of English letters and customs similar to that of *Polite Learning:* a

discussion of the superiority of French dramatic theory (III, 237), an examination of the "moroseness" of the English character (III, 248), an account of
the defectiveness of the English stage (III, 250)—all recurring issues in
Goldsmith's periodical work. The figure of Voltaire, as Goldsmith presents
him by pointed selection from the French author's articles and letters, also
looms large in the *Bee*. The translated article "On the Contradictions of the
World" contains a Goldsmith-like juxtaposition of contraries concerning the
English national character: "The English serve their kings upon the knee; but
they are often found to depose them, to imprison them, and bring some of
them to the scaffold" (I, 467). A translated letter enumerates instances of
political cruelty and remembers England's most vehemently debated controversy of 1757: "I know not whether the English yet find any remorse for
theirs [of cruelty] to Byng" (I, 392). Another letter, previously cited,
rehearses stereotypical views on Prussian militarism (I, 369)—a theme central to the last completed book of Goldsmith's *Memoirs*. At least for the
greater part of 1759 Goldsmith frequently uses Voltaire to lend substance and
prestige to his own pattern of cultural comparison.

Throughout his periodical career, Goldsmith persistently praises the
culture of France at the expense of English manners. In "On Our Theatres"
the Parisian actress Mademoiselle Clarion, "the most perfect female figure I
have ever seen upon any stage," is contrasted with the "ridiculousness" of
Mrs. Cibber in her role of Belvidera in *Venice Preserved* (*Bee*, I, 389). The
French woman is "a perfect architect in dress" while her English counterpart
is among the most ill-dressed in the world (*Bee;* I, 374). The English
"gloomy reserve" is contrasted with the French "easy affability" (*Bee;* I, 490).
And in a theme he repeats in essays for the *Weekly* and the *Lady's,* the
inadequacy of the English manner of preaching and its inferiority to the
sublimity of French sermonizing contributes to the vulgarity and ignorance
of the English lower class, "the most barbarous and the most unknowing of
any in Europe" (*Bee,* I, 480).

Goldsmith's comparisons between these rival nations are not intended
principally as paeans to French achievement, any more than his Chinese
Letters celebrate Oriental culture; they are a formulaic means of advancing his
own complaints, both mild and harsh, against English society. The genial
"Citizen of the World," though endowed (as Goldsmith admitted in his
preface) with the author's own colloquial ease, nevertheless furnishes Goldsmith with another persona to effect specious cultural comparisons and
sincere social criticism. Lien Chi Altangi first appears in the pages of the
Public Ledger as a "stranger to [English] manners" (II, 16) with comic naïveté
and objectifying distance. He questions the luxuriousness of the English,
their "universal passion for politics" (II, 29), the foolishness of their journalists and critics, and the shallowness of their morals. His letters expand on
the serious critique Goldsmith had made in "Upon Political Frugality," in

another of his sweeping cultural summaries: "There is not, perhaps, in the world a people less fond of this virtue [i.e., frugality] than the English, and of consequence there is not a nation more restless, more exposed to the uneasiness of life, or less capable of providing for particular happiness" (*Bee*, I, 435). This generalization summarizes the two related complaints the author repeats most frequently in this work: the "luxurious" English have lost the virtue provided by a simple life, and they have become generally unhappy or "morose."

Much of Goldsmith's prose written in this vein is unsophisticated and imitative. It is, nonetheless, lively and timely; its usual tone of gentle disapproval and its stylistic ease are characteristic of his later writing. Further it affords scholars an incomplete but useful means of classifying the first third of Goldsmith's authorial career, a classification more specific than Wardle's "Tinker? Tailor?" tag or identifications of Goldsmith as a "laughing comedy" playwright, "sentimental" novelist, or reform-minded poet.[29] In his "foreign correspondent" role Goldsmith began his career, set up his own periodical, published *Polite Learning* and *The Citizen,* wrote essays for a variety of periodicals, and collected and reprinted much of his anonymous work in *Essays by Mr. Goldsmith* (1765). In this capacity he met Griffiths, Smollett, and Johnson and made his entrée into the London publishing world.

Essays and Editorial Policy

Another accommodation Goldsmith made to survive in the journalistic profession was to match his style and moral content to the stated goals of the journals for which he wrote. Even though the *Monthly* and *Critical* were not as philosophically opposed as their frequent and well-publicized quarrels would indicate, Goldsmith's ability to write for both Tory and Whig editors implies his adaptability to the ideologies and concerns of his employers. He displayed a similar ability in his contributions to the magazines and newspapers for which he worked. He adopted what Alvin Sullivan calls an "urbane, tongue-in-cheek" tone suitable for the *Busy Body* and its "cultured observations on the British scene."[30] To the *Weekly* he contributed humorous and didactic biographical sketches, a genre frequently reappearing in the weekly miscellanies, and he echoed the journal's moderate, balanced position in the ongoing "ancients versus moderns" literary controversy. For the conservative, patriotic *Royal* he wrote his "Comparative View" series extolling patriotic virtue; for the *British Magazine,* which Spector describes as the most aesthetically conservative journal of its time, Goldsmith wrote "moral tales" and expressed contempt for modern fashions in learning.[31]

While editing the *Bee* in October 1759 Goldsmith also contributed to the short-lived *Busy Body* (9 October 1759 to 3 November 1759), managed by

Edward Purdon, a printer, and the bookseller Israel Pottinger. A throwback to the era of single-essay periodicals, it was the only such journal to which Goldsmith contributed. Only two essays and two poems in this series can be confidently attributed to Goldsmith, but the tone, narrative stance, and themes are strikingly similar to those of the *Bee*. In its gently satiric treatment of London society and in its development of a well-delineated first-person narrative, the *Busy Body* was indebted to the *Spectator* and the *Connoisseur*, as Goldsmith was in "A Description of Various Clubs." The fourth number, unattributed, reflects both the self-mocking persona common in Goldsmith's light essays and the character of the traveler/correspondent:

> I received from nature a genius so active and enterprising, that a single kingdom appeared a sphere too narrow for the exertion of abilities, which heaven certainly endowed me with, for the emolument of my fellow-creatures. . . . This my ardent passion for travelling, as it sprung from a laudable desire to promote the general happiness of Europe, will certainly meet with the approbation of the generous and noble-minded.[32]

The writer, broadly ironic, bemoans the poor public reception the *Busy Body* had received. Short-lived as this periodical was, it was one of the more amusing efforts of its time. For example, in a burlesque of advertising, the *Busy Body* appealed for contributions: "Wanted, to read and apply the character of the Busy Body, a person of consummate assurance, possessed of a prodigious rapidity of expression, without any solid sense.—As several pretenders have been already rejected, it is hoped no person will apply, who is not well versed in the art of scandal."[33] This tongue-in-cheek appeal, implying the need for contributors and the difficulty of the task at hand, may have attracted Goldsmith and his developing talent for light satire. In another vein, the *Busy Body* published Goldsmith's poignant "On Public Rejoicings for Victory." Reprinted in his *Essays* (1765), this essay, one of his most memorable, is an impassioned appeal for lasting peace and reconciliation.

Little is known about Pottinger, but an anecdote that William Cooke attributed to Hugh Kelly, who had worked with Pottinger on the *Lady's Museum* and *Court Magazine,* may help explain the rapid demise of the *Busy Body:* "He [Pottinger] was a man who dashed at any thing in the temporary way, and was at one time getting a good deal of money, though he afterwards fell into great indigence."[34] Though Goldsmith contributed two of his finest essays to the journal, and its essays were consistently witty and stylish, the *Busy Body* was conceptually outmoded and vanished even more rapidly than the *Bee*. It may, indeed, have been an idea of Pottinger's "dashed at . . . in the temporary way."

From December 1759 to September 1760 Goldsmith contributed to at least five different journals, each distinctive in format, but each concerned to some degree with aesthetic criticism, didacticism, and foreign affairs. For a second Pottinger publication, the *Weekly Magazine, or Gentleman and Lady's Polite Companion,* Goldsmith contributed a variety of essays: his typical "foreign correspondent" letters; brief biographies, including a hilarious account of Theophilus Cibber that might have been subtitled "Three Ways of Getting into Debt"; and several pieces of criticism. Spector cites the *Weekly* for its atypical attacks on prescriptive critical rules; certainly Goldsmith's "The Futility of Criticism" notably contributed to the paper's challenge to a rule-governed aesthetic.[35]

For the conservative, patriotic *Royal Magazine, or Gentleman's Monthly Companion,* begun in July 1759 by John Coote, a business associate of John Newbery, Goldsmith celebrated England as a "nation of philosphers" in his "A Comparative View of Races and Nations" series.[36] Tailoring his series to fit the ideology of the *Royal,* Goldsmith carefully avoided the sort of harsh criticism of England that typified much of his "foreign correspondent" work. One of his more artful contributions to the *Royal* was an Eastern tale, "The Proceedings of Providence Vindicated," reprinted in *Essays* (1765). Using a genre popular throughout the 1750's in the essay-periodicals, Goldsmith constructed an allegorical attack on the spirit of national defeatism and a thinly disguised appeal for love of country.

In 1760 Goldsmith wrote prolifically for the two journals that probably had more impact on his later career than any others to which he contributed: Newbery and Smollett's *British Magazine* and the *Public Ledger, or Daily Register of Commerce and Intelligence.* The nature and importance of Goldsmith's association with the *Public Ledger,* as with the *British,* has been, to a degree, overlooked and misunderstood. The *Ledger* is remembered chiefly for printing Goldsmith's 119 Chinese Letters from 24 January 1760 to 14 August 1761. In fact, the Letters were a relatively small and somewhat anomalous part of this daily. The newspaper was dominated by accounts of military operations, port and domestic news, and advertisements (it published an extensive index to advertisements in the other dailies and weeklies). The only major variable in its format was its lead, left-hand column.

Goldsmith's fictional letter writer, irregularly published, was only one of a number of fictional and nonfictional personae occupying this column in the *Ledger.* Another semiregular pseudonymous column was "The Visitor" by "Philanthropy Candid, Esq.," who often excoriated the English public for its moral shortcomings. The *Ledger* published other miscellaneous pieces of varying seriousness, including one from "Will Frankly" on the danger of imprudent wives (7 July 1760). Just as often, though, this column was filled with material more directly appropriate to the periodical's purpose, as stated in its subtitle. The issue for 1 July 1760, for example, published a letter recounting proudly the triumphant siege of Quebec. Often, too, the column was used for listing ships "taken or re-taken" in the war.

Within the context of this predominately serious and topical newspaper, which was concerned (as were most periodicals of that time) with foreign intelligence, a political reading of the Letters must be considered. Although Robert Hopkins presents a plausible analysis of *The Citizen* as political satire, most scholars have seen the Letters as genial social criticism rather than as timely political documents appropriate to a "Daily Register of Commerce and Intelligence."[37] To avoid political commentary entirely in such a vehicle and for such an audience would have been nearly impossible. But in the preface to his eight contributions to the *Ledger* not related to the Chinese Letters, Goldsmith portrayed his essays as apolitical, as a respite from the glut of foreign news filling the dailies:

> In fact, the reader of a modern news-paper has some right to expect a little refreshment of this nature; we have fought over the German battles even to satiety, Pondicherry and Mocomogo are now our own; it is but just that same page which is stained with blood and slaughter, should also refresh us with the exertions of benevolence or wisdom. (III, 158–59)

While not overtly related to contemporary events, this new series—again of the "foreign correspondent" variety—examined England's progress in the arts and sciences vis-a-vis that of its European neighbors. His tough assessments of English arts and manners, quite unlike the *Royal* essays in tone, must be considered at least implicitly political.

Goldsmith's association with the *Lady's Magazine* remains relatively obscure. Percy's *Memoir* mentions that Goldsmith was its editor for a time, and he published in it his unfinished *Memoirs of M. de Voltaire* in monthly installments from February to November 1761. Two essays reprinted in *Essays* (1765) first appeared in the *Lady's*: "Of the Assemblies of Russia" and "Some Remarks on the Modern Manner of Preaching." Friedman accepts Crane's attribution of "A Lady of Fashion in the Times of Anna Bullen Compared with One of Modern Times," but rejects three other Crane attributions as inconclusive (Introduction, III, 143–44). There is insufficient evidence to decide whether Goldsmith, in effect, became "Caroline Stanhope," the ostensible publisher of the *Lady's,* as some have claimed. But he was certainly a principal contributor in 1761 and styled his rather frothy essays to suit his conception of a female readership.

"The Indigent Philosopher"

By October 1761 Goldsmith had significantly broadened the scope of his authorial work. Miscellaneous projects for Newbery included history writing, prefaces, translations, anthologies, and a variety of full-length non-fiction work. By this time the styles, themes, and theories that generated later productions such as *The Vicar, The Deserted Village, The Traveller,* and his two comedies had been well-established. Though he was still a relatively obscure figure because of the anonymity of his contributions, he had at least improved both his financial circumstances and his reputation among publishers.

In the middle of 1760, he left Green Arbour Court for a more comfortable dwelling in Wine Office Court, Fleet Street, where he probably lived with a relative or acquaintance of Newbery.[38] Among his companions there were Percy, Smart, Francklin, Murphy, and the playwright Isaac Bickerstaffe.[39] While living at Wine Office Court and completing his Chinese Letters, Goldsmith first met Johnson (according to Percy) on 31 May 1761.[40] This new association certainly improved Goldsmith's visibility as a public figure and member of "The Club," and Johnson was instrumental in arranging the publication of *The Vicar* and *The Traveller.* But the friendship with Johnson also inevitably invited unfair comparisons—the appellations "Doctor Minor" and the diminutive "Goldy" he so detested.[41] The accounts of Boswell, Thrale-Piozzi, Reynolds, Murphy, and others portray Goldsmith as the "idiot savant" educated by Johnson, the tolerant "Master." Garrick's famous "epitaph,"

> Here lies poet Goldsmith, for shortness call'd Noll,
> Who wrote like an angel, but talked like poor Poll

epitomizes the attitude of Goldsmith's contemporaries, who gave as much attention to the "poor Poll" characterization as to the "angelic" writer. The first of Johnson's comments on Goldsmith, as recorded by Boswell, expresses the same paradox: "Dr. Goldsmith is one of the first men we now have as an authour, and he is a very worthy man too. He has been loose in his principles, but he is coming right."[42] Johnson's analysis came at a time, 25 June 1763, when Goldsmith's accomplishments had been chiefly limited to his journalistic work. Nonetheless, he had already laid a substantial foundation for his literary career by the time he met his mentor.

Toward the end of 1761, Goldsmith conceived of a project that seems to suggest a political motivation for his writing the Chinese Letters. He appealed to Lord Bute, who had risen to ministerial control under George III, for funding of a tour of the East to study Oriental arts and sciences; the appeal was denied.[43] If Goldsmith had aspirations of becoming one of Bute's "Tory pensioners," as Johnson was to become a year later, his hopes were short-lived.

His plans to further his career as a scholar of the Orient having failed, Goldsmith apparently turned to Newbery once more in January 1762, and he was assigned to write a series of essays as "The Indigent Philosopher" for

Lloyd's Eveninig Post, of which Newbery was a principal shareholder.[44] His philosopher admits:[45]

> Indigence be my motive for this publication, yet I have taken Honesty for my guide: I am one of those characters who being always poor, have been ever receiving advice from their friends and acquaintance. . . . I intend, for the benefit of these good advising friends, in this public manner to dose them with part of it back. (III, 183)

He issued an ironic promise to "shew [his] philosophy" by commenting on the "crucial" topics of the day: the Cock Lane Ghost, the construction of the Blackfriars bridge, and the "Machine to carry Fish," a plan to procure fish for London and Westminster by land carriage (III, 183n).[46]

In some respects, *Lloyd's* was a less ambitious version of the *Ledger*—it appeared triweekly instead of daily, and had a three-column format instead of a six-column format. Like the *Ledger,* it featured foreign and domestic news, advertisements, letters to the editor, and occasional book reviews (by the pseudonymous "Benevolus"). The distinctive quality of this series was its self-reflexiveness: its essays were replete with comical and cynical observations about the journalistic enterprise. Goldsmith's contributions were topical. Two of them described such events and controversies then attracting *Lloyd's* readers as the Cock Lane Ghost and the recently declared war against Spain. But they also allowed the author another chance to pillory the profession.

The "Indigent Philosopher" was a world-weary newspaper hack who, in the first number (20–22 January 1762), bemoaned the death of a friend and his own ignoble occupation: "Alas! how ill do I support the dignity of a Scholar or a Gentleman, by thus consigning my little acquirements to the same vehicle that must too often necessarily convey insipidity and ignorance!" (III, 182). After updating his *Busy Body* essay "A Description of Various Clubs" for the second number (25–27 January 1762), Goldsmith returned to his self-reflexive mode. For the third number (29 January–1 February 1762), he composed an addition to Smollett's *History* in which he evaluated several of London's periodicals. He reserved highest kudos for the *Gentleman's* but also praised "the sensible British Magazine"; "the Royal Magazine, written by a Society of Gentlemen"; and "the Lady's Magazine, by a Lady of very high quality" (III, 188).

The last word of the "Indigent Philosopher" on journalism came in the 8 February 1762 issue of *Lloyd's,* with his satirical "Magazine in Miniature." In making a distinction between an essayist and a "magaziner," he reflected humorously on his own miscellaneous productions of the preceding two-and-a-half years:

> We Essayists, who are allowed but one subject at a time, are by no means so

fortunate as the Writers of Magazines, who write upon several. If a Magaziner be dull upon the Spanish War, he soon has us up again with the Ghost in Cock-lane; if the Reader begins to doze upon that, he is quickly rouzed by an Eastern Tale; Tales prepare us for Poetry, and Poetry for the Meteorological History of the Weather. The Reader, like the Sailor's Horse, when he beings to tire, has at least the comfortable refreshment of having the spur changed. (III, 191)

Actually, Goldsmith had been both essayist and "Magaziner" and his remarks reflected ironically on the miscellaneous nature of his own career in the diverse periodicals for which he wrote. Ironically, Goldsmith may, in fact, have published a pamphlet on the Cock Lane Ghost incident, *The Mystery Revealed,* on 23 February 1762, less than two weeks after this satirical mention of the controversy appeared in *Lloyd's.* Certainly he had contributed his share of Eastern tales and topical poetry, though we have no record of his remarking on the Spanish War or meteorological history.

The brief parody in *Lloyd's* contained a miscellany of garbled addresses, a hodgepodge of clichés, a set of ridiculous "rules for behavior," and "a mock translation"—in short, it was an absurd and perhaps even angry attack on his profession (III, 191–95). While such parodies were commonplace in the essay-periodicals and newspapers, Goldsmith's disillusionment with the profession may have been genuine: he was gradually turning away from periodical authorship and training his sights on a more independent authorial course.

In June he contributed his last essay for *Lloyd's,* "The Revolution in Low Life," which Crane has called "the 'Deserted Village' in prose."[47] The paper was Goldsmith's first vehement protest against the Enclosure Laws, and in its nostalgic and sentimental tone it clearly anticipated the author's famous poem, completed in 1769 and published in 1770. He may also have returned to *Lloyd's* in November to publish an anonymous defense of his *Life of Richard Nash* (published 14 October 1762). Complaining about the ignorance of critics, the author of the defense observed that even "the little books for children, written by Mr. Newbery, have not escaped censure and abuse, though they have done so much service to the rising generation" (III, 395). Attribution of this piece to Goldsmith is uncertain; Friedman offers plausible if not definitive evidence (III, 392–4). If it were written by Goldsmith, the piece would be a fitting salute to the publisher so instrumental in helping him achieve literary notice.

Scholars have been unable to identify precisely when Goldsmith composed *The Vicar,* although it was almost certainly written during the later stages of his journalistic career.[48] An autobiographical impulse bleeds into almost all of his work at this period, and in *The Vicar,* the story of George Primrose's disillusionment with the profession of authorship becomes a vehicle for autobiographical reflection. The first six pages of Chapter 20, in which

George narrates the "history of a philosophic vagabond," are almost entirely a compilation of reflections Goldsmith had made in letters and in his journalism. George is the optimistic young man arriving in London, where "abilities of every kind were sure of meeting distinction and reward" (IV, 107). He considers work as an usher at a boarding school, but Goldsmith reuses his advertisement from the *Citizen* (II, 35) to demonstrate the virtual impossibility of this career choice. Considering a career as author, George paraphrases Goldsmith's letter to Hodson (31 August 1758): "You have read in books, no doubt, of men of genius starving at a trade: At present I'll shew you forty very dull fellows about town that live by it in opulence" (IV, 108). Similarly, George echoes Goldsmith's initial optimism and ambitiousness, his confidence in placing himself in the "great tradition" of English letters: "I thought it my glory to pursue a track which Dryden and Otway trod before me" (IV, 109). Later discouraged with this prospect, as Goldsmith seemed to be when the *Bee* failed to attract an adequate readership, George, like Goldsmith, attempts a different strategy: "The jewels of truth have been so often imported by others, that nothing was left for me to import but some splendid things that at a distance looked every bit as well" (IV, 109). Here Goldsmith, through George Primrose, identifies himself as "importer of truth"—the foreign correspondent identity by which he had largely sustained his journalistic career. With great expectations George takes on "the whole learned world," but finds himself ignored.

Bemoaning his fate—in a coffeehouse, of course—he is persuaded to "write for bread" (IV, 110–11). His reflections on this course of action, again, derive almost verbatim from Goldsmith's comments in the *Bee,* in his Chinese Letters, and in other miscellaneous essays. They also provide the basis for his later introduction to his collected essays:

> But I was unqualified for a profession where mere industry alone was to ensure success. I could not suppress my lurking passion for applause; but usually consumed that time in efforts after excellence which takes up but little room. . . . My little piece would therefore come forth in the mist of periodical publication, unnoticed and unknown. The public were more importantly employed, than to observe the easy simplicity of my style, or the harmony of my periods. Sheet after sheet was thrown off to oblivion. (IV, 111)

Thus George Primrose, in describing the failure of his learned "paradoxes," identifies a central paradox in Goldsmith's journalistic career: the same features of periodical publication that enabled a talented unknown to enter the profession, develop a recognizable style and appealing personae, and establish himself as one of its principal participants, also enforced anonymity and poverty. In large measure, the record of Goldsmith's journalism—itself obscured from the view of historians by the protective veil of anonymity—is that of an author's attempt to reconcile himself to this system. He tried to take advantage of the opportunities it presented, while abhorring its lack of moral and aesthetic foundation; to appeal to the coffeehouse tribunal, while protesting its vulgarity and injustices; and to establish an enduring place in a belletristic tradition that seemed to be vanishing.

8

"Arrant Tories" and "Soure Whigs": The Political Context of Goldsmith's Journalism

> You must understand, gentlemen, that I was born a poet: this, I think, I may say without vanity; yet, when I commenced author, I received the same answer from every bookseller to whom I offered my service in the poetical way. "Poetry does not sell, Sir," was the tune with them all. I was therefore obliged to check my poetical fire, and bring myself down to politicks and criticism.
>
> —"The Distresses of an Hired Writer"

Little attention has been paid to Goldsmith's politics and even less to the political nature of his journalistic career.[1] Goldsmith's careful crafting of a reputation for being apolitical may be partly responsible for this neglect. Even in his review work, he portrayed partisan politics as a barrier to authorial objectivity and to a writer's prospects for lasting fame. Responding to a pamphlet on military operations in North America, he noted that impartiality is the "first great quality of a historian," and he complained of the author: "We are too much led to suspect him of having an interested attachment to one party, implicitly to believe all he says against the other" (I, 37). Lien Chi Altangi complains about the pretentiousness of writers for the "Daily Gazettes": "You must not, however, imagine that they who compile these papers have any actual knowledge of the politics, or the government of a state; they only collect their materials from the oracle of some coffee-house" (II, 29). This professed impartiality frequently disguises political statement. Reviewing *A Compleat History of England* for Griffiths, Goldsmith criticizes the politics of Smollett, his editor's rival and his own future ally: "In private life, he should have the character of being free from Party, and his former writings ought always to have shewn the sincerest attachment to truth" (I, 50). Accusing Smollett of bias, Goldsmith himself became a combatant in the political rivalry between the journals.

Donald Davie writes of Goldsmith's politics that "all the contemporary accounts agree: Goldsmith was ingenuous, a naïf."[2] Most subsequent commentary has, by and large, oversimplified the problem of identifying the author's complex and often inconsistent ideological stances. R. W. Seitz traces the Irish origins and development of Goldsmith's "conventional Tory" partisanship—certainly an important but not exclusive strain in Goldsmith's writing.[3] Historians, following Seitz, have cast Goldsmith as a typical Anglo-Irish patriot, an "outsider" in English society who adopted an orthodox, paternalistic view of politics and society.[4] Again, Goldsmith's views, as expressed in his journalism, resist such simple categorization. His gentlemanly English persona avoided any hint of his Irish roots, and on one of the central "Irish issues"—inclusion of the Irish in the Militia Bill—he was conspicuously silent.[5]

Wardle, also of the "conventional Tory" school, does not give much weight to Goldsmith's own description of his politics in a letter to Bennet Langton (7 September 1771):

> They begin to talk in town of the opposition's gaining ground, the cry of Liberty is still as loud as ever. I have published or Davis has published for me an Abridgement of the History of England [*The History of England from the Earliest Times to the Death of George II,* published 6 August 1771] for which I have been a good deal abused in the newspapers for betraying the liberties of the people. God knows I had no thoughts for or against liberty in my head. My whole aim being to make up a book of a decent size that as Squire Richard says would do no harm to nobody. However they set me down as an arrant Tory and consequently no honest man. When you come to look at any part of it you'l say that I am a soure Whig.[6]

Wardle agrees with Balderston's suggestion that Goldsmith's Tory sentiments in his *History* are more prevalent than this disclaimer would suggest.[7] Still, the letter indicates that Goldsmith abhorred the ambiguous *Tory* label. It also reveals his ambivalence toward popular "liberty": he viewed it as the disruptive cry of reformist Whig factions and radicals like John Wilkes, but steadfastly refused to be seen as its opponent. And this letter reveals the paradoxical nature of Goldsmith's approach to politics: his writing was political while professing not to be; he defended the common man yet was appalled by the "mass" of his countrymen; he championed reform, yet often opposed "liberty," at least as Wilkes and his followers understood it. To Goldsmith, the supremacy of the masses unchecked by the crown was a threat to English security.

As little as his contemporaries thought of his political awareness, as much as scholars have downplayed his role as political commentator, as frequently as the author himself denied the political content of his writing, this "foreign correspondent" unavoidably contributed to the political dialogue which dominated the press during the war. A selective reading of his contributions could support either a "Tory Royalist" or a "Republican" interpretation. Davie has described the difficulty of reconciling Goldsmith's fervent support of a strong monarch with his appeals for reform in *The Traveller* and in *The Deserted Village*.[8] Many other critics have debated the political ramifications of *The Vicar of Wakefield*, though their task is complicated by the nature of the novelist's persona.[9] This same difficulty is inherent in studying the politics of Goldsmith's journalism: his narrative voices shift to suit his purposes as a writer and the political views of the journals to which he is contributing. Still, his periodical work, with all its complexity and inconsistency, offers a broader basis for analysis than any of his later works.

Given the nature of the radically changing journalistic climate of the age, completely avoiding political commentary would have been nearly impossible. During a "slow" journalistic period, Edmund Burke commented to Elizabeth Montagu (6 October 1759): "We have very little News either Political or Literary; the one of these has always some influence on the other."[10] Even the act of refusing to discuss many of the hotly disputed controversies had political implications. In fact, his protestations to the contrary notwithstanding, Goldsmith concerned himself with many of the critical issues of the period: the nature of party politics, royal and ministerial prerogative, the role of the press and the decline of patronage, the democratization of the "middling classes," and the proper relationship between law and personal authority. He may have been neither astute nor especially original as a political observer, and this role may have contributed little to the development of his literary reputation. Nonetheless, it is an important feature of his journalism that provides some perspective both on his own development and on a particularly turbulent period of English history.

Griffiths' Whig-for-Hire?

Attempts to identify Goldsmith with partisan views are frustrated by the essential ambiguity of the terms "Whig" and "Tory" as applied to the shifting political alliances of the High Georgian era, an ambiguity of reference by no means unique to this period.[11] Radical changes in the politics of the 1750s and the 1760s, brought about in part by the war, ministerial crises, and the accession of George III, make allusion to particular Whig or Tory positions especially difficult. Even the posture of nonpartisanship, taken by many journalists such as Goldsmith, might be interpreted politically. The "extinction of party" was one of the stated goals of Bute and the court of George III, and was partly an attempt to undermine the dominance of Whig coalitions.[12] Despite these semantic ambiguities, recognizing the competing philosophies in the context of a rapidly changing political arena contributes to our understanding of the climate in which Goldsmith developed as an author. Though historians sometimes attempt to eliminate party labels altogether in their discussions of the politics of the war period, the terms, however ambiguous, were part of the contemporary journalistic vocabulary. As William Shenstone noted in December 1762, "I am sorry to find that *Whig* and *Tory* are like to become as fashionable as ever."[13]

Historians have rightly challenged the notion of a unified Whig hegemony, controlled initially by Walpole, dominating English politics before the accession of George III in 1760. But the collapse of Whig ministerial control and the further factionalization of the party, the subsequent challenge to royal authority, and the emergence of the periodical press as a major factor in political debate brought a new degree of political destabilization to the late 1750s and 1760s. John Brewer accepts, at least in part, what he calls the Whig view of history: the perception of 1760 as a sort of watershed, when the Whig party faced its "imminent demise," and the Tory advocates of increased royal authority were rewarded by the crown.[14] Citing the end of single-party government, the decline of parliamentary patronage, and the proliferation of political journalism, Brewer argues: "The importance of the 1760s to the historian lies in the fact that all of these prerequisites of political stability were in some way challenged, modified or altered during that stormy decade."[15] Just as Goldsmith was reaching the peak of his productivity as a journalist, England underwent what George Nobbe calls "an unparalleled reversal." Nobbe notes that with the resignation of Newcastle on 24 May 1762, "The Whigs had been turned completely out of office just nineteen months after George III became King of England."[16]

One factor undermining Whig control was the gradual disappearance of the Jacobite threat.[17] For Goldsmith in 1759 the "threat" existed primarily in the minds of the "vulgar" and was an object of contempt. Eveline Cruickshanks notes that the "death of Jacobitism" by the time of the accession enabled George III "to be the king of all his people"—to include Tories as an active part of the political process.[18] But the term "Tory" still carried Jacobite associations and had long been a term of almost universal reproach—hence Goldsmith's refusal to describe himself as an "arrant Tory." In his *Busy Body* essay "On Public Rejoicings for Victory," his narrator notices a poor tradesman and his wife among the mobs of people celebrating in the streets of London: "The husband, who was, it seems, a journeyman shoemaker, damned her for being a Jacobite in her heart; that she had not a spice of loyalty in her whole body; that she was as fond of getting drunk one day as another" (III, 18–19). Ten years earlier, when Fielding described Squire Western's hatred for the "*Hannover* Rats," the Whig ministry used the more immediate Jacobite threat to gain leverage with the crown.[19] The second number of the *Monitor* (1755–65), a journal critical of both the king and the ministry, proclaimed this political strategy to be obsolescent: "You know the grand delusion, in regard to the king and people, has been to stigmatize all patriots with the odious name of Jacobites, or enemies to the present establishment, and family on the throne; and every opposition or censure of the ministry, with the obsolete name of Jacobitism."[20] Robert Rea accurately observes that by 1760, "the Jacobite threat was dead, or no more than an undergraduate toast at Oxford."[21]

In 1756, the loss of Minorca to the French and the resignation of Newcastle signaled the further disintegration of the "Whig coalition." The political centerpiece of this event—and the single greatest preoccupation of the periodical press for nearly a year—was the court-martial of Admiral Byng. The press had become newly empowered by virtue of the Act of 1757. Attempting to control the press with increased taxation, parliament uniformly fixed tax rates on all periodicals regardless of their size. Journals were thus encouraged to increase the number of their pages and could add space for advertisements and political commentary.[22] Not only could newspapers and magazines increase their revenues, but they could insert themselves squarely into the political process. And one of the first manifestations of this power was the near-mythologizing of the Byng court-martial.

Those journals supporting Newcastle argued for Byng's personal responsibility in fleeing the disaster at Minorca; his cowardice, not the ineptness of Newcastle and Secretary of State Henry Fox, was to blame for the English defeat. Arthur Murphy's *Test* (1756–57) defended the fallen Newcastle administration and attacked William Pitt, the dissident Whig who had become virtual prime minister and administrator of the war effort. Owen Ruffhead, Goldsmith's colleague on the *Monthly* staff, established the *Con-Test* (1756–57), which defended the Pitt administration and blamed the Newcastle administration for the Minorca defeat. The *Monitor* also supported Pitt and his coalition. Created by Richard and William Beckford, the journal perceived Newcastle as the representative of a decadent Whig aristocracy and saw Pitt as representative of the rising merchant class.[23]

The *Monthly* and *Critical* inevitably entered the controversy as well. Spector argues that the responses of both journals were similar in their fairly conciliatory tones. The *Critical* reviewers supported Pitt as a challenger to Whig aristocracy and saw continuation of the controversy as a challenge to Pitt's authority; James Ralph, who reviewed much of the Byng material for Griffiths, also favored a moratorium on further public debate on the justice of the trial.[24] Newly appointed to Griffiths' staff, Goldsmith was assigned three short Monthly Catalogue entries (May 1757) relating to the Byng affair. Although each entry was only one sentence long, and his position on the controversy was almost certainly dictated by the opinions of Griffiths and Ralph, this "Tory Monarchist" clearly supported the Newcastle Whigs in his first periodical writing.

The first of these entries (May 1757) dismisses "a vindication of the Admiral" on the grounds that "the public may, by this time, wish to have done with" the controversy (I, 17). While his remark echoes those made by

Ralph in reviews which appeared almost every month from October 1756 to April 1757, it clearly rejects a pamphlet which maintained that the court-martial was unjust, an assumption which was one of the bases of Pitt's taking power. Another notice seems to contradict his implication that further discussion of the Byng controversy would be pointless. Goldsmith refers to a pro-Newcastle pamphlet as "a well written defence of the twelfth article of war, upon which the sentence against Admiral Byng was founded; and of the justness of that unhappy Commander's punishment" (I, 26). Here Goldsmith further establishes his partisan support for the prominiserial forces defending the execution of Byng. He clearly opposes the so-called Tory position, championed by Smollett and others, which viewed Byng as a scapegoat for an incompetent Newcastle administration.

A third notice is even more surprising in the light of Goldsmith's later support for strong monarchical authority, for it is an attack on Tory loyalism: "this garland seems to have been composed by some loyal Soul, who we doubt not, would, upon occasion, be equally ready to testify his zeal at a *bonfire*, by *flourishing his hat*, and *huzzaing for* HIS MAJESTY KING GEORGE!" (I, 22). However trite and sensational the poem he reviewed might have been, Goldsmith's irreverent mention of the king seems utterly uncharacteristic—evidence, perhaps, of the flexibility of his political views in suiting his editor's requirements. Even though Goldsmith may have been reflecting the editorial biases of his employer, these apparently insignificant examples of Goldsmith's support for the ministry, heretofore unmentioned by Goldsmith scholars, force at least a partial modification of the "Tory Royalist" view. Not a single piece that Goldsmith wrote for Smollett, either for the *Critical* or for the *British,* even remotely concerned politics. Whether this circumstance was merely coincidental, or whether Goldsmith's inclinations steered him away from politics at this time, or whether Smollett, in fact, viewed Goldsmith as a potential ideological opponent, cannot be ascertained.

The Accession and Goldsmith's Royalism

Another event further eroding the dominance of the Whig aristocracy occurred midway through Goldsmith's journalistic career: the death of George II on 5 November 1760 and the accession to the throne of his grandson, George III. The coming to power of the new king virtually ended Whig domination of government appointments and helped foster the reinvigoration of the Tory party, a process culminating in the appointment of the Tory Lord Bute as prime minister. The reestablishment of Tory authority; the concomitant demise of Whig hegemony; periodic economic crises, particularly the drought of 1762; the political and social problems stemming from the war with France—all helped produce what Brewer calls the "focussed radicalism of the 1760s."[25] These issues, fully debated in the London press, polarized the periodicals of the late 1750s and early 1760s.

Both the so-called Whig and Tory views of history correctly identify a vital issue in the years following the accession of George III: the legitimate constraints that might be placed on both royal and ministerial authority, that is, the proper balance between the traditional privileges of the king and the constitutional authority of Parliament. On this issue, Goldsmith was unwavering, at least after his departure from the *Monthly*. His support for greater royal power, based on tradition—and for corresponding restraint on legal and ministerial authority—was one of the prevalent political themes in his journalism. His writings at the time of the accession honored the memory of George II, expressed confidence in the new monarch, and implied suspicion of the Pitt ministry. Several months before the death of George II, Goldsmith's Chinese philosopher had praised the aging king's sense of justice and argued that its fair dispensation could be preserved only by a monarch with the power to transcend strict legal interpretations of it. The context of this argument was the king's upholding the recent execution of Laurence Shirley, fourth earl of Ferrers, for the murder of his steward (II, 163n):

> Yet think not that battles gained, dominion extended, or enemies brought to submission, are the virtues which at present claim my admiration. Were the reigning monarch only famous for his victories, I should regard his character with indifference. . . . The virtue in this aged monarch which I have at present in view, is one of a much more exalted nature . . . a strict administration of justice, without severity and without favour. (II, 162)

Goldsmith maintained the view he had earlier enunciated in his *Bee* essay "Customs and Laws Compared": a nation is wiser to "abridge than encrease" laws; custom and royal authority are better safeguards than law (I, 483–86).

His Chinese Letter of 5 November 1760 chided participants in the coronation celebration who had failed to mourn properly for the death of George II (II, 386). Yet Goldsmith quickly turned his attention to the new king and his controversial dismissal from power of the "old guard." In an article ostensibly advising George III to simplify his regal title, he indirectly offered support to the new king's political housecleaning:

> The young Monarch of this country has already testified a proper contempt for several unmeaning appendages on royalty; . . . the whole tribe of *necessary people*, who did nothing, have been dismissed from further services. A youth who can thus bring back simplicity and frugality to a court, will soon probably have a true respect for his own glory, and while he has dismissed all useless employments, may disdain to accept of empty or degrading titles. (II, 467–68)

Goldsmith's advice extended beyond the frugality of a simple title or praise for George's asserting his will in the royal court; it implied that the new king would be wise to keep the basis of his authority simple: a personal and traditional prerogative uncomplicated by rival ministerial factions vying for governmental power. A constitutional system dominated by parliament would be less "frugal" than strong monarchical government. And Goldsmith applauded the early manifestations of royal power, even those of a largely symbolic nature.

Goldsmith's support for royal prerogative should not be construed as his favoring a particular social class. Ricardo Quintana sees as the essence of Goldsmith's "Toryism" the idea of balanced interests among the Crown, Lords, and Commons, and distrust for the upper-middle class.[26] Goldsmith's attacks on "luxury" stemmed partly from his distaste for commercialism in English life; but he was equally disdainful, when it suited his purposes, of the "merchant" classes, the poor, the "middling classes," and the luxurious aristocracy.[27] At least in his journalistic writing, Goldsmith's political philosophy was "unbalanced," in that the king was usually portrayed as the just, rational, and stabilizing force in English politics, whereas the people and their representatives were frequently capricious, excessively mercantile, and even "barbarous." As the cry of "Liberty" came to symbolize opposition to the crown, Goldsmith portrayed the word as the mindless utterance of a people incognizant of its own self-interest:

> Pride seems the source not only of their national vices, but of their national virtues also. An Englishman is taught to love his king as his friend, but to acknowledge no other master than the laws which he himself has contributed to enact. . . . Liberty is echoed in all their assemblies, and thousands might be found ready to offer up their lives for the sound, though perhaps not one of all the number understands its meaning. (*The Citizen*, II, 27–28)

At a time when Burke and Wilkes among others championed the cause of "Liberty," Goldsmith's was a clear and consistent opposing voice. In perhaps his most unequivocal argument for preserving royal prerogative, Goldsmith's Chinese Philosopher asked, "What is an Englishman's freedom?" (19 June 1760). The answer was, his freedom consists in [his] enjoying all the advantages of democracy with this superior prerogative borrowed from monarchy, *that the severity of [the] laws may be relaxed without endangering the constitution*" (II, 210). Goldsmith found the philosophical basis for strong monarchy in the need for "an *effective* power superior to the people, capable of enforcing obedience, whenever it may be proper to inculcate the law either towards the support or welfare of the community" (II, 211). Responding directly to challenges to that power in the press, Goldsmith argued that "every diminution of the regal authority is, in fact a diminution of the subjects freedom; but every attempt to render the government more popular, not only impairs natural liberty, but even will at last, dissolve the political constitution" (II, 212). Goldsmith distrusted not only the "upper-middle classes" but all Englishmen who in their "pride" mistakenly believed that their essential freedom was derived from a source other than the crown.

Another Chinese Letter has an important bearing not only on Goldsmith's political thinking but also on our understanding of *The Deserted Village*. His Letter CI (5 January 1761) reminds his readers, in the wake of George II's death, that "all cannot be rulers, and men are generally governed by a few" (II, 399). He presents an allegorical tale about a Chinese prime minister, besieged by imaginary grievances from a people who fail to appreciate how well the nation has been governed. His queen responds to these invented public grievances by banishing the minister, who requests to be sent to a "ruined town, or desolate village in the country [he has] governed" (II, 401). In fact, not a single such village can be found and the minister's governance is thereby vindicated: *"How can that country be ill governed which has neither a desolate village, nor a ruined town in it?"* (II, 401). This simple exemplum delivers an immediately applicable political message: popular protest is untrustworthy, and a system which is effective should not be altered in response to public pressure. Times are prosperous: "The empire of England now happily finds itself in the most glorious circumstances it has hitherto ever experienced; more formidable abroad, and more united at home" (III, 30). Any radical alteration of such a system, he argues, would threaten that prosperity. By 1769, however, when he published *The Deserted Village*, Goldsmith had become keenly aware of England's "desolate villages" and "ruined towns," which were the result of drought, enclosure, and depopulation. The forced social change over the course of the economically turbulent 1760s altered his view of England's essential prosperity and social justice.

Scholars have identified the depopulation theme in *The Traveller* (1764) and in "The Revolution in Low Life" for *Lloyd's* (14–16 June 1762).[28] But the implied link between ineffective ministry and abandoned villages in this Oriental tale suggests that it should be considered as one of the conceptual origins of *The Deserted Village*. Goldsmith's Chinese Philosopher made the desolate village a metaphor for inadequate ministerial government. The minister in this tale was exonerated; those in the real world responsible for rural poverty and depopulation, by implication, should not be spared. As Goldsmith's essay implies, proper punishment for the inept minister would be banishment to one of his own deserted villages.

A number of explanations have been offered for Goldsmith's "Tory Royalism." Seitz speculates that Goldsmith had hopes of receiving a pension from George III.[29] In his *Life of Johnson*, Boswell writes: "The accession of George the Third to the throne of these kingdoms, opened a new and brighter prospect to men of literary merit, who had been honoured with no mark of royal favour in the preceding reign."[30] Through the intercession of Alexander Wedderburne, Lord Loughborough, and the Earl of Bute, Johnson received his pension in 1762. Goldsmith may have expected that he, too, would be pensioned, but his relative anonymity before 1764 worked against such a prospect, and in any case he was not recognized as a political journalist.[31]

A more satisfactory explanation is Seitz's theory of the Irish origins of Goldsmith's politics and his often-discussed contempt for English mercantilism.[32] As an Irishman, and thus an outsider, he was denied access to the London elite, denied a physician's practice, and held captive—in his view— by an exploitative publishing industry. Biographical accounts by Boswell, Reynolds, Thrale-Piozzi, and others stress the "ridiculous" lengths to which Goldsmith went to be accepted into Johnson's circle. To one so dispossessed, coming from a nation of the dispossessed, the new king may have represented a new possibility for enfranchisement and the dissolution of a government hostile to "have-nots" and "outsiders."

America and the War

Goldsmith's position on the Seven Years' War is more complex than some scholars have acknowledged. Ralph Wardle's assessment of Goldsmith as man of peace restates the generally accepted critical view. Of Goldsmith's work for the *Public Ledger* Wardle writes:

> Because the *Public Ledger* was a daily newspaper, Goldsmith inevitably approached political topics in his Letters, which must have served, in part at least, as a statement of editorial policy. And although the war with France was still in progress, he appealed always for peace—and contented acceptance. . . . War, conquest, colonization, all are evidences of restlessness, of discontent, of failure to accept life as it is; and all are doomed to end in failure.[33]

Many of Goldsmith's writings support such an interpretation. In Letter XVII (13 March 1760), he provided an ironic assessment of the war's origin: "The pretext of the war is about some lands a thousand leagues off; a country cold, desolate, and hideous; a country belonging to a people who were in possession for time immemorial" (II, 73). Indeed, Goldsmith's repeated warnings about excessive colonization, first articulated in *Polite Learning,* appeared in a variety of narrative forms in the *Public Ledger* and the *Busy Body.* He wrote frequently about establishing a just and merciful peace with the French.

Goldsmith's position, however, should not be viewed purely as antiwar idealism. A close examination of his political positions reveals a fear of ministerial authority and his calls for peace served as veiled warnings or protests to Pitt and the ministry responsible for carrying out the war. While supporters of Pitt enjoyed their "public rejoicings for victory" and reveled in the economic promise of an expanding empire, Goldsmith sounded a note of cautious dissent.

Goldsmith's *Weekly* contribution "Some Thoughts Preliminary to a General Peace" (29 December 1759) seems to be a nonpartisan, idealistic, antiwar statement. Underlying his argument, however, is a distrust of the Pitt leadership. He celebrates England's triumphs in battle, but fears that the popular ministry will become self-interested and autocratic: "I cannot without admiration think that we have a minister, who in the midst of the success of his schemes, and surrounded with conquest and glory, should still so far prefer the interests of mankind to his own as to make the first propositions. . . . I hope our present glorious ministry will not comply with the mercenary or the vulgar in this respect" (III, 31, 34). Another appeal for peace, in Chinese Letter XVII (13 March 1760), contains a similar veiled warning to Pitt: "It should seem the business of the victorious party to offer terms of peace; but there are many in England who, encouraged by success, are for still protracting the war" (II, 74). This unmistakable reference to Pitt, who indeed wished to "pursue and extend" the war, is one of Goldsmith's more direct attacks on the ministry.[34] With his military successes and growing popularity, Pitt and his war effort became a potential threat to royal authority. Recognizing Pitt's growing power and popularity, Goldsmith's Lien Chi Altangi directs an even more forceful and somewhat less disguised warning to George II (19 June 1760): "If then, my friend, there should in this country, ever be on the throne a King who, thro' good nature or age, should give up the smallest part of his prerogative to the people, if there should come a minister of merit and popularity.—But I have room for no more" (II, 213). Not so subtly omitted is the explicit description of the disaster such an event would bring.

The reattribution of a *British Magazine* piece to Goldsmith, however, complicates this view. "A Parallel between the Gracchi and the Greatest Man of the Present Age" (January 1760) is unabashed puffery for Pitt: "We know not a character of antiquity which can be produced as a rival to that of the present minister." The minister is honored for his "eloquence, integrity, and zeal for the interests of the commonwealth."[35] Although the piece certainly seems hyperbolic in its praise, it provides little other evidence to suggest ironic intention. Pitt is the model of "patriotic humanity." The essay does remark on Pitt's "universal popularity," a factor that may have motivated the writer. If, indeed, the piece is Goldsmith's, it certainly does not conform to views he expresses elsewhere, although it is consistent with the nationalistic line of the *British*. Perhaps the piece is another example of the influence of editorial ideology, and it serves as further warning against facile political labeling.

This anomalous essay aside, he consistently expressed disdain for the commercial implications of the war—and Pitt was popularly perceived as the champion of those interests. Goldsmith argued for an immediate, conciliatory peace on reasonable terms with the French, not continuation of a war fought so that Britain's "merchants may furnish Europe with tobacco and raw silk" (*Weekly*, III, 33). Donald Greene argues that the Pittites "were distinctly the spokesman for the business community, and the tendency of the policies they advocated were always in the direction of aggressive commercial and imperial expansion."[36] These forces were precisely the ones Goldsmith opposed in his *Weekly* article. In his political journal, George Bubb Dodington, adviser to Bute, cites the commercial motivation for continuing the war: "Trade then no doubt has greatly flourished during this war (and the merchants more, by dipping in all the combinations and monopolies for every sort of furnishment for carrying it on)."[37] Deliberately prolonging the war for commercial gain was to Goldsmith another symptom of English luxuriousness, and as such represented a threat to national security.

In his opposition to Pitt and to England's interest in the war, Goldsmith generally stood apart from the Tory "party line." For many Tories, Pitt represented the patriotic ideal and the party's resurrection as a political force. Cruickshanks notes: "The Tories could identify with the policies of the elder Pitt, and his use of sea-power, and could feel a genuine pride at England's victories."[38] For Goldsmith, these victories were suspect. If, as Linda Colley argues, "acquiring and consolidating overseas territory and markets was consonant with old-style tory enthusiasm for a patriotic war," much of Goldsmith's journalistic writing departed from the "Tory position."[39]

Some of Goldsmith's early writings, however, offer at least limited support for England's participation in the war and the nation's defense of its interests in North America. In the August 1757 issue of the *Monthly*, he reviewed John Mitchell's book *The Contest in America Between Great Britain and France, With Its Consequences and Importance,* which urged that Great Britain "root the French out of America altogether."[40] Complaining about the inactivity of British soldiers in America, Mitchell argues that the colonies "know surely, that their welfare depends upon the prosperity of Britain. . . . Our colonies seem to be very desirous and tenacious of their liberties and priviledges: but how long do they expect to maintain them if the French come among them? They can never expect them from a French yoke."[41] Goldsmith responds with his customary disdain for "the transitory politics of the day" and for the "national partiality" of the author. But his conclusion warns that the French "will hardly ever let us be at rest in America, while we have so much to be robbed of there, and they have so little to lose" (I, 107–9).

Further, his little-known compilation *The History of the Seven Years' War,* parts of which were written and published while the war was still being fought, supported the war, so long as it tended toward increasing the authority of European monarchy.[42] Borrowed, in part, from articles published in the *Literary* and attributed to Johnson, *The History* argues that war is a necessary agent vitalizing and strengthening a nation. It defends and celebrates England's victories in this war, "the most important of any recorded in modern history," chastises its critics, and examines the competing motives of England, France, Prussia, Germany, and Spain.[43] The terms of peace the treatise proposes are based purely on expediency: if England will permit a circumscribed French presence in America, that presence will serve as a deterrent to American colonial revolt. To this end, a victorious England should preserve the French monarchical system, though it should be "disabled" from beginning a new war.[44] Goldsmith and the authors from whom he borrowed see great advantage in supporting Prussia's king and argue that Germany is weak because its emperor is weak: "The so much boasted liberty of the Germanic body is nothing more than the exercise of arbitrary power which a small number of men happen to enjoy, while the emperor is incapable of preventing them from oppressing the people; who are reckoned as nothing and used like slaves."[45] Again, Goldsmith's assessment of foreign culture, like his judgment of the war, is colored by his own monarchical bias. War, he feels, is justifiable to the extent that it brings greater security and more genuine liberty, both of which inhere in royal authority.

In one important respect, Goldsmith was far less "patriotic" than many of his contemporaries. At a time when the newspapers and magazines were filled with denunciations of the French, Goldsmith remained comparatively evenhanded in his discussions of England's enemy. He relied heavily on French sources, held up Voltaire for admiration, and praised French culture throughout *Polite Learning* and his essays. In the *Bee,* he ridiculed the fervent nationalism of the *Literary,* which had added "Anti-Gallican" to its title before expiring in 1758 (I, 418). His mild treatment of the French can be understood in the context of his antiwar professions, his declared political neutrality, and his attempt to create an international persona. This strain in his writing differentiates him from his contemporaries, though many of his other political statements were nothing more than well-rehearsed orthodoxies.

The example of Goldsmith provides an important exception to John Sainsbury's view of the early 1760s as a time of virtual unanimity in English support for colonial expansion and tighter control of the American colonies. Sainsbury traces English discontent with colonial policy from the unpopular Treaty of Paris in 1763, John Wilkes's attacks on government throughout the 1760s, and the formation of the "Real Whigs," a radical circle that saw a connection between tighter colonial control and rising parliamentary despotism.[46] Actually, some "Tory" journalists, writing well before the conclusion of the war, expressed the same concerns. Greene demonstrates that Johnson was one of the early opponents of the war and Pitt's conduct toward the American colonies. He says, "He was as uniformly and bitterly hostile to the whole of Pitt's ambitious enterprise as Swift had been to Marlborough's."[47] However, Johnson was not entirely, as Greene claims, "a one-man crusade."[48] Goldsmith, too, opposed Pitt's policy, though he was neither as vehement nor as unequivocal as Johnson. Goldsmith was no political crusader. Rather, his writings on the dominant political issue of the period reveal an ideological inconsistency and complexity that has not been fully recognized.

Conservatism and the Man of Feeling

Obviously, Goldsmith's conservatism did not exclude a recognition of the need for social reform. Though some of his journalistic writing addressed itself to the comparatively superficial issues of dress and manner, it also tackled some of the most pressing social issues of the era. To blame for the barbarousness of the English commoners, he thought, were two of his favorite targets for satire and reproach: teachers and ministers. Social reform, he believed, should begin with education, which had failed to "teach us to become useful, sober, disinterested and laborious members of society" (*Bee,* I, 436). The "chief object of politics," though, he thought to be the establishment of a "truer and firmer bond of the *Protestant religion*" (*Bee,* I, 482). In matters of religion, Goldsmith's views were orthodox: the maintenance of social order depended on the efficacy of the Church of England. The liberal theological challenge to Church doctrine and the assertion of the primacy of reason were clearly unacceptable to him. He believed that preserving the morality of a "vulgar" public depended upon the vitality and "enthusiasm" of the church and its ministers, just as maintaining obedience and loyalty depended on the strength of the educational system.

Goldsmith was certainly not alone in his social conservatism. Spector cites him as an example of a prevalent attitude among periodical writers of this time: "If skepticism of man's natural benevolence and human reason indicates conservatism, most of the writers in the essay-journals were conservative. Only those in the *Con-Test* and *Monitor,* advocates for the London commercial classes, presented an optimistic view, and their optimism was more economic and political than philosophical."[49] Lance Bertelsen may be betraying a Whig bias when he argues that Smollett deserved the abuse he received for his "consistently derogatory view of the great majority of the middling people."[50] Goldsmith's view of "frugality"—belief in governmental restraint and opposition to the extension of the franchise—was hardly unique. The "rise of the middle class," described in studies such as Ian Watt's *The Rise of the Novel,* represented a threat to those who had perceived themselves as the rightful arbiters of taste and dispensers of privilege.[51] An expanding reading public represented for many, including Goldsmith, an uncontrollable assault on the long-held conventions of taste and morality.

Such essays as "On Justice and Generosity" in the *Bee* (I, 405–8), which rose to the defense of the "miser" and opposed false generosity and sentimental charity, are difficult to reconcile with the popular view of the charitable and good-natured author of *The Vicar* and *The Traveller*. In fact, Goldsmith himself seems to have had difficulty reconciling his philosophic opposition to charity with his own tenderness toward the poor—the conservative with the man of feeling. This problem manifested itself in *Citizen* with the appearance of the "Man in Black," whose history and viewpoints closely parallel Goldsmith's.[52] The first account of the "Man in Black" and his excursion into the country epitomize the author's contradictory approach to poverty and social reform.

Letter XXVI (3 April 1760) introduces this character "with some instances of his inconsistent conduct," the inconsistency being the difference between his philosophic claims about human nature and charity and his actual behavior when confronted with the poor (II, 108–12). Goldsmith says his character "seemed amazed how any of his countrymen could be so foolishly weak as to relieve occasional objects of charity, when the laws had made such ample provision for their support" (II, 109). Charity, he argues, "encourages idleness, extravagance, and imposture" (II, 109–110), an argument the author had made in the *Bee* and earlier in his Chinese Letters. Then, in the sort of partly satiric, partly sentimental progression that became a staple of fiction in the 1760s and 1770s (in Laurence Sterne's *A Sentimental Journey* [1768] and Henry Mackenzie's *The Man of Feeling* [1771], for example), the "Man in Black" is confronted with a series of touching scenes of poverty, to which he gradually succumbs, eventually finding himself relieved of every shilling in his pocket.

As foolishly "luxurious" as Goldsmith may have considered this type of behavior, he apparently found it natural and almost unavoidable for a "man of sentiment." Such a man narrates the meditative *Bee* essay, "A City Night-Piece." Here, the author sets aside his reservations about charity and describes in pathetic detail the plight of the poor: the wretchedness of orphans, the disease-ridden misery of the homeless, the vulnerability of "poor shivering females" to prostitution. The poor are "persecuted by every subordinate species of tyranny, and [find] enmity in every law" (I, 432). John Sekora recognizes the tension in Goldsmith's *Citizen* between the dangers of "luxurious" treatment of the poor and a partial acceptance of some forms of luxury.[53] Most frequently, though, Goldsmith used the term "luxury" to inveigh against the decadent values of the poor and aspiring "middling" class, much as Brown and Smollett had applied it before him. He saw in those classes a vulgar, commercial appetite that threatened England's cultural standing.

Appeals for reform, at least in Goldsmith's early work, are atypical. He was certainly not a vocal advocate of legal reform, though in a review for the *Monthly* he states his support for the reform of debtors' prisons, a theme which would become important in *The Vicar* (*Consideration upon the Present Increase of Civil Prisoners and Debtors in England,* I, 18). Clearly, though, he was cognizant of poverty and sympathetic to the plight of the rural poor (the "vulgar masses" he described were generally city dwellers). Perhaps this sympathy was part of his royalist philosophy—his belief that a benevolent king, with dutiful subjects, should be more powerful than inflexible law and legislatures that were unsympathetic, partisan, and transitory. The fault of the English people was that they had all tried to be politicians, and thereby failed to recognize that their essential liberty rests in their allegiance to the crown. In his *Bee* essay on Charles XII of Sweden, he claimed that "a peasant who does his duty is a nobler character than a king of even middling reputation" (I, 382). In this mutual responsiveness between monarch and subject Goldsmith placed his faith in the potential for social justice.

On two of the most urgent political controversies of his age, Goldsmith was noticeably silent. Walter J. Shelton suggests that the most vital concern for England's poor in 1757 was the passage of the new Militia Act and the prospect of military conscription to serve overseas.[54] Goldsmith only scoffed at journalistic preoccupation with the issue (*Bee,* I, 418). On the hunger riots of 1756–57 and the well-publicized agrarian unrest of the early 1760s in his native Ireland, the poet of *The Deserted Village* was silent as a journalist. Though not unsympathetic toward the plight of the poor, his gentlemanly persona steadfastly avoided direct reference to these events. Whether or not his silence on these issues was a product of his social conservatism or of his effort to maintain a reputation for being "above the fray," Goldsmith as journalist was more cautious in his treatment of social issues than he would be as poet.

"An Anarchy of Literature": The Politics of Authorship

Goldsmith was fairly reticent about the need for social reform in comparison with his frequent pronouncements about the decadence and vulgarity of the English press. In almost every periodical for which he wrote and in most of his independent publications during this period, Goldsmith addressed the politicization of the press and the changing nature of authorship. Whether frustrated by the slow progress of his career, disappointed in not receiving a pension, or bitter over his treatment by editors such as Griffiths, Goldsmith became one of the harshest critics of the periodical press during its revolutionary changes of the war years. To some extent the press was associated, as Brewer suggests, with "extraparliamentary radicalism" and as such became a natural target for Goldsmith's conservatism.[55]

One manifestation of the debate over the proper role of the press was the controversy over the legitimacy of authorship as a profession. In some ways the prototypical professional author of the period was James Ralph, who spearheaded a challenge to the anti-Grub Street attacks of men like John Brown and, later, Goldsmith. Ralph had established a long string of Grub Street credentials: collaborator with Fielding on *The Champion* (1739–40); propagandist for George Bubb Dodington; journal editor; reviewer; pamphleteer; and so on. Spector places him politically with those who furthered the political aspirations of the merchant class, though he might fairly be called a pen for hire.[56] J. C. D. Clark points out, for example, that as editor of the antiministerial *Protester* in 1753, Ralph was "bought off" with a pension by Newcastle.[57] He later advised Lord Bute in the minister's attempts to use the press as a means of shaping public opinion.[58]

Ralph's book *The Case of Authors* is an *ex post facto* recognition of an evolutionary change in the nature of authorship: the "Voluntiers" or "Gentleman-Writers," as Ralph called them, were a vanishing breed. Survival as an author depends on acceptance of the rules of professional authorship. Writing for money, he argued, is historically, morally, and aesthetically defensible; attempts to oppose the commercialization of authorship, a *fait accompli*, would be futile. Philip Stevick recognizes Ralph's contribution to our understanding of the nature of authorship in the late 1750s. He calls *The Case of Authors* "a sharply reasoned recognition of the fact that the paternalistic days of the Tory nostalgia are gone forever, that a mass audience and a class of professional writers is here to stay, and that this phenomenon can be understood not by facile moralizing and shrill polemics but by critical discrimination, historical understanding and clear-eyed social observation.[59] Ralph's nonjudgmental acknowledgment of the growing power of the press and his defense of professional authorship were atypical, though the *Monthly* wholeheartedly affirmed his arguments.[60] Most professional authors scorned the industry which supported them; satires on periodicals and periodical readers filled virtually every magazine, regardless of political affiliation. Essay after essay created the paradoxical image of periodical readers, congregated in coffeehouses, eagerly devouring satirical essays on periodical readers in coffeehouses. Lien Chi Altangi observed: "This universal passion for politics is gratified by Daily Gazettes. . . . You must not, however imagine that they who compile these papers have any actual knowledge of the politics, or the government of a state; they only collect their materials from the oracle of some coffee-house, which oracle has himself gathered them the night before from a beau at a gaming table" (II, 29). The coffeehouse, for Goldsmith, was the source of groundless literary opinion of the sort that made and broke reputations:

A great man says, at his table, that such a book *is no bad thing*. Immediately the praise is carried off by five flatterers to be dispersed at twelve different coffeehouses, from whence it circulates, still improving as it proceeds, through forty-five houses, where cheaper liquors are sold, from thence it is carried away by the honest tradesman to his own fire-side, where the applause is eagerly caught up by his wife and children, who have been long taught to regard his judgment as the standard of perfection. (II, 236-37)

The satire implies that in this corrupt state of letters, literary fame was ephemeral, echoing thoughtlessly in the coffeehouses and residing, finally, in the parlors of a growing class of common readers.

Goldsmith was certainly not alone in decrying the politicization and commercialization of the press, while at the same time using the industry for his own political and financial ends. In the *Bee* he complained: "Literary fame I now find like religious, generally begins among the vulgar" (I, 417). Ralph, though, effectively responded to this bit of "Tory nostalgia" by asking essentially, "What other avenue can the 'Gentleman-Author' take?"

The Voluntier, then, by a sufficient Manifestation of Intelligence, Principle, and the Art of improving every Hint that offers to the Service he undertakes, must be in Possession of the Public, before he can hope for such Connections and Confidence, as alone can put him in the Situation above described [i.e., ministerial support or pension]—And for a Man to raise himself out of Obscurity so as to become this Object of public Notice and public Favour, is so hard a Task, that a very few Instances will serve for half an age."[61]

A writer such as Goldsmith, socially unconnected and relatively impoverished, had no choice but to achieve public recognition through such vehicles as the periodical press if he hoped to attain governmental sponsorship. Distasteful as he made this process appear, Goldsmith's only means of achieving literary fame was through Grub Street and the approbation of his readers.

Goldsmith's *Bee* essay "An Account of the Augustan Age of England" is especially relevant to this discussion, not only because of its treatment of patronage and the press, but also because Georgian analyses of party politics during the reign of Queen Anne were often interpreted as a key to the author's own political affiliation.[62] Goldsmith argues that the pinnacle of English letters occurred during or "some years before" the reign of Queen Anne, during which time "there seemed to be a just balance between patronage and the press" (I, 498–99). He maintains that contemporary publishing was dominated by two groups ill-qualified to recognize genius: booksellers and the public.

The article then attempts to provide a balanced view of the history of political writing. To what extent this history reflects Goldsmith's own views is uncertain, because this section is largely excerpted from a *Literary Magazine* article of May 1758.[63] Sir Roger L'Estrange, described in the essay as a Tory apologist, has "generally the worst side of the argument," but is nonetheless admirable for his courage and literary style (I, 499). Another Tory, Lord Bolingbroke, is admired for his "writings against Sir Robert Walpole, . . . incomparably the best parts of his works" (I, 502). Directly contrasting the central political writers of Queen Anne's time, the author concludes: "Mr. Walpole, Mr. Addison, Mr. Mainwaring, Mr. Steele, and many members of both houses of parliament, drew their pens for the whigs; but they seem to have been over-matched, tho' not in argument, yet in writing, by Bolingbroke, Prior, Swift, Arbuthnot, and the other friends of the opposite party" (I, 503–4). At this point in the essay Goldsmith's direct borrowing stops, and he adds a qualified defense of the Whig partisans: "They who oppose a ministry, have always a better field for ridicule and reproof, than they who defend it" (I, 504). Again, Goldsmith carefully avoids being associated with a particular party or faction; he concludes the essay with another attack on the London reviews, which by "giving an epitome of every new publication, must greatly damp the writer's genius" (I, 505).

Goldsmith specifically blames the commercialization of authorship for the decline of English letters; for him the concept of "luxury," expressive of both the materialism and growing political power of the "middling classes," epitomizes modern corruption. London periodicals and booksellers foster this decay: "The press, and every other method of exhortation, seems disposed to talk of the luxuries of life as harmless enjoyments" (*Bee,* "Upon Political Frugality," I, 436). It is a political argument disguised through the voice of a neutral outsider, a dispassionate observer who has no pretensions toward party or royal patronage. By using the voices of the foreign correspondent or Chinese Philosopher Goldsmith tries to objectify his positions and distance them from the sullying influence of partisan dispute. In fact, in the context of Ralph's defense of professional authorship, the growing power of the merchant classes, and public debate over the extension of suffrage and the conduct of the war, Goldsmith's writing is not as politically naive as some of his contemporaries mistakenly believed.

Goldsmith's solution for reforming the press is somewhat ambiguous. He is opposed to returning to a system based exclusively on patronage. A "Club Satire" for the *Public Ledger* (Letter XXX, 2 May 1760) portrays one of the victims of such a system, an author cheated by "the earl of Doomsday." "A nobleman, cries a member, who had hitherto been silent, is created as much for the confusion of us authors as the catch-pole" (II, 132). Perhaps the solution can be inferred from a complaint issued by the Chinese Philosopher (Letter XX, 20 March 1760): "Thus, instead of uniting like the members of a commonwealth, they are divided into almost as many factions as there are men; and their jarring constitution instead of being stiled a republic of letters should be entitled, an anarchy of literature" (II, 85). A properly run press should be unified, strictly controlled by a hierarchical order. Implicit in this position is Goldsmith's faith in centralized authority as opposed to the chaos of factionalism. For Goldsmith, factionalism, favoritism, and disorder were inherent in republican philosophy, order and justice the results of a strong monarchy.

Johnson, Murphy, and Smollett: Political Journalists Compared

Goldsmith was not the political innocent some perceived him to be, but by preserving the illusion of nonpartisanship and maintaining relative anonymity, he escaped the political price contemporaries such as Murphy and Smollett had to pay—public ridicule for their political views and frequently biased treatment of their literary productions. Nor did Goldsmith receive the reward for services rendered that Ralph and Johnson enjoyed. One characteristic that distinguished Goldsmith from many of his conservative colleagues was his avoidance of overt political debate in the press and active participation in ministerial conflict. He was certainly not alone in realizing the lasting damage party affiliation could wreak on a literary career. Murphy excised his political writings from his own collected works, much as Goldsmith had omitted such material from his collected essays, but could not fully escape the lifelong enemies he had made supporting Henry Fox in the *Test* and Lord Bute in the *Auditor* and the *Briton*.[64] Hawkesworth was rather ludicrously accused of "furious Jacobitism" for defending Johnson's receiving a pension.[65] Hume and Smollett both understood what Goldsmith had suggested about political objectivity as central to their reputations as historians. Both vehemently denied any attachment to party or faction, but were attacked, nonetheless, for partisanship.[66] Only when he turned to history writing himself was Goldsmith accused of partisanship.[67] At least in his journalistic efforts, Goldsmith alone among these writers preserved a politically neutral reputation.

How did Goldsmith's political stance differ from those of his important contemporaries? An obvious beginning, albeit difficult and ultimately unfair, is a comparison with Johnson's political philosophy. By 1757 Johnson had been engaged in various forms of political dialogue for almost twenty years. The complexity of Johnson's political philosophy and the sheer voluminousness of his political writing obscure Goldsmith's; the Tory royalism of "Dr. Minor" is rendered trivial by any comparison to the celebrated monarchism of his mentor. But their basic political philosophies were similar. Greene notes that the essence of Johnson's philosophy is contained in *The False Alarm* (1770), in which he expresses support for a strong, paternal monarch and suspicion of factionalism.[68] Goldsmith, too, argued for the primacy of royal prerogative over laws and factions. But, difficult as it is to differentiate Goldsmith's views from Johnson's, on at least a few issues they disagreed in substance or approach.

On the Byng controversy, they took opposite positions: Johnson was a steadfast defender of Byng and opponent of Newcastle, while Goldsmith was convinced of Byng's guilt—or at least content to repeat the party line of Griffiths' *Monthly*. Perhaps a more significant difference is in their respective treatments of actual kings. Greene observes: "His [Johnson's] 'monarchism' he maintains concurrently with a striking lack of reverence for monarchs."[69] At the time of George III's coronation, Johnson, like Goldsmith, complained about the excessive pomp of the festivities; but unlike Goldsmith, he admitted to being "weary of our old King."[70] Both writers were enthusiastic about the new king and the promise of what Greene calls a sort of "New Deal."[71] But Goldsmith was careful to commend the career of George II and complained about the lack of respect accorded him during the coronation ceremonies. Generally, Goldsmith displayed unmitigated respect for England's reigning kings in his periodical writing, and in his history writing he attempted a balanced and respectful portrayal of past monarchs.

The most obvious difference, though, between Goldsmith's politics and Johnson's was in their respective attitudes toward the enterprise of political writing itself. Green notes that "Even in the narrowest sense of the word 'politics,' there were few periods in Johnson's life when he was not close to the political life of the day."[72] Throughout his career Johnson threw himself unabashedly into political controversy, from his invectives against Robert Walpole in the late 1730s to his defense of the North ministry's taxation of the American colonies in 1775. Unlike his "mentor," Goldsmith generally belittled political writing as beneath the writer who aspires to fame. He maintained his distance from party politics, even while betraying party bias. An instance of this stance appears in Goldsmith's preface to *The History of England* (1771), largely an abridgment of Hume's *History*. Immediately after taking Hume to task for partisanship, he launches into his own political diatribe, defending royal prerogative and implicitly attacking "republicanism":

It is not yet decided in politics, whether the diminution of kingly power in England tends to increase the happiness or the freedom of the people. For my own part, from seeing the bad effects of the tyranny of the great in those republican states that pretend to be free, I cannot help wishing that our monarchs may still be allowed to enjoy the power of controlling the encroachments of the great at home. A king may easily be restrained from doing wrong, as he is but one man; but if a number of the great are permitted to divide all authority, who can punish them if they abuse it?[73]

He concludes by asserting that such a position does not make him guilty of political bias, and he hopes "the reader will admit [his] impartiality."[74] By contrast, Johnson was less reluctant to admit to political conviction and less reticent about participating in political journalism.

Another revealing comparison could be made between Goldsmith and his fellow Irishman Murphy. Like Johnson and Goldsmith, Murphy upheld the powers of the crown and, as Spector notes, feared the "democratic fervor" of the masses.[75] From November 1756 to July 1757 he edited the *Test,* sponsored by Henry Fox; he defended the policies of Newcastle and, as Goldsmith had done, blamed Byng for the disaster at Minorca. In 1762, when Lord Bute replaced the popular Pitt, Murphy joined Smollett in defending the new Bute administration.

Murphy's political tactics and literary techniques in his pro-Bute organ the *Auditor* (15 July 1762 to 16 May 1763) closely resemble Goldsmith's. He adapted the "foreign correspondent" point of view to satirize his political opponents. He even wore the mask of a Chinese philosopher, as well as an Indian primitive, to gain the same strategic advantage Goldsmith had achieved in his writings for the *Public Ledger* and elsewhere: the objective perspective provided by an outsider who is untouched by factionalism and bias. While this technique had been developed earlier in the century by Steele in the *Tatler* and *Spectator,* Goldsmith's use of the foreign observer in the *Public Ledger* had achieved considerable circulation and was a probable source for Murphy's "Chinese Philosopher" in the *Auditor.*

In his biography of Murphy, Spector argues convincingly that Murphy suffered permanent damage to his reputation as a result of his political activities. Having been attacked, for example, for dedicating *The Orphan of China* to Lord Bute and having suffered personal attacks from John Wilkes in the *North Briton,* Murphy bore permanently the scars of political dueling.[76] Goldsmith was able to avoid the consequences of such conflict. Prior says of Goldsmith's attitude toward anonymity in his journalism of that "being unknown as having produced any thing of popular interest, he was unwilling to make his first appearance in small things when conscious of powers capable of accomplishing almost the greatest."[77] For Murphy, who had already received recognition both as playwright and polemicist, the luxury of anonymity was not an option.

Smollett, too, paid a price for his publicly acknowledged participation in political journalism. His contributions to the *Briton* in support of the Bute ministry are still almost universally reviled. Despite their shared allegiance to royal prerogative and their mutual participation in the *Critical* and the *British,* Goldsmith and Smollett appeared to be on opposite sides of the ministerial crises of the late 1750s and 1760s. Smollett used the *Critical* to defend Byng and blame the Newcastle ministry for the defeat at Minorca—thereby opposing, at least initially, the *Monthly's* attempts to bury the controversy. He was also, at least initially, an ardent supporter of Pitt. In the same month (December 1759) that Goldsmith issued his ministerial attack, "Some Thoughts Preliminary to a General Peace," for the *Weekly,* Smollett wrote to John Harvie (10 December 1759): "The people here are in high spirits on account of our successe and Mr. Pitt is so popular that I may venture to say that all party is extinguished in Great-Britain. That Minister is certainly in this respect the most surprising phenomenon that ever appeared in our hemisphere."[78] A month later Smollett's glowing tribute to Pitt appeared in the dedication of the *British.*

By agreeing to take on the defense of the Bute ministry in the *Briton* (1762), Smollett was forced to repudiate his support for Pitt, a move which proved disastrous to his reputation and subjected him to public ridicule. His onetime friend and correspondent John Wilkes became a vicious opponent in the *North Briton.* By all accounts, Wilkes, writing in support of Pitt, got the better of the argument, and Smollett was replaced by Murphy as editor of the *Briton.* Historians are nearly unanimous in proclaiming Smollett's work for the *Briton* a failure. Spector is more generous than most in acknowledging the near impossibility of Smollett's task of defending an unpopular ministry, whose handling of the war was inevitably compared unfavorably with Pitt's.[79] The rhetoric of the *Briton* was that of bitter assault, rather than of patriotic advocacy. The first two numbers (29 May and 5 June 1762) ridiculed the efforts of the *Monitor;* the third and fourth (12 and 19 June 1762) attacked the *North Briton.* Smollett's unfortunate entry into the ministerial crisis and his changing affiliations made his early protestations of being "wholly impartial and disinterested" ring hollow.

Perhaps responding to Goldsmith's criticism of his *History,* Smollett wrote to William Huggins, 'I have flattered no individual; I have cultivated no Party. I look upon the Historian who espouses a Faction . . . as the worst of Prostitutes."[80] Having engaged in political journalism, Smollett made himself a target for those challenging his objectivity. Even Goldsmith, twice Smollett's literary associate, returned to the subject of Smollett's *History* and its politics four-and-a-half years after initially reviewing it for Griffiths. The "Indigent Philosopher" relates to readers of *Lloyd's* his mortification at finding "that most of the Writers he [Smollett] mentions as doing honour to the present age, are Scotchmen." He continues, "I am the more uneasy at his seeming partiality, as I am informed that Doctor Smollet is himself a native of Cornwall" (III, 187).

Like Murphy, and like Johnson to the degree he sustained personal attacks upon receiving his pension, Smollett paid a personal price for his political "hack work." Goldsmith avoided paying this price by steering clear of the *Test* and *Con-Test* controversy, by preserving his anonymity, and by cultivating a nonpartisan image, while expressing his political philosophies through the fictionalized voices of innocents and outsiders. One consequence of Goldsmith's public neutrality and his apparent political reticence is that scholars have failed to take the author's politics seriously. As prominently situated as Johnson and Smollett are in discussions of the politics of era, Goldsmith's monarchism and his opposition to the war and commercialism are generally regarded as minor features of his work. Virtually unnoticed is his attack on the Pitt administration and his participation in the debate over the nature of authorship.

That Goldsmith's collected essays were published in France with the misleading titles *Contes moraux de Goldsmith* and the ludicrous *Essais d'education et de morale à l'usage de la jeunesse* suggests the prevalent and misleading attitude many of his contemporaries held toward his journalistic writing.[81] The dominant early nineteenth-century image of Goldsmith as a morally instructive and sentimental author did not include the political polemicist. And even recent biographies and critical studies have done little to consider his politics seriously. Perhaps, at least with respect to his politics, Goldsmith achieved exactly the sort of fame for which he had hoped.

9

"Paternoster Row Is Not Parnassus"

Distress drove Goldsmith upon undertakings, neither congenial with his studies, nor worthy of his talents. I remember him, when in his chamber in the Temple, he showed me the beginning of his "Animated Nature"; it was with a sigh, such as genius draws, when hard necessity diverts it from its bent to drudge for bread, and talk of birds, and beasts, and creeping things, which Pidcock's show-man would have done as well. Poor fellow, he hardly knew an ass from a mule, nor a turkey from a goose, but when he saw it on the table. But publishers hate poetry, and Paternoster Row is not Parnassus.

—Memoirs of Richard Cumberland

A satisfactory history of British journalism in the eighteenth century has yet to be written. Scholars such as Robert D. Spector, Jeremy Black, and Robert R. Rea have certainly begun the process with important insights into the politics of the press; Robert L. Haig, Derek Roper, and others have traced the development of individual periodicals; Robin Myers and Michael Harris have contributed significantly to our understanding of the eighteenth-century book trade; and Alvin Kernan has demonstrated the connectedness of changes in printing technology and British letters. The present study, like Basker's of Tobias Smollett, focuses on a figure already ensconced in the belletristic tradition, so as to isolate him somewhat from that tradition and show him as a "professional" formed by and rebelling against powerful commercial and political forces. It considers his journalistic output not as subliterary ephemera but as biographical, historical, and journalistic texts.

One of the strategies of the "New Historicism" has been to blur the distinction between literary work and historical artifact. In an essay for H. Aram Veeser's influential collection *The New Historicism* (1989), Stephen Bann proposes "the need for a historical view which will include both the amateur and the professional . . . the historical novel and the text edited by the Public Record Office—rather than insisting that they differ like chalk and cheese."[1] Advertisements in the London dailies, marked copies of printers' proof sheets, and plagiarized translations become as essential to this undertaking as the graceful, satiric essays in *The Bee*. Lien Chi Altangi becomes, simultaneously, the genial, reflective persona of a literary classic, *The Citizen of the World,* and the recurring journalistic mask of a newspaper columnist.

In an essay for the same anthology, Frank Lentricchia defines historicism, "old and new," as the "assumption that all cultural phenomena, especially selves, like all natural phenomena, are to be understood as effects produced by imperious agents of causality (cultural traditions, institutions, race, ethnicity, relations of gender, economic and physical environments, dispositions of power)."[2] Clearly, Goldsmith's journalistic career was shaped by the genteel tradition of the Addisonian essay, the burgeoning publishing industry, his Irish roots and English disguises, a still-prevalent Tory paternalism, his inescapable poverty, the economic and political contest among the journals for readership, and their collective rebellion against aristocratic sanctioning of literary taste. It is equally important, in Goldsmith's case, to acknowledge the reciprocal effect of these agents; in his journalistic work Goldsmith not only responded to these shaping forces but constructed and reconstructed them to define a literary self. Collectively, they become a monolithic antagonist against which the unknown hero must struggle and eventually come to terms. The stakes in this contest, as Goldsmith defines them, are literary fame or perpetual invisibility. In a grander sense, at stake is the soul of polite learning in England.

Emergence from Anonymity

Four months after Goldsmith wrote his last Chinese Letter for the *Public Ledger,* and five months before the first edition of *The Citizen of the World* was published (1 May 1762), his name appeared in the London press, apparently for the first time. The *Court Magazine,* a monthly miscellany less ambitious than the *Gentleman's Magazine* but structurally similar to it, published "The Motives for Writing: A Dream" (December 1761), in which the author imagines England's foremost writers as prisoners before the court of Apollo. The "compelling motives" of fifty-six authors are revealed. The list of those whose motives are found incriminating include Arthur Murphy ("ignorance, hunger, and pride"), Tobias Smollett ("imaginary abilities and virulence unparalleled"), George Colman ("the hope of unmerited applause"), Samuel Foote ("impudence and the folly of the public"), and "Mr. John Newberry, bookseller and quack" ("avarice and a chariot"). Included in the list of those exonerated are Edward Young ("exalted genius and universal philanthropy"), Samuel Johnson ("the benefit of mankind and the greatest abilities"), and Goldsmith ("taste and understanding").[3] Though the author of the piece is unknown—Hugh Kelly, the editor of the *Court,* is a likely candidate—and his judgments are obviously biased, the fact that Goldsmith should be mentioned publicly in such company is remarkable. It means at least one journalist, reasonably well acquainted with English letters, placed Goldsmith, a "hack" with only four years of experience, among England's best writers.

William Rider's anonymous pamphlet, extolling Goldsmith's virtues as a stylist, followed in 1762. While his biographical account of England's best authors is factually unreliable and his judgments often questionable (he lavishes praise on his own work, for example), his work reveals an intimate knowledge of several of his subjects, including Johnson, Smollett, Sterne, and Goldsmith. As an "insider," a contributor to the *Gentleman's*, Rider knew, for example, that Thornton and Colman had written the *Connoisseur*;[4] and he recognized Cleland as the author of *Memoirs of a Woman of Pleasure*, praising it as "the most picturesque of any Work of the Kind."[5] In spite of its unreliability, Rider's work provides further evidence that by this time Goldsmith was beginning to achieve public recognition.

Although he reviewed Brookes's *Natural History* for both the *Critical* and the *Monthly* in August and October 1763 respectively (he had written a general preface and an introduction to each of Brookes's first four volumes), and his *Belles Lettres* series for the *British* extended into 1763, Goldsmith's career as an active journalist essentially ended in 1762. In 1763 he was occupied by Newbery with longer works such as *An History of England, in a Series of Letters from a Nobleman to His Son* (26 June 1764) and a variety of prefaces. In December 1764, his poem *The Traveller* was published. Though he received only twenty guineas for it, the poem finally earned him public acclaim.

The following year he published his collected *Essays by Mr. Goldsmith* (1765), which he revised for a second edition in 1766. Unfortunately for scholars, Goldsmith chose most frequently essays from *The Bee* and *The Citizen of the World*, sources that would not in any event have posed problems in attribution. To some extent, Goldsmith's preface to the 1765 edition and his selections for it represented his final words on his journalistic career.

Some scholars have refused to believe that Goldsmith abandoned a productive periodical career after 1762. Prior, for example, argues that Goldsmith contributed essays to the *Christian's Magazine* in 1764—a claim for which little evidence exists.[6] Morris Golden has consistently advocated expanding the accepted canon. He attributes articles in the *Universal Museum, and Complete Magazine* (1764–65) to Goldsmith, based primarily on verbal parallels. While he does demonstrate how frequently the *Universal Museum* reprinted perviously written essays of Goldsmith's, Golden's attributions are not substantiated with external evidence and have not been widely accepted.[7] Available evidence suggests the tentative conclusion that with the publication of *The Citizen* and *The Traveller* Goldsmith became a public figure who actively promoted his literary reputation and hoped for enduring fame.

Further anonymous work in the periodicals could not enhance his reputation, and his complaints in the preface to *Essays* about plagiarisms of his work and their meager public reception lend credence to the theory that he saw little to gain in continuing as a journalist.

Friedman accepts into the canon only one essay written between 1762 and 1773, when Goldsmith briefly returned to journalism by contributing four essays to the *Westminster Magazine*. An "Essay on Friendship," which first appeared in an issue of *Owen's Weekly Chronicle* (no longer extant), was reprinted in Hugh Kelly's *Babler* (1767) and in the *Universal Magazine* (1774). A characteristic exemplum on the virtue of "true friendship," the essay reiterates warnings about the false expectations for lasting friendship and love that his contemporary novelists typically propagated.

According to William Cooke, whose "Table Talk" anecdotes for the *European Magazine* (1793) provide fairly reliable details on several of the leading figures of the 1760s and 1770s, Goldsmith may have edited the *Gentleman's Journal,* an undertaking which "hardly lived to its sixth month."[8] The journal was apparently printed by William Griffin, publisher of *The Good Natur'd Man* (1768). If Cooke's account is correct, Goldsmith teamed up with two of his chief rivals: Hugh Kelly, whose comedy *False Delicacy* competed with *The Good Natur'd Man* in 1768, and William Kenrick, whom Forster calls Goldsmith's "evil genius" because of their ongoing literary disputes.[9] Unfortunately, no known copies of the *Gentleman's Journal* survive, nor does any other source confirm this improbable collaboration.

As for the *Westminster* contributions, they may have been, in part, "dashed off for the ready cash that they would yield," as Wardle argues.[10] "The History of a Poet's Garden" (January 1773) is a brief "Reverie" on the mutability of beauty and the poet's contented acceptance of life's disappointments. "The History of Cyrillo Padovano, the Noted Sleep-Walker" (February 1773) recounts the tale of a monk who commits crimes in his sleep, and "A Register of Scotch Marriages" is a letter, supposedly written by a landlady at a Scottish inn, warning young women of the consequences of elopement. These three essays are, for the most part, variations on themes and methods established in Goldsmith's earlier writings. As such, they are probably set pieces for the one essay Goldsmith had the clearest motivation to write.

"An Essay on the Theatre; or, A Comparison between Laughing and Sentimental Comedy" is more than a catchpenny. As Robert D. Hume points out, the essay is "a puff to prepare the way for *She Stoops to Conquer,*" first produced at Covent Garden on 15 March 1773.[11] At the time the essay was published, Covent Garden's manager George Colman, whose *Connoisseur* had favorably impressed Goldsmith at the beginning of his career, was quarrelling with the playwright over possible revisions of the comedy;[12] as Friedman suggests, the manager had little confidence in the play and wished to delay it, but was more or less pressured into accepting it for production (V, 89).

"An Essay on the Theatre" implicitly defends the comedy against Colman's objections.

Goldsmith calls for the production of "laughing comedy," of which his play, by implication, is an example. This type of comedy, he says, is both amusing and appropriate to classical definitions of the genre. Opposed to it is "sentimental comedy," a "bastard" genre replete with maudlin dialogue and void of any production value. Hume points out the extent to which Goldsmith's generic classifications are misleading—more a tool for promoting his own play than an accurate assessment of the type of comedies being produced.[13] Nevertheless, Goldsmith's analysis of the transition from "sentimental" to "laughing" comedy became the standard critical view for almost two centuries.

Such, then, is the basic shape of Goldsmith's journalistic career, to the extent that it can be reconstructed. Hired as "foreign correspondent" by *Monthly* editor Griffiths, he learned "the Trade" and formed initial judgments about authorship in his capacity as reviewer. After having broken his first contract with Griffiths, he wrote his *Polite Learning,* a work that can be seen as a bridge between his reviewing and magazine careers. He then returned to book reviewing, his assignment with the *Critical* being more strictly "literary" than his work for Griffiths. Getting acquainted with a number of booksellers and allying himself with a "syndicate" of printers and publishers, he edited his own magazine and offered his services—primarily as a social satirist and commentator—to a variety of London periodicals. The leading figure in that "syndicate," John Newbery, invited him to participate in two innovative projects, the *British Magazine* and the *Public Ledger,* the relative success of which assured him steady employment. After 1762 he gradually withdrew from periodical work to pursue fame in the more "respectable" role of poet, while continuing his productive affiliation with Newbery. He returned for a final, brief journalistic assignment before his death in 1774.

Goldsmith's periodical work can be seen as a career in itself—perhaps the only phase of his career that can be isolated for such an analysis—and not merely a preparatory phase. As such, it was a product of a changing profession. It began at a time of widespread reexamination of the nature of authorship and of England's position as a military and intellectual leader; it flourished during a period of preoccupation with the war, ministerial conflict, and the coronation of a new king; and it ended at a time when journalism had become, to a great degree, an organ for partisan debate. Not only did these conditions make his career possible, but they became the author's primary material, out of which he constructed a narrative of authorial survival.

In a sense, there is no unifed "later career" to speak of. Goldsmith's poetic output was slight, for example. How do we classify the author of long, partly derivative historical compilations and natural histories, except with the vague appellation of "miscellaneous writer"? Do two plays make a playwright? If the pattern of his journalistic career was that of trial and error and six years of struggle, the record of his novel, poems, and plays is one of almost unequalled success, given their relatively anomalous place in his corpus. His one novel enjoyed phenomenal public success and critical attention for almost two centuries, before changing aesthetic sensibilities began to weaken its hold on the popular imagination. One of his two plays remains, more than two hundred years later, a repertory favorite. *The Traveller* and *The Deserted Village,* among a meager poetic canon, have become staples of academic anthologies. Goldsmith did not live long enough to enjoy fully the fruits of this success nor to redefine himself, retrospectively, as a successful artist. He did, however, provide such a self-definition for his journalistic career.

Essays by Mr. Goldsmith (1765)

By 3 June 1865, when Newbery published the first collected edition of Goldsmith's essays, the author's professional stature had greatly altered: he had developed an intimate relationship with Johnson; he had written a series of prefaces for Newbery, as well as a two-volume *History of England* that achieved a wide circulation; and he had received immediate public recognition for *The Traveller,* published 19 December 1764. As his friend Joshua Reynolds noted, "His *Traveller* produced an eagerness unparalleled to see the author. He was sought after with greediness."[14] Pressed financially, he decided to capitalize on the success of *The Traveller* by editing some of his anonymously published essays. But his preface to *Essays by Mr. Goldsmith* (1765) suggests another motivation for publishing the collection. Having achieved a measure of literary success, he wanted to canonize his periodical work, much of which had been reprinted frequently and plagiarized. Confident of future literary fame, as his letters indicate he had been as early as 1758, he clearly wanted his periodical writing to be judged as part of his oeuvre. The collection sold well enough to merit a second edition, *Essays by Oliver Goldsmith* (1766), and earned reviewers' plaudits in the *Critical* and *Lloyd's,* where he was acclaimed as one of the England's foremost essayists. (The *Monthly* continued its practice of scorning Goldsmith's efforts.) Further, the relative success of the collection may have helped encourage Francis Newbery to publish *The Vicar of Wakefield* (27 March 1766), four years after Goldsmith had sold his manuscript to Francis's uncle John.

The collection of essays provides one obvious benefit for scholars: it certifies the attribution of a significant part of Goldsmith's periodical work. For those essays republished in the *Essays* (1765) and the two added to *Essays* (1766), Goldsmith's authorship is certain. A second and largely overlooked benefit of having such a collection is the perspective it provides on Goldsmith's own assessment of his journalistic career. The comments with which Goldsmith prefaces the edition are revealing in themselves. They include his complaints about the poor public reception of essay-periodicals, his claims for the originality of his humor, his defense of the form against charges of triviality, and his stated confidence in receiving eventual recognition. Even more revealing, however, are the particular choices he made of which essays to include and which to exclude.

One surprising pattern in the collection is the omission of most of Goldsmith's "foreign correspondent" essays. For some of the essays, the reasons for this editorial decision are apparent. A series such as his four-part "Comparative View of Races and Nations" for the *Royal* would probably have been too long for such a collection. Many other essays of this type were highly derivative from French sources; none of the Voltaire translations were included. Others of the "foreign correspondent" genre, such as his "literary essays" for the *Ledger* in 1761, had become dated by 1765. These explanations, however, account for only a portion of Goldsmith's essays of this type. What the systematic exclusion of this type of essay from the collection suggests is that Goldsmith was finally abandoning his "philosophic vagabond" persona by 1765. With a few exceptions, notably the satiric essay "On the Assemblies of Russia," his discussions of foreign nations are also excluded. The prevailing voice in the collection is that of a lightly moralizing English humorist, not of a foreign affairs commentator.

Goldsmith's elimination of his cultural analyses may be based on his recognition of their inherently political nature. Throughout his journalistic career he had denigrated political writing and, clearly, his intention in collecting his essays was to establish an enduring reputation beyond the transitory fame of many political journalists. As he had written in a *Monthly* review at the beginning of his career: "The Author who engages in the transitory politics of the day, may be compared to a Sportsman shooting flying;—while he is taking aim, the object in view often gains too great a distance, and escapes the meditated blows. Such Writers are generally obliged to sacrifice ornament to opportunity; and, in order to catch the present hour, give up all hopes with regard to posterity" (I, 105–6). Many other types of essays were generally excluded from the collection: his anthropological speculations, his "state of learning" essays, and most of his short fiction. Even more noticeably, all of his literary and dramatic criticism was omitted. Even the well-known "Fame Machine" essay in the *Bee,* with its allusion to Johnson, did not appear in the collection. Whether or not Goldsmith had changed his mind about many of his early literary and dramatic critical judgments is difficult to assess. The collection's contents, however, do suggest a reason for excluding much of his serious aesthetic and political commentary.

Most of the selected essays are of two types: light social satire and gently didactic essays treating immutable concerns such as "happiness," "worldly grandeur," "education," and "Providence." Seventeen of the twenty-five essays published in the 1765 edition are from the *Bee* and *The Citizen*. His first essay is the introduction to the *Bee,* in which Goldsmith established his persona of the inexperienced and apologetic writer who promised vivacity if not wit. The essay also complements Goldsmith's satirical reflection on the magazine trade which he furnishes in his preface to the collection. In an age when magazines were "not the result of any single man's industry" (I, 354), Goldsmith casts himself as a throwback to the nobler days of single-author periodicals. Most of the remaining selections taken from the *Bee* are simple exempla illustrating recurrent themes: the danger of luxuriousness, the pleasure of a rural retreat, the virtue of generosity, the mutability of fame. His selections from the Chinese Letters are mostly social satires gently ridiculing facets of English life. The remaining selections, garnered from six other sources, are of the same type. In establishing his corpus and projecting the image of himself as essayist, Goldsmith returns to his initial conception of the ideal form. As he had written in his review of the *Connoisseur,* the essential traits of an ideal essay are "good taste" and "good humour," and the proper tone is "perfectly satyrical, yet perfectly good-natured." Still enjoying his first real flush of literary acclaim, he crafts his collection in hopes of securing a place as a worthy successor to Addison and Steele.

Goldsmith and His Contemporaries

Like Johnson with his *Rambler,* John Hawkesworth with the *Adventurer,* and Arthur Murphy with the *Gray's Inn Journal,* Goldsmith probably hoped to offset the meager sales of his essays with a collected edition. Walter Graham notes that "authors and publishers had come, by Hawkesworth's day, to realize that a series of essays must make itself popular with the reading public first, if any wide sale was to be expected for it in book form."[15] Goldsmith apparently hoped, instead, to rely on the recognition he began to receive after his periodical career was over, rather than on the initial popularity of his essays. While his periodical career had earned him a steady flow of "hack" jobs from London publishers, it was his first major poetic effort which earned him the fame upon which rested his hopes for his *Essays* (1765). In December 1764, John Hawkesworth reviewed *The Traveller* for the *Gentleman's Magazine;* he strongly recommended "a new author so able to afford refined pleasure to true taste," and Goldsmith fully emerged from relative anonymity.[16]

The purpose of the collected edition, however, was not purely pecuniary. Goldsmith had learned from and adapted models provided by his great predecessors, Addison and Steele, and by contemporaries such as Johnson,

Murphy, Hawkesworth, Bonnell Thornton, and George Colman. With his newly found recognition, and after nearly six years of experience, he felt ready to take his place in the periodical tradition. Keenly aware of his predecessors and unreluctant to borrow, Goldsmith adapted elements from all of these journalists to his own style and method. Like so many other imitators of the *Tatler* and *Spectator,* Goldsmith borrowed the fictional author and his "lightly moralizing note," as Graham describes it. Most notably, this is the tone of Lien Chi Altangi in the Chinese Letters.[17] By 1759, however, the once-conventional single-essay periodical and its identifiable persona were nearly extinct. The periodicals for which Goldsmith wrote were miscellanies or reviews such as the *Bee* and *Busy Body,* lengthy and diverse magazines such as the *British,* or newspapers such as *Lloyd's.* While he admired the *Rambler* and the *Connoisseur,* both six-page, single-essay serials, he avoided this format, which had generally failed to attract large readerships in the 1750s. And other than his "Chinese Philosopher," and perhaps his "Indigent Philosopher" there is no recurring character in Goldsmith's essays analogous to Johnson's dignified "Mr. Rambler," Murphy's "Charles Ranger" *(Gray's Inn Journal),* Edward Moore's "Adam Fitz-Adam" *(World),* or Thornton and Colman's "Mr. Town" *(Connoisseur).*

Edward Cave's *Gentleman's Magazine,* the dominant periodical miscellany since its inception in 1731, set the tone for magazine formats in the late 1750's; most of the periodicals for which Goldsmith wrote were structurally similar to the *Gentleman's.* As John Abbott writes: "The publication was marked at the outset by the catholicity of its contents—it was truly a magazine, or storehouse, of materials, including news summaries; lists of births, deaths, promotions, bankrupcies; stock and weather reports; historical, scientific and political articles; commentary on religion; and, increasingly, literature and literary criticism."[18] The success of the *Gentleman's* could not have failed to attract the attention of other publishers and editors. Its imitators were of two principal types: those that relied primarily on light, topical essays and those that focused on politics and current events. Murphy's *Gray's Inn Journal* (September 1753–September 1754), an example of the former type, included satiric "club" essays; imaginary letters; dream visions; and Oriental, romantic, and allegorical tales—the common stock of material well-worked by essayists in the early 1750s.[19] (These forms were a staple of some of the last significant single-essay journals such as the *Adventurer,* the *World,* and the *Connoisseur.*) The *British,* the *Bee, Busy Body,* and *Weekly* expanded on this basic concept.

The second type spawned by the success of Cave's periodical was the political or historical miscellany, of which the *Literary* could be considered an example. This journal, for which Johnson probably acted as editor in its first year (1756), allowed Johnson to vent his antiwar sentiments and "country Tory bias." Although the *Literary,* because of its unpopular stances, reached only about one-seventh the readership of the *Gentleman's* in 1756, its political emphasis exemplified a growing number of new periodicals after the advent of war with France.[20] The *Universal Chronicle,* a newspaper miscellany to which Johnson contributed his *Idler* columns, displayed a similar emphasis. When Johnson began his column on 8 April 1758, the *Idler* filled approximately two-and-a-half of the three columns on the first page of the *Universal.* The balance of its seven pages were devoted to news and commentary, stock reports, lists of new publications, and advertisements. The *Public Ledger* and *Lloyd's,* to which Goldsmith contributed, were miscellanies of this type, featuring news and political observations.

To some extent, Johnson's journalistic career mirrored the changing trends in periodical publication to which Goldsmith tried to adjust. Johnson's biweekly *Rambler,* with its classical mottoes, serious moral tone, and omission of advertisements, was outsold by the *World,* a lighter, mildly didactic periodical featuring social satire and avoiding serious ethical discussions. Johnson subsequently contributed to the *Adventurer,* which was leavened by Thornton's "pantomime" contributions under the name of "Harlequin Hercules." With the outbreak of war and the proliferation of newspapers and political magazines, Johnson contributed increasingly political essays to the *Literary* in 1756, the *London Chronicle* in 1757, and the *Universal Chronicle* in 1757.

By 1759, single-essay periodicals such as the *Rambler* and the *Connoisseur* had proved themselves financially unsuccessful. Goldsmith turned, instead, to the more diverse light miscellany to gain public acceptance. He rejected the moralistic tone frequent in some of the *Spectator* essays and in Johnson's early periodical writing. The passage Goldsmith quoted in his review of the *Connoisseur* may have reflected his own views: "I purposely avoided the worn-out practice of retailing scraps of morality, and affecting to dogmatize on the common duties of life. In this point, indeed, the Spectator is inimitable: Nor could I hope to say any thing new upon these topics, after so many excellent moral and religious Essays, which are the principal ornament of that work" (I, 15). Like Johnson in the later part of his career, Goldsmith used the periodical as a vehicle for expressing short, ironic reflections on English society. While he avoided the more obviously political shifts of Johnson and Smollett in their journalism, he did cater to the public demand for commentary on European affairs.

Of the major periodical writers in the late 1750s and early 1760s, Goldsmith has been one of the most difficult to characterize. Some have been most readily associated with their political ideology. Smollett, in addition to his editorship of the *Critical,* achieved notoriety as the defender of George III and John Stuart, earl of Bute, in the *Briton.* Although Murphy established himself as both playwright and "literary" journalist with early essay sheets such as the *Gray's Inn Journal,* he devoted himself from 1756 to 1763 to political journalism. His *Test* attacked the Pitt ministry while defending the ousted Newcastle, and his *Auditor* served the policies of Lord Bute. Another political journalist, John Wilkes, is remembered for his ironic attacks on the Bute administration in the *North Briton.*

Other journalists have been chiefly identified with a specific periodical. Despite his famous and ambiguous connection with the publication of Cleland's *Memoirs of a Woman of Pleasure,* Ralph Griffiths' name is nearly synonymous with the *Monthly.* Although also recognized as the chronicler of Captain James Cook's voyages, John Hawkesworth is rightly remembered for his thirty-two year connection with the *Gentleman's,* for which he reviewed Johnson's *Dictionary;* Goldsmith's *The Traveller, The Good Natur'd Man,* and *The Deserted Village;* Sterne's *Tristram Shandy;* and Smollett's *Humphrey Clinker.*[21] And discussions of Johnson's journalism usually focus on the *Rambler* or the *Idler* essays, though his career was nearly as diverse as Goldsmith's.

The locus of Goldsmith's periodical career is not within a particular journal, though the *Bee* has certainly received more critical attention than his other contributions. Nor is he easily identified with a particular political affiliation, though Goldsmith is not as apolitical as the critical neglect of his ideology might imply. In some respects, Goldsmith's attempt in his *Essays* (1765) to portray himself as a humorist has succeeded. Those relatively few scholars who continue to study Goldsmith's work despite its declining critical reputation argue about his use of irony and his varied satiric techniques by drawing selectively from his periodical work. Neither his self-appointment as "foreign correspondent"—an element at least as prevalent in the journalism as his "amiable humorist" stance—nor his remarkable range has been duly considered a distinguishing characteristic.[22] In fact, the sheer number of periodicals for which he was engaged in a relatively short period and his frequent posture as cross-cultural critic may be the most characteristic features of Goldsmith's journalism.

For purposes of comparison, the Irishman Hugh Kelly might be considered Goldsmith's journalistic successor.[23] When Kelly is mentioned in connection with Goldsmith, the occasion is almost always the theatrical rivalry in which the two were involved. The success of Kelly's comedy *False Delicacy* (1768), which was playing at Drury Lane when *The Good Natur'd Man* opened at Covent Garden, is said to have provoked Goldsmith's jealousy and, ultimately, an irreparable breach between those onetime friends.[24] Goldsmith had contributed an essay for the *Babler,* Kelly's column in *Owen's Weekly Chronicle* from 1763 to 1767, and the two may have joined forces to produce the *Gentleman's Journal.*[25]

Forster, perhaps the most eminent of Goldsmith's late-nineteenth-century biographers, deplored Kelly's "sentimentalism" and noted that the author "has not survived to our time."[26] Kelly's continuing obscurity is compounded by the fact that little documentary evidence remains concerning his career.[27] Attribution problems make a detailed analysis of his periodical writing nearly impossible; however, his editorship of several of London's important periodicals in the mid-1760s has been well-established, and he was clearly one of the most prolific journalists of the decade. An Irishman escaping poverty and coming to London in 1760—three years after Goldsmith's arrival—Kelly launched a dramatic career after establishing himself as a versatile essayist and editor; he was active until his death in 1777—three years after Goldsmith's. Prior comments: "Hugh Kelly was one of those men, of whom there are several in the history of letters, who starting into life under serious disadvantages, found nothing in his progress through it but his own industry to help him on his way, and who unable to attain a place in the first rank of genius, received little credit for the talents he really possessed, or the difficulties he overcame."[28]

According to William Cooke, who claimed to have known him well, Kelly began his journalistic career much as Goldsmith had—as a "drudge" for a printer/bookseller. Kelly's duties, however, were even less "literary" than Goldsmith's. He was "engaged as a Paragraph-Writer to one of the Daily Papers" and "had it in his choice to have either a settled salary of a Guinea per week, or so much for every Paragraph."[29] Like Goldsmith, Kelly successfully made the transition from "drudge" to periodical essayist, though at a much younger age. At twenty-one, he procured a position as a contributor to Charlotte Lennox's *Lady's Museum* (March 1760–January 1761). He then attracted the attentions of Israel Pottinger, who had recruited Goldsmith for the *Busy Body* in 1759, and was appointed editor of the *Court Magazine* in September of 1761. Whether Kelly knew Goldsmith personally at this time is not known; but the *Court* certainly followed Goldsmith's preoccupation with the state of polite learning, and its praise for Goldsmith's "taste and understanding" in the fourth issue was consistent with its primary focus.[30] The *Court* intended, like *Polite Learning* and many of Goldsmith's essays for the *Public Ledger,* to help counteract England's literary and cultural decline.

Kelly's association with Pottinger was more fruitful than Goldsmith's; the *Court* survived under Kelly's editorship until 1765. When Goldsmith was withdrawing from journalism, Kelly was reaching his peak: in 1762, he contributed to the *Royal Chronicle* and wrote political correspondence for the *Gazetteer,* in addition to his work for the *Court.*[31] According to Haig, letters from journalists like Kelly were vital to the success of the *Gazetteer* in the 1760s.[32] On 12 February 1763, he began his *Babler* in *Owen's Weekly Chronicle,* which endured until 5 June 1767—making the series, as Robert Bataille notes, one of the longest-running of the century.[33] Adopting a frivolous title—a risk, considering the failure of the *Bee,* the *Busy Body,* and others of that type during the war—Kelly filled the *Babler* with essays much like Goldsmith's in the *British.* They were mostly didactic tales aimed at young people and light social satire. Cooke paid the *Babler* a backhanded tribute when he noted that though the essays "possess none of the deep recesses of knowledge and morality which are to be found in the Spectator [and] Rambler . . . we have more than once heard this question asked with some impatience at the Coffee-houses, 'Well, what does the Babbler say to-day?' "[34] Though Kelly may, indeed, have seldom reached the level of sophistication that Goldsmith achieved in *The Citizen,* he was considerably more successful as a journalist in establishing an enduring popularity with his readers.

Kelly also enjoyed considerably more success than Goldsmith as an editor. In 1765 he assumed the editorship of the *Public Ledger,* which Goldsmith had helped popularize with his Chinese Letters. Under his direction until 1772, the *Ledger* became an important defender of George III and an enemy of Wilkes. Clearly, Kelly was a worthy successor to Goldsmith. Unlike Goldsmith, he never deserted the profession, even while writing six plays.[35] He also actively joined in the political controversies of the 1760s, in a manner for which Goldsmith expressed distaste, and became well-known as a polemicist. As famous as Kelly became in his time, posterity has reduced his career to a footnote in periodical history. But his career as a journalist affords a revealing comparison to Goldsmith's—and reminds us that remarkable success as a periodical editor and writer does not ensure lasting recognition. Would Goldsmith have been remembered by literary historians solely on the basis of his periodical writing—apart from his successful poetry, *The Vicar, She Stoops to Conquer,* and the inestimable aid of Johnson? The relative obscurity of Kelly makes it seem unlikely.

A Place in the Tradition

By the time Edward Young published his *Conjectures on Original Composition* in 1759, his view of authorship had become antiquated. He had the perspective of a living anachronism, a survivor from an age of literary patronage, gentlemen-authors, and genteel readers:

To Men of Letters, and Leisure, it [composition] is not only a noble Amusement, but a sweet Refuge; it improves their Parts, and promotes their Peace: It opens a back-door out of the Bustle of this busy, and idle world, into a delicious Garden of Moral and Intellectual fruits and flowers; the Key of which is denied to the rest of mankind. . . . How independent of the world is he, who can daily find new Acquaintance, that at once entertain, and improve him, in the little World, the minute but fruitful Creation, of his own mind?

  These advantages *Composition* affords us, whether we write ourselves, or in more humble amusement peruse the Works of others. While we bustle thro' the thronged walks of public Life, it gives us a respite, at least, from Care; a pleasing Pause of refreshing Recollection.[36]

Young's "modern" models of originality were Swift, Pope, and Addison, who addressed readers seeking amusement, instruction, and solace in their "delightful bowers" of retirement.[37] Of course, Paternoster Row in the late 1750s was vastly different from the world of letters Young described—and the one for which John Brown longed nostalgically in 1757. Authors could not afford the luxury of being "independent of the world" at a time when discussions of politics, wars, and fashion were the principal products of the press and the preferred fare of London readers. The "volunteer" author, independent of booksellers and public taste, had become virtually extinct.

For a talented and aspiring author in 1757, the path leading to literary fame was, in some respects, narrowly circumscribed. Twenty years after the Licensing Act of 1737, London theatres were still producing few new mainpieces; even after establishing himself as a well-known author, Goldsmith had great difficulty getting his two comedies staged. The prospects for an unknown author's establishing a career as dramatist were decidedly bleak. Prospective poets faced a similarly daunting challenge. Cumberland's remark, "publishers hate poetry," certainly applied to mid-century England.[38] Though poets such as Gray, Smart, and Thomas Warton enjoyed a following among the literati, poetry publication was an unprofitable venture, attracted relatively little notice in the press, and promised even the most skillful of its practitioners a meager existence as best. Nor was becoming a "novelist" a practicable or respectable option. The genre was ill-defined and, more often than not, reviled in the press as an inferior and corrupting form. With the important exceptions of Richardson, Fielding, and Smollett, none of whom depended on the sale of their fiction for sustenance, novelists faced almost certain obscurity, if not public ignominy.

The most promising route available for the new class of aspiring professional authors—for many, the only route—was the periodical press. None of the scholars who have written about Goldsmith—from biographers of the "poor Goldsmith" school to admirers of his "major" work—have fully appreciated the degree to which his career was enabled and shaped by an extraordinary confluence of historical and professional circumstances. A poor yet ambitious Irishman who had failed to establish a medical practice, he met Ralph Griffiths at a time when he had little more to recommend him than a stock of observations about European culture, an aptitude for translating French, and, presumably, the kind words of the schoolmaster John Milner. Already in his late twenties, he had published nothing, unlike most of Griffiths' other reviewers, nor had he achieved any sort of recognition in another field. Yet, because of Griffiths' pressing need for reviewers, prompted in part by expanding competition, and because public demand created the need for greater coverage of "foreign news," Goldsmith was fortunate enough to gain employment with one of London's leading publishers. Keenly aware of the fierce competition between Griffiths and Smollett, he took advantage of the "battle of the reviews" to launch his career and to make the professional connections that would sustain him as a periodical author.

Throughout his journalistic career, Goldsmith complained about the very circumstances that had made his career possible: the inescapable rules of journalistic publication and the "mechanization" of authorship. In his *Conjectures,* Young may have been transmitting a common criticism of journalistic writing when he noted: "*Imitations* are often a sort of *Manufacture* wrought up by those *Mechanics, Art,* and *Labour,* out of pre-existent materials not their own."[39] Ironically, the journals themselves probably provided the most incisive and relentless attacks on periodical publication, the "mechanization" of authorship, and the threat to genius posed by the commercial press. An anonymous letter printed in the *Court* rehearsed these complaints succinctly:

> If we consider the republic of letters as a commercial state, and look upon the different professors as a kind of mechanics, we must undoubtedly be very much surprized at the insolent claims, every little pretender to genius, shall make to the character of a gentleman from the writer of an humble Acrostic in the Daily Gazetteer, to the sensible compiler of an Evening's Essay in the St. James's Chronicle. . . .
>
> This imaginary importance were indeed a little excusable, in the generality of our modern writers, if their performances had any pretension to a tolerable degree of merit; but where the quantity, and not the quality of the work, is the principal consideration of both the author and the bookseller, the one must find himself disappointed in his hopes of admiration, and the other mistaken in his expectations of a fortune.[40]

The author concluded his letter by relating his outrage at having been insulted at the Bedford Coffee House by a self-proclaimed expert on foreign affairs, who, he later discovered, was no more than a "paragraph maker to a News-Paper."

The proliferation of journals during the Seven Years' War period, most of them devoted heavily to reporting foreign news, made imitation and mechanization a necessity. The difficulty writers faced in creating appealing personae; the pressing deadlines for daily, weekly, or monthly copy; and the limited number of genuinely newsworthy events—all forced journalists to borrow from previously published sources and to rework their own ideas. This practice led Goldsmith to the development of his most clearly identifiable journalistic persona: the "foreign correspondent," or "citizen of the world." The fictional role first assigned him by Griffiths provided him a reliable vehicle through which to comment on the state of English politics, learning, morals, and manners, as compared with those of her European neighbors.

Attempting to categorize meaningfully a career as multifaceted as Goldsmith's has proven an elusive task. Those who have studied Goldsmith as a satirist have debated ironic intention in *The Vicar;* critics of Goldsmith as a social commentator have discerned ideological differences between *The Traveller* and *The Deserted Village;* critics of Goldsmith as a "good-natured man" have defined him as an "amiable humorist."[41] None of these definitions applies satisfactorily to the first six years of Goldsmith's authorial career. To see Goldsmith as a journalist responding to the demands of his profession and social changes brought on by the war and England's redefinition of itself as a nation—such an approach best defines the first six years of his seventeen-year career as an author and helps to explain his rise from obscurity and anonymity, even before he met "Doctor Major."

The first years of his literary career correspond roughly to those of England's participation in the Seven Years' War. Donald Greene argues that the latter might best be called the "Great War for Empire": "It did indeed bring the British Empire into being, adding the two great subcontinents of Canada and India to Britain's territorial possessions, and it provided Britain with easy access to markets and sources of raw materials throughout the world and so laid the foundations of Britain's amazing commercial prosperity in the nineteenth century."[42] Although scholars may be tempted to see Goldsmith as aloof from politics and isolated from its influence, the war was probably the single most important factor shaping his journalistic career. He first came to London at a time when Newcastle had resigned in the face of heated debate about the conduct of the military. Events such as Admiral Byng's retreat from the French forces at Minorca provoked a spirit of national insecurity and doubt about England's status as a dominant world power. Authors like Brown and his imitators in the press became purveyors of doom, chroniclers of the political, literary, and religious decline of the nation.

In his capacity as a reviewer, Goldsmith commented on the literary productions of England's neighbors and launched an attack on popular novels, which he found morally defective and symptomatic of England's literary decline. Behind a veil of anonymity, he added his voice to a growing number of London reviewers; though fearful of the power inherent in such a position, he influenced the literary careers of many of England's foremost writers. Collecting many of the observations he had made as a reviewer in his *Polite Learning,* he cast himself as an authority on European letters and the state of scholarship in England. Like Brown's *Estimate,* the book deplored England's intellectual decline, and it expressed disgust with the *Monthly,* the *Critical,* and London's "critical news-papers and magazines without number" (I, 289). Though, like many of his colleagues, he protested against what he felt was the bookseller's unwarranted authority and the author's enslavement to economics and popular fancy, he survived admirably in such a system and laid a foundation for a career as poet, novelist, and playwright.

By the time Goldsmith moved from reviewing to essay writing and compiling in 1759, London's magazines and newspapers had become, to a great extent, outlets for political expression. The pseudonymous "Thomas Touchit," writing about the "Advantages from Political Writing" in the *Literary,* articulated an increasingly common function for journalists: "to convince the public that a political watchman is absolutely necessary for the safety and security of this great city."[43] Goldsmith expressed little interest in becoming such a watchman. Instead, he attempted, with his *Bee,* to carve out a place for himself as successor to the great humanistic essayists of the century—echoing in tone and substance the *Tatler, Spectator, Rambler,* and *Connoisseur.* When the *Bee* failed, as so many of its type had in the first years of the war, he recast himself in the role first designed for him as a reviewer. As the worldly and objective "foreign correspondent," he compared England's progress in culture and government to that of other nations. This "citizen of the world," free from partisanship and national prejudice, attempted to preserve an apolitical posture; such a task, for journalists in the late 1750s and early 1760s, was nearly impossible.

Goldsmith has been viewed either as apolitical or as a simpleminded royalist. While he frequently argued for absolute monarchical authority, he also opposed George II on the king's most urgent agenda late in his reign. Speaking to both houses of Parliament on 4 July 1757, the king declared: "The succour and preservation of my dominions in *America* have been my constant care. And, next to the security of my kingdoms, they shall continue to be my great and principal object."[44] Goldsmith was skeptical of English colonialism and the commercial motivation underlying the struggle in America. Many of his essays addressed a paradox articulated by Soame Jenyns: "Trade and wealth are the strength and the pursuit of every wise nation, yet these must certainly produce Luxury, which no less certainly must produce their destruction."[45] Amid the celebrations for English military triumphs in 1759, Goldsmith urged caution.

Compared to contemporaries like Murphy and Smollett, however, Goldsmith did remain aloof from ministerial politics—and may have paid a price for doing so. As Alexander Andrews noted, "The writers for the ministry, after all, got the best of it as far as substantial reward goes."[46] Anti-ministerial writers frequently profited as well. Smollett lamented: "The Truth is there [is] no Author so wretched but he will meet with Countenance in England if he attacks our Nation in any shape."[47] Goldsmith hoped for more permanent rewards, apart from the political sphere. As the preface to his *Essays* (1765) suggests, he wished to be recognized by future scholars as an important and independent author—to paraphrase Cumberland, to make the unlikely leap from Paternoster Row to Parnassus.[48]

When Goldsmith's contemporaries talked about the writer's genius—usually in the same breath with an anecdote revealing his personal foolishness—they mentioned, foremost, his grace and good humor as a stylist. Boswell was probably echoing Johnson's opinion when he wrote of Goldsmith: "His mind resembled a fertile, but thin soil. There was a quick, but not a strong vegetation, of whatever chanced to be thrown upon it. No deep root could be struck. The oak of the forest did not grow there; but the elegant shrubbery and the fragrant parterre appeared in gay succession."[49] If Goldsmith did, indeed, lack Johnson's intellectual prowess, the quickness and versatility to which Boswell alludes served him well as a journalist. The first manifestation of his "genius," as his career in the periodicals demonstrated, was his unusual ability as a "compiler," or what might now be called a "popularizer." He was an astute observer of innovations in his profession; he carefully noted his contemporaries' popular successes and failures; he adapted to the demands of a changing profession; and he crafted his own observations and "whatever chanced to be thrown" in his way from other sources. In short, he had precisely the sort of "genius" needed to establish a successful career as a journalist.

At present, scholarship on Goldsmith appears to be virtually moribund, if the paucity of entries in recent bibliographies is an indication of critical interest in the author. He is still considered at least a "major minor," whose works (particularly *The Deserted Village, The Traveller, The Vicar of Wakefield,* and *She Stoops to Conquer*) remain ensconced in the established canon. Yet, in the aftermath of the controversy over ironic intention in *The Vicar* that briefly enlivened scholarship in the late 1960s and early 1970s, no polarizing debate or unifying constructs have helped invigorate Goldsmith studies. Portraits of the author as an "amiable humorist" or "good-natured man" or "sentimentalist" have been effectively challenged as incomplete, as has the view of Goldsmith as an "Augustan" satirist.

With the publication of successful contextual studies of other prominent eighteenth-century figures, Goldsmith becomes an obvious candidate for analyses of the interrelationship between his work and his milieu. This book has attempted to move discussion of the author in such a direction. Concentration on his journalistic career has several advantages. First, it removes the author from his place in the "Johnson Circle," in which role he has become obscured by "Doctor Major" and trivialized by anecdotal treatment. In fact, before he came under Johnson's influence, Goldsmith had written *The Citizen of the World,* one of his finest works; he had edited his own periodical; and he had established himself as an important reviewer and prolific essayist. A second advantage to such an approach is that it capitalizes on a great deal of exciting research being done on the eighteenth-century periodical. The availability of a large number of mid-century newspapers and magazines provides a rich source of details about the profession in which Goldsmith engaged as an apprentice writer. Finally, new approaches to history promise a more thorough integration of documentary "texts" with biography and the traditional boundaries of literature.

In contributing to the journals of his period, Goldsmith laid the theoretical and stylistic groundwork for many of his later productions. This study has found in his reviews and essays early intimations of *The Vicar, The Traveller, The Deserted Village,* and *She Stoops to Conquer.* But it has focused more fully on the journalistic work as a separable part of his career. Studying the later works in isolation, scholars have found disparate images of Goldsmith as an author: the sentimental or satirical novelist, the poet clinging to the "Augustan" tradition, the playwright of "laughing comedy." A focus on the journalistic career produces a more unified view. He can be seen as an author who was both a product of and contributor to the literary, social, and political controversies of his age; as an opportunist, grudgingly adapting to the demands of a newly emerging profession; as an objective "outsider" comparing English culture with that of foreign nations; and as a political writer who had evolving and often contradictory observations on the war, the crown, and ministerial politics. Posterity, to whom Goldsmith appealed in the preface to his collection of essays, has helped him make the unlikely climb from Paternoster Row to Parnassus. But the prominent features of his journalistic career—the requisite adaptability, the sensitivity to a changing readership, the impatience with any single genre—played an unmistakable role in defining and assuring, at least in some measure, an enduring literary reputation.

Notes

Preface

1. James G. Basker, *Tobias Smollett: Critic and Journalist* (Newark: University of Delaware Press, 1988). For his treatment of the proposed additions to the Goldsmith canon, see pp. 194–96.

2. Oliver Goldsmith, *Essays and Criticism,* ed. Isaac Reed and Thomas Wright, Vol. 2 (London: J. Johnson, 1798). For confirmation of Thomas Wright's apprenticeship to Archibald Hamilton (1758–66), see D. F. McKenzie, ed., *Stationers' Company Apprentices, 1701–1800* (Oxford: The Oxford Bibliographical Society, 1798), 154.

3. Fanny Burney, *Cecilia* (1782; London: Virago Press, 1986), Book VII, 720.

4. Useful treatments of Johnson's periodical career include Paul Fussell's "The Anxious Employment of a Periodical Writer" in *Samuel Johnson and the Life of Writing* (New York: Harcourt Brace Jovanovich, 1971), 143–80; Donald J. Greene, *Samuel Johnson: Political Writings,* vol. 10, Yale Edition of the Works of Samuel Johnson (New Haven: Yale University Press, 1977); James L. Clifford, *Dictionary Johnson: Samuel Johnson's Middle Years* (New York: McGraw-Hill, 1979); and Donald D. Eddy, *Samuel Johnson: Book Reviewer in the "Literary Magazine, or Universal Review," 1756–1758* (New York: Garland, 1979). Murphy's dramatic career has attracted more notice than his journalism, but discussions of the latter are included in Arthur Sherbo, *New Essays by Arthur Murphy* (East Lansing: Michigan State University Press, 1963) and in Robert Donald Spector, *Arthur Murphy* (Boston: Twayne, 1979). The best treatment of Hawkesworth's career is John Lawrence Abbott, *John Hawkesworth: Eighteenth-Century Man of Letters* (Madison: University of Wisconsin Press, 1982).

5. Ronald S. Crane, *New Essays by Oliver Goldsmith* (Chicago: University of Chicago Press, 1927).

6. See, for example, John Forster, *The Life and Times of Oliver Goldsmith,* 2 vols. (London: Bickers & Son, 1877) and Austin Dobson, *Life of Oliver Goldsmith* (London: Walter Scott, 1888).

7. Scholars have been unable ultimately to determine Goldsmith's year of birth; in the Goldsmith family Bible, notation of the year has been torn away, though the exact day, November 10, has been preserved. Most nineteenth-century biographers argued for 1728; Katharine C. Balderston, editor of the *Collected Letters,* presented some evidence for 1730 and persuasively demonstrated why 1728 was an unlikely candidate ("The Birth of Goldsmith," *Times Literary Supplement* [7 March 1929]: 185–86). Ralph Wardle notes that he has "nothing to add to the vexed subject" (Wardle, 300). For the most thorough presentation of available evidence, see R. S. Crane's review of Balderston's article in *Philological Quarterly* 9 (1930): 190–91. Crane suggests 1729 as the probable date.

8. Balderston, *A Census of the Manuscripts of Oliver Goldsmith* (New York: Brick Row Book Shop, 1926).

9. Temple Scott, *Oliver Goldsmith, Bibliographically and Biographically Considered* (New York: Bowling Green Press, 1928).

10. R. W. Seitz, "Goldsmith and the *Literary Magazine,*" *Review of English Studies* 5 (October 1929): 410–30. Seitz demonstrates that several contributions to the *Literary Maga-*

zine, long assumed to Goldsmith's, had been attributed to him on insufficient or erroneous grounds. Morris Golden, in "Goldsmith's Attributions in the 'Literary Magazine,'" *Notes & Queries* 201 (October 1956): 432–35, argued for reinclusion of these essays in the canon, but failed to convince either Crane or Friedman.

11. Elizabeth Eaton Kent, *Goldsmith and His Booksellers* (Ithaca: Cornell University Press, 1933).

12. Though inadequately cross-referenced and vexingly incomplete, Nangle's index is a convenient and still virtually untapped source.

13. Although he incorporates the scholarship of Crane, Seitz, and Balderston, Wardle contributes relatively little new information and relies heavily on Prior. The text of Friedman's edition is generally reliable. His attributions are laudably cautious, though separate inclusion of some long-maintained, doubtful attributions would have been helpful. Lamentably, he excludes all of Goldsmith's histories and long compilations, some of which are included in the edition of J. W. M. Gibbs, *The Works of Oliver Goldsmith,* 5 vols. (London: George Bell and Sons, 1884–86).

14. Ricardo Quintana, *Oliver Goldsmith: A Georgian Study* (New York: Macmillan, 1967).

15. John Ginger, *The Notable Man: The Life and Times of Oliver Goldsmith* (London: Hamish Hamilton, 1977), 362.

16. Samuel H. Woods, "The Goldsmith 'Problem,'" *Studies in Burke and His Time* 19 (Winter 1978): 47–60.

17. Ibid., 50–51, 60.

18. Woods, *Oliver Goldsmith: A Reference Guide* (Boston: G. K. Hall, 1982).

Chapter 1. Journalist by Profession

1. Bonnell Thornton and George Colman, *The Connoisseur,* 3d ed. (London: Baldwin, 1757), 18.

2. Goldsmith used the term in a similar vein in Chinese Letter XX (20 March 1760): "But lest you should think the French alone are faulty in this respect, hear how an English journalist delivers his sentiments of them" (II, 87).

3. Anon. [Samuel Johnson], "Of the Duty of a Journalist," *Universal Chronicle* (8 April 1758): 1. The essay appeared in the first number, one week before Johnson introduced the *Idler.*

4. Magali S. Larson, *The Rise of Professionalism: A Sociological Analysis* (Berkeley: University of California Press, 1977), 4–5.

5. Johnson, *The Rambler,* ed. W. J. Bate and Albrecht B. Strauss, vol. 3, Yale Edition of the Works of Samuel Johnson (New Haven: Yale University Press, 1969), 46–50.

6. For a valuable discussion of Brown's *Estimate,* see Spector, *ELP,* 63–65.

7. John Brown, *An Estimate of the Manners and Principles of the Times,* 2d. ed., 2 vols. (London: Davis and Reymers, 1757), II, 75–76. For parallels in Goldsmith's writing see *Polite Learning* (I, 290, 319).

8. See, for example, reviews of Brown's *Estimate* in the *Critical Review* 6 (April 1757): 346; *Monthly Review* 16 (June 1757): 522.

9. Sixteen such responses are noted by Donald D. Eddy, *A Bibliography of John Brown* (New York: Bibliographical Society of America, 1971), 142.

10. Richard Steele, *The Tatler,* ed. Donald F. Bond, 3 vols. (Oxford: Clarendon Press, 1987), I, 32.

11. Anon., "Essay upon the Most Remarkable Periods of English Literature," *Court Magazine* 1 (September 1761): 16.

12. *Tatler,* I, 104.

13. Isaac Disraeli, *The Calamities and Quarrels of Authors,* ed. Benjamin Disraeli (1812–14; London: Frederick Warne, 1867): 8–9.

14. Ibid., 15.

15. Samuel Foote, *The Author,* in *The Plays of Samuel Foote,* ed. Paula R. Backscheider and Douglas Howard (New York: Garland, 1983): 5.

16. George Lyttleton, *Dialogues of the Dead* (1760; rpt. New York: Garland, 1970), 306–7.

17. Ibid., 310. Brown responded to some of Lyttleton's arguments in *An Additional Dialogue of the Dead, Between Pericles and Aristides* (London: Davis and Reymers, 1760). See Eddy, *A Bibliography of John Brown,* 85–86.

18. Washington Irving, *Oliver Goldsmith: A Biography* (1849), in *The Complete Works of Washington Irving,* vol. 17, ed. Elsie Lee West (Boston: Twayne, 1978). Irving's sentimental account of Goldsmith's "servitude" to bookseller Ralph Griffiths influenced much subsequent critical commentary on Goldsmith's first journalistic assignment: "Such was the literary vassalage to which Goldsmith had unwarily subjected himself. A diurnal drudgery was imposed on him . . ." (50).

19. Robert W. Kenny, "Ralph's *Case of Authors:* Its Influence on Goldsmith and Isaac D'Israeli," *PMLA* 52 (March 1937): 104.

20. James Ralph, *The Case of Authors by Profession or Trade,* 1758; rpt. intro. by Philip Stevick (Gainesville, Florida: Scholars' Facsimiles & Reprints, 1966), 6.

21. Stevick, "Introduction," *The Case of Authors,* ix–x.

22. Ralph, 8.

23. See, for example, Robert H. Hopkins, *The True Genius of Oliver Goldsmith* (Baltimore: Johns Hopkins Press, 1969). Hopkins contrasts Brown's "militant tone and boldly stated thesis" with Goldsmith's "coolly detached and seemingly philosophical approach" (29).

24. Robert W. Kenny, in his "Ralph's *Case of Authors,*" briefly acknowledges Ralph's influence on Goldsmith in *Polite Learning,* but the debt may be even more considerable than he suggests. Consider, for example, the parallel arguments in the two authors' comparisons of "holiday writers" with professionals. Ralph writes: "But the Voluntier-Writers of our Times are Holiday-Writers indeed.—That is to say,—They write just enough to shew They can read; and, having so done, throw away the Pen.—Whereas, by the very Malice of his Star, the Writer by Trade is for ever obliged to write on; and thereby obtains that Mastery in Matter, Method, Stile and Manner, which is hardly to be obtained any other Way" (Ralph, 8–9). Goldsmith's version says: "But be assured, by friend, that wit is in some measure mechanical, and that a man long habituated to catch at even its resemblance, will at last be happy enough to possess the substance; by a long habit of writing he acquires a justness of thinking, and a mastery of manner, which holiday writers, even with ten times his genius, may vainly attempt to equal" (II, 377). Goldsmith's description of the fiddler in the theater orchestra who winds up with more money than the author (Letter LVII, II, 238) is probably borrowed from the same illustration used by Ralph (42). And like Ralph, Goldsmith cites Dryden and Otway as examples of prominent "writers for bread" (II, 376 and Ralph, 24).

25. Such a narrative stance is consistent with Boswell's description of Goldsmith's deportment as "that of a scholar aukwardly affecting the easy gentleman" in *Life of Johnson,* I. 413.

26. Lance Bertelsen, *The Nonsense Club: Literature and Popular Culture, 1749–1764* (Oxford: Clarendon Press, 1986), 136.

27. Brewer, 16.

28. The reviews he wrote late in 1763, at a time when he had abandoned full-time periodical writing, were in support of his work as a compiler and writer of prefaces. Similarly, his last four essays for the *Westminster Magazine* (1773) were written at least partly to promote his theatrical work. Morris Golden, in "Goldsmith and the *Universal Museum* and *Complete Magazine,*" *Notes & Queries* 202 (August 1957) argues: "I believe that he did not abandon the fairly lucrative labors of the magazines in 1762, and I shall try to show his connection with at

least one periodical in 1764–5 and point out some new essays written for it" (340). Ultimately, Golden proves only that Goldsmith's essays were, as the author himself had pointed out in his *Essays* (1765), borrowed without acknowledgement by a variety of magazines throughout his career.

29. Robert L. Haig, *The Gazetteer, 1735–1797: A Study in the Eighteenth-Century English Newspaper* (Carbondale: Southern Illinois University Press, 1960), 42.

30. Soame Jenyns, *A Free Inquiry into the Nature and Origin of Evil,* 2d ed. (London: Dodsley, 1757), 128–29.

31. Ibid., 140.

32. For an account of the history of the *North Briton* and of Wilkes's arrest, see George Nobbe, *The "North Briton": A Study in Political Propaganda* (New York: Columbia University Press, 1939; rpt. New York: AMS Press, 1966).

33. Prior, I, 350.

Chapter 2. Goldsmith's Hiring and Its Periodical Contexts

1. *Connoisseur* (15 April 1756): 91–92.

2. *Letters,* 21.

3. Ibid., 28.

4. John Triplet [pseud.], "The Distresses of an Hired Writer, Addressed to the Authors of the *British Magazine,*" *British Magazine* 2 (April 1761): 198–200. The mistaken attribution of this piece to Goldsmith was corrected by Morris Golden in "Goldsmith and 'The Distresses of an Hired Writer,'" *Notes & Queries* 200 (April 1955): 165.

5. Boswell writes that at this time Goldsmith supplemented his income by working as Samuel Richardson's "corrector of the press"—a claim for which there is no corroborating evidence (*Life of Johnson,* I, 411).

6. See *Percy's Memoir,* 16. Wardle follows biographers who have written that the agreement was to include a salary of one hundred pounds (Wardle, 76). In the manuscript of Goldsmith's biographical narration to Bishop Percy (28 April 1773), however, "100 Pd. per annum" is overwritten with "some pecuniary stipend."

7. For a discussion of this "war" and Johnson's first contacts with Cave, see Thomas Kaminski, *The Early Career of Samuel Johnson* (New York: Oxford University Press, 1987), 3–23.

8. Ibid., 4.

9. For example, Elizabeth Eaton Kent fictionalizes: "As Dr. Milner at times contributed to *The Monthly Review,* the conversation turned to literary criticism, and Goldsmith's remarks attracted the attention of Griffiths, who asked the usher for some specimens of his critical writing" (Kent, *Goldsmith and His Booksellers,* 22). In fact, we have no evidence to suggest that Milner contributed to the *Monthly.* We do know, however, that Griffiths had reviewed a collection of Milner's sermons in the *Monthly* (Nangle, 159).

10. *Letters,* 68.

11. Nangle, xi. Norman Oakes has further demonstrated the care with which Griffiths maintained ideological homogeneity on his staff in his unpublished dissertation, "Ralph Griffiths and the *Monthly Review,*" Columbia University, 1961.

12. Brewer, 143.

13. Samuel Johnson, *The Idler and The Adventurer,* ed. W. J. Bate and Albrecht B. Strauss (New Haven: Yale University Press, 1963), II, 23.

14. Prior, I, 226.

15. Nangle, 10, 39.

16. Ibid., viii.

17. Alvin Sullivan, ed., *British Literary Magazines,* vol. 1, *The Augustan Age and the Age of*

Johnson, 1698–1788 (Westport, Conn.: Greenwood Press, 1983), I, 231.

18. Anon., "To the Authors of the *Monthly Review*," *Monthly Review* 6 (May 1757): 402–3.

19. Graham, 209.

20. Grainger, Review of *The Fleece*, *Monthly Review* 16 (April 1757): 328–40.

21. Graham, 212.

22. Ibid., 214.

23. Anon., Review of *A Letter to Tobias Smollett, M.D.*, *Critical Review* 7 (February 1759): 141–58.

24. Nangle, viii–xi. See also Lewis M. Knapp, "Ralph Griffiths, Author and Publisher," *The Library* 20 (September 1939): 197–213.

25. Nangle, x.

26. Tobias Smollett, *The Letters of Tobias Smollett*, ed. Lewis M. Knapp (Oxford: Clarendon Press, 1970), 46.

27. Derek Roper, "Smollett's 'Four Gentlemen': The First Contributors to the *Critical Review*," *Review of English Studies* n.s. 10 (February 1959): 38–44.

28. Knapp provides a biographical account of Armstrong in "Dr. John Armstrong, Littérateur, and Associate of Smollett, Thomson, Wilkes, and Other Celebrities," *PMLA* 59 (December 1944): 1019–58.

29. *Life of Johnson*, I, 455.

30. Smollett, *Letters*, 57; Roper, "Smollett's 'Four Gentlemen,' " 40.

31. Smollett, *Letters*, 47–48.

32. Ibid., *Letters*, 58.

33. Ibid., *Letters*, 65.

34. Ibid., *Letters*, 60.

35. Nangle, viii.

36. *Life of Johnson*, II, 40.

37. Ibid., III, 32.

38. Prior, I, 293–94.

39. Aubrey Hawkins, "Some Writers on the *Monthly Review*," *Review of English Studies* 7 (April 1931): 170.

40. Anon. [William Kenrick], Review of *Polite Learning*, *Monthly Review* 21 (November 1759): 381–89.

41. Anon. [Griffiths?], advertisement, *Monthly Review* 1 (May 1749): 1.

42. Ibid.

43. William Black, *Goldsmith* (London: Macmillan, 1909), 29.

44. Unfortunately, Hopkins ignores Goldsmith's reviews, some of which could have given support to his placing the author in the satiric tradition of Swift and Pope.

45. Quintana, 21.

46. *Percy's Memoir*, 16.

Chapter 3. The "True Critic"

1. Ginger, 102.

2. The list includes the following: *The Impetuous Lover* (I, 15–16), *The History of Two Persons of Quality* (I, 16), *The Unfortunate Beauty* (I, 16), *Memoirs of Sir Thomas Hughson* (I, 16–17), *True Merit, True Happiness* (I, 17), *An Address to the Gentlemen* (I, 56), *The History of Cleanthes* (I, 57), *Memoirs of Harriot and Charlotte Meanwell* (I, 57–58), *The Ghost of Ernest* (I, 58–60), *The Mother-in-Law* (I, 82), *The Fair Citizen* (I, 82), and *Jemima and Louisa* (*Critical*, I, 205–6). Of these, only *The Ghost of Ernest* is praised.

3. Henry Fielding, *Amelia* (1751), ed. Martin C. Battestin (Middletown, Conn.:

Wesleyan University Press, 1983), bk. 8, ch. 5, 329.

4. *Rambler,* III, 19–21.

5. Ioan Williams, ed., *Novel and Romance, 1700–1800: A Documentary Record* (New York: Barnes & Noble, 1970), 13.

6. Robert D. Mayo, *The English Novel in the Magazines, 1740–1815* (Evanston, Ill.: Northwestern University Press, 1962), 193.

7. Anon. [Griffiths], Review of *The Memoirs of Fanny Hill, Monthly Review* 2 (March 1750): 431.

8. Ibid.

9. James Raven, *British Fiction, 1750–1770: A Chronological Check-List of Prose Fiction Printed in Britain and Ireland* (Newark: University of Delaware Press, 1987), 132–40.

10. Anon, *The Bubbled Knights; or, Successful Contrivances* (London: Francis Noble, 1757).

11. Anon., *The History of Miss Katty N——* (London, Francis Noble, 1757).

12. Anon., *Memoirs of B—— Tracey* (London: J. King, 1757).

13. Anon., *The Prostitutes of Quality; or, Adultery À-La Mode* (London: J. Cooke and J. Coote, 1757). Goldsmith later contributed to Coote's *Royal Magazine.*

14. *Letters,* 60. See also Chinese Letter LXXXIII: "I say with them, that every book can serve to make us more expert except romances, and these are no better than instruments of debauchery" (II, 340).

15. Anon., *True Merit, True Happiness: Exemplified in the Entertaining and Instructive Memoirs of Mr. S——* (London: Francis Noble, 1757).

16. Sven Bäckman cites this review as an important early expression of Goldsmith's views on romance novels: "But his chief objection to their way of dealing with love between the sexes was that their readers were given a false and exaggerated picture of the happiness that love could bring." *This Singular Tale: A Study of "The Vicar of Wakefield" and Its Literary Background* (Lund, Sweden: C. W. K. Gleerup, 1971), 24.

17. Hopkins, 6.

18. William St. Pierre, *The History of two Persons of Quality, taken from memoirs written in the reign of Edward IV* (London: Francis Noble, 1757).

19. Anon., *Memoirs of Sir Thomas Hughson and Mr. Joseph Williams, With the Remarkable History, Travels, and Distresses, of Telemachus Lovet. The whole calculated for the Improvement of the Mind and Manners, and a becoming and useful Entertainment for the Youth of both Sexes* (London: "Printed for the Author," 1757).

20. Anon., *A New Battledore for Miss in her Teens, For the Use of Boarding Schools* (London: M. Cooper, 1757), xi.

21. Ibid., 15.

22. Ibid., 37.

23. Robert DeMaria, Jr., *Johnson's "Dictionary" and the Language of Learning* (Chapel Hill: University of North Carolina Press, 1986), 18.

24. Charlotte Bellmour, *The Fair Citizen: or The Real Adventures of Miss Charlotte Bellmour* (London: T. Lownds, 1757).

25. Anon. ["Miss Cassandra"], *An Address to the Gentlemen under the Denomination of Old Batchelors* (London: "Printed for the Author," 1757).

26. Charlotte Lennox, *Memoires for the History of Madame de Maintenon, and of the last Age* (London: Millar, 1757).

27. Clifford, 90, 191, 232.

28. Lennox had herself been an early purveyor of warnings against the dangers of popular fiction. The final chapter of *The Female Quixote* (1752), announced as "Being in the Author's Opinion, the best Chapter in this History," described the evils incumbent upon those innocent readers subjected to "Romantick Heroism" (rpt. New York: Garland, 1974: II, 299).

29. Felicity A. Nussbaum, *The Autobiographical Subject: Gender and Ideology in Eighteenth-Century England* (Baltimore: The Johns Hopkins University Press, 1989), 137.

30. *Letters,* 8.

31. The Reverend Mr. [Vicesimus] Knox, *Essays Moral and Literary,* 2 vols. (London: Dilly, 1779), II, 311.

32. According to Prior, Goldsmith translated for Griffiths French novels such as *Memoirs of My Lady B* (Prior, I, 279).

33. For further discussion of this issue, see Richard C. Taylor, "Goldsmith's First Vicar," *Review of English Studies* 41 (March 1990), 191–99.

34. The *DNB* incorrectly lists 1767, instead of 1757, as the date of publication.

35. John Leake, *A Dissertation on the Properties and Efficacy of the Lisbon Diet-Drink: A Medicine, for many Years, successfully used in Portugal, in the cure of the Venereal Disease and Scurvy* (London: Clarke, 1757), 3, 6.

36. Antonia Forster, "From 'Tasters to the Public' to 'Beadles of Parnassus': Reviewers, Authors and the Reading Public, 1749–1774," unpublished dissertation (University of Melbourne, 1986), 32.

37. Ginger, 102.

38. *Bibliothèque des sciences et des beaux-arts* 6 (October–December, 1756): 285–303. Caroline F. Tupper demonstrates Goldsmith's "fidelity to the French summary and also the grace of his translation" in "Oliver Goldsmith and 'The Gentleman Who Signs D,'" *Modern Language Notes* 45 (February 1930): 71–77.

39. For example, he reused the "Conquerors" simile cited above in Chapter 5 of his *Polite Learning* (I, 278).

40. "The Distresses of an Hired Writer," 198.

41. Spector, *ELP,* 14.

42. Captain Augustus Hervey gives a valuable account in his *Journal* (1746–59); one of the best modern accounts is by Donald Greene, *Samuel Johnson: Political Writings,* 213–60.

43. Boswell remarks: "The generosity with which he [Johnson] pleads the cause of Admiral Byng is highly to the honour of his heart and spirit" (*Life of Johnson,* I, 314).

44. Anon., Review of *The Works of David Mallet, Monthly Review* 20 (May 1759): 464.

45. L. B. Namier, *The Structure of Politics at the Accession of George III,* 2 vols. (London: Macmillan, 1929), I, 283; II, 536.

46. Wardle, 76–77.

47. Prior, I, 220.

48. Anon., Review of *Douglas, Critical Review* 3 (March 1757): 258.

49. Anon., Review of *The Tragedy of "Douglas" Analyzed, Critical Review* 3 (March 1757): 287.

50. None of Home's subsequent productions—*Agis* (1758), *The Siege of Aquileia* (1760), *The Fatal Discovery* (1769), or *Alonzo* (1773)—met with much success.

51. Spector attributes the quick demise of the *Connoisseur* and other "non-political essay-journals in the *Spectator* tradition" to the popular preference for political and military news in the late 1750s (Spector, *ELP,* 14 and passim).

52. Bertelsen, 34.

53. The following are previously unnoticed instances of Goldsmith's probable indebtedness to the *Connoisseur:* "On Dress" (*Bee,* I, 374–79) and "A Lady of Fashion in the Times of Anna Bullen Compared with One of Modern Times" (*Lady's Magazine,* III, 147–49) closely parallel *Connoisseur* No. 36, "On Dress: Fashions in Queen Elizabeth's Days Compared with the Present"; "A Description of Various Clubs" (*Busy Body,* III, 6–16) and "The Author's Club" (*Lloyd's Evening Post,* III, 184–87) echo remarks made in *Connoisseur* No. 1; and Goldsmith's "The Futility of Criticism" (*Weekly Magazine,* III, 51–53) borrows from *Connoisseur* No. 83. Thornton and Colman's "The Character of Toby Bumper" (No. 132, 5 August 1756, 214–15) is probably a prototype for Goldsmith's character Tony Lumpkin in his Colman-produced comedy *She Stoops to Conquer.* Other sources, such as those proposed by J. H. Smith, "Tony Lumpkin and the Country Booby Type in Antecedent English Comedy," *PMLA* (1942):

1038–49, lack the close verbal and thematic parallels present in these two characterizations.

54. See especially *Connoisseur*, No. 71. Of all the works Goldsmith reviewed for the *Monthly* and *Critical*, only Brookes's *Natural History* (1763), for which he wrote a preface, and the four-volume collected edition of the *Connoisseur* were in his own collection sold at auction 12 July 1774. Also in his collection were an eight-volume edition of the *Spectator* (1729) and editions of the *Idler* and *World*. (See "A Catalogue of the Household Furniture" in Prior, II, 579–86.) At the time of his death, Goldsmith owned copies of none of the rest of the books he reviewed—a fact that suggests his booksellers had lent rather than given him review copies, or that he sold most of the copies he had received.

55. Stephen Gwynn, *Oliver Goldsmith* (New York: Henry Holt, 1935), 98.

56. Wardle, 77.

57. Clifford, 184.

58. Ibid., 185.

59. *Life of Johnson*, II, 122.

60. *Letters*, 63.

61. *Polite Learning* argued that Rabener merited "the highest applause" (I, 286).

62. G. W. Rabener, *Satirical Letters*, 2 vols. (1752; London: Linde, 1757), I, xv.

63. Ibid., I, 3.

64. Note Goldsmith's application of this satiric precept in Chinese Letter XXVI, "The character of the man in black; with some instances of his inconsistent conduct" (II, 108–12).

65. William Wilkie, *The Epigoniad* (1757; London: J. Murray, 1759), i–xlviii.

66. Anon., *A Critical Essay on the "Epigoniad", Wherein the Author's horrid Abuse of Milton is Examined* (Edinburgh, 1757), 5, 6, 12.

67. Thomas Gray, *Odes by Mr. Gray* (Strawberry-Hill, Pall-Mall: Dodsley, 1757), 12.

68. According to Boswell, Johnson was considerably less charitable in his attitude toward Gray's *Odes;* he referred to them as "forced plants raised in a hot-bed; and they are poor plants" (*Life of Johnson*, IV, 13).

69. Goldsmith's opinion of Gray's *Odes* apparently remained consistent, at least through his periodical career. In his journal entry for 25 December 1762, Boswell quotes Goldsmith as saying, "They are terribly obscure. We must be historians and learned men before we can understand them" (*Boswell's London Journal*, 106).

70. George Colman and Robert Lloyd, *Two Odes* (London: H. Payne, 1760), 6, 13.

71. Prior, II, 465.

72. Ibid., 464–65.

73. John Witherspoon, *The History of a Corporation of Servants* (Glasgow: Gilmour, 1765), 3.

Chapter 4. In the Rival Camp

1. For a convincing account of the collapse of Goldsmith's plans to secure a position as civilian physician for the East India Company, see Balderston, *Letters*, xxx–xxxiii.

2. Basker, 39–64. Basker asserts that Goldsmith's connection with the *Critical* began in 1757 (45), but does not supply evidence for his assertion, which contradicts Prior and Friedman.

3. Nangle, 96.

4. Forster, I, 125.

5. Prior, I, 220–21.

6. Letter to Edward Mills, 7 August 1758, *Letters*, 34. R. W. Seitz cautions that since *Polite Learning* was not published until 2 April 1759, Goldsmith's claim to Mills that the book was already in the press was probably untrue, "but it indicates at least that he had been working on the book before that time" (Seitz, "Goldsmith and the *Literary Magazine*," 430n). In a letter to Robert Bryanton of 14 August 1758, Goldsmith wrote: "You see I use Chinese

names to show my own erudition, as I shall soon make our Chinese talk like an Englishman to show his" (*Letters*, 39–40). Goldsmith creates the character of the "Chinese Philosopher" to lampoon the subject of literary reputation. R. S. Crane argues that such a use does not prove, as Balderston and Seitz had suggested, that Goldsmith was at work on his Chinese Letters (review of Seitz, "Goldsmith and the *Literary Magazine*," *Philological Quarterly* 9 [1930]: 192).

7. *Letters*, 39–40.

8. Ibid., 46.

9. Seitz, "Goldsmith and the Literary Magazine," 430.

10. *Letters*, 51.

11. Wardle, 88.

12. Prior, I, 285.

13. *Letters*, 66–68.

14. The Voltaire memoir was finally published serially in the *Lady's Magazine*, beginning with the February 1761 issue.

15. William Kenrick, Review of *Polite Learning*, *Monthly Review* 21 (November 1759): 381. Kenrick took over for Goldsmith as Griffiths' "foreign correspondent."

16. Griffiths, *Monthly Review* 51 (1774): 161.

17. Graham, 196–97.

18. Graham, 199–200.

19. Anon., advertisement for the *Critical Review, London Evening Post* (15–18 January 1757): 3.

20. Anon., "To the Authors of the *Court Magazine*," 1 (November 1761): 125.

21. Anon. [Smollett?], "To the Old Gentlewoman Who Directs the *Monthly Review*," *Critical Review* 4 (November 1757): 469–72.

22. See, for example, advertisement for the *Critical Review*, London Evening Post (1–4 January 1757): 2.

23. Anon., advertisement for the *Centinel, London Evening Post* (6–8 January 1757): 2.

24. Anon., advertisement for the *London Magazine, London Evening Post* (1–4 January 1757): 3.

25. Spector, *ELP*, 159.

26. Tupper, 71–77.

27. Anon. [Griffiths?], advertisement for the *Monthly Review, London Evening Post* (5–8 February 1757): 3.

28. Anon. [Griffiths?], advertisement; letter from Correspondent "D", *Monthly Review* 16 (February 1757): 140.

29. James Grainger, Review of *Contemplations on the Night, Monthly Review* 16 (April 1757): 289.

30. Grainger, Review of *The Fleece, Monthly Review* 16 (April 1757): 328.

31. Graham, 217.

32. Anon., Review of *Douglas, Critical Review* 3 (March 1757): 258–68.

33. Anon., Review of the *Connoisseur, Critical Review* 3 (April 1757): 314–15.

34. Anon., advertisement for Smollett's *Compleat History, Lloyd's Evening Post* (20–22 January 1762): 3.

35. Anon. [Smollett?], Review of *A Letter to Tobias Smollett, M.D., Occasioned by His Criticism on a Late Translation of Tibullus by Dr. Grainger, Critical Review* 7 (February 1759): 141–58.

36. Rose, who was Griffiths's brother-in-law, had been an active contributor to the *Monthly* staff since its founding in 1749 (Nangle, 37; Prior, I, 226).

37. Hume, *Letters*, I, 304.

38. Lewis Melville, *The Life and Letters of Tobias Smollett* (Boston: Houghton Mifflin, 1927): 135.

39. Prior, I, 241.

40. Brown, II, 75.

41. Anon., *The Battle of the Reviews* (London: Marriner, 1760): 58.

42. Ibid., v–vi.

43. Ibid., 37.

44. Ibid., 42.

45. Nangle, ix.

46. *The Battle of the Reviews*, 46.

47. Derek Roper offers a valuable discussion of the political differences between the *Monthly* and *Critical* in "The Politics of the *Critical Review*, 1756–1817," *Durham University Journal* n.s. 22 (March 1961): 117–22. He reasserts the position associated with Sir Lewis Namier *(The Structure of Politics)* that "Whig" and "Tory" labels are almost meaningless in the context of the factional disputes in 1750s and 1760s.

48. *The Battle of the Reviews* seems to confirm the partnership between Cleland and Griffiths in first setting up the *Monthly* (76).

49. In 1759 Smollett was arrested for libel against Admiral Charles Knowles.

50. Prior, I, 236.

51. *Percy's Memoir*, 16.

52. Sullivan, *British Literary Magazines*, I, 72–76. See also Friedman, "Goldsmith's Contributions to the *Critical Review*," *Modern Philology* 44 (1946): 23–52; Claude E. Jones, "Contributors to the *Critical Review*, 1756–1785," *Modern Language Notes* 61 (1946): 433–41; Jones, "The *Critical Review*'s First Thirty Years (1756–1785)," *Notes and Queries* n.s. 3 (1956): 78–80; and Roper, "The Politics of the *Critical Review*, 1756–1817."

53. Wardle, 92.

54. *Letters*, 57.

55. Wardle, 93.

56. Despite the efforts of Friedman, Morris Golden, and others, attribution of reviews in the *Critical* remains problematic. Given the absence of marked copies for 1759, scholars have relied primarily on early collected editions and internal evidence. My conclusions about Goldsmith's *Critical* contributions are necessarily tentative and are based on Friedman's inclusions in the *Collected Works*.

57. Thomas Marriott, *Female Conduct: Being an Essay on the Art of Pleasing. To be practiced by the Fair Sex, Before, and After Marriage* (London: W. Owen, 1759), 18.

58. Ibid., 176–77.

59. Ibid., viii.

60. Nangle, 25.

61. Ibid., 45–6.

62. John Pike Emery, *Arthur Murphy: An Eminent English Dramatist of the Eighteenth Century* (Philadelphia: University of Pennsylvania Press, 1946), 48–49. See also *The Plays of Arthur Murphy*, ed. Richard B. Schwartz, 4 vols. (New York: Garland, 1979), I, viii.

63. Another of Goldsmith's acquaintances, Thomas Percy, was working on his Chinese novel, *Hau Kiou Choaan*, at this time. Goldsmith apparently learned of Percy's project on 26 February 1759, when Percy read part of his novel to his publisher, Robert Dodsley. Goldsmith alluded to Percy's novel in a note to his review: "A specimen of this kind [a "Chinese" novel] will probably appear next season at Mr. Dodsley's, as we are informed" (I, 171). Dodsley published the novel in its final, four-volume form on 14 November 1761 (Bertram H. Davis, *Thomas Percy* [Boston: Twayne, 1981], 38).

64. Clifford, 243–44.

65. William Dunkin, *An Epistle to the Right Honourable Philip, Earl of Chesterfield. To which is added Lawson's Obsequies: An Eclogue* (Dublin: Faulkner, 1759), 3.

66. Ibid., 10.

67. Ibid., 17–18.

68. Ibid., 19.

69. See, especially, *Thraliana: The Diary of Mrs. Hester Lynch Thrale (Later Mrs. Piozzi), 1776–1809,* ed. Katharine Balderston, 2 vols. (Oxford: Clarendon Press, 1942), I, 80–84.

70. He also satirized this critical position in Chinese Letter XX: "Other critics contradict the fulminations of this tribunal, call them all spiders, and assure the public, that they ought to laugh without restraint" (II, 88).

Chapter 5. The "Weekly Historian"

1. John Sitter, *Literary Loneliness in Mid-Eighteenth-Century England* (Ithaca: Cornell University Press, 1982), 9.

2. Sitter, 30.

3. Alvin Kernan, *Printing Technology, Letters & Samuel Johnson* (Princeton: Princeton University Press, 1987), 81.

4. Spector, *ELP,* 13.

5. Ibid., 14.

6. Ibid.

7. Anon., "The Life of the Right Hon. Joseph Addison, Esq." *British Magazine* 2 (March 1761): 124. The three-part series ran in January (36–40), February (89–93), and March (121–24).

8. Goldsmith had also borrowed from Johnson's essays in the *Literary;* see, for example, Chinese Letter XVII (II, 74n).

9. Clifford, 73.

10. See Goldsmith's tribute to the *Rambler* in his preface to a seven-volume translation of *Plutarch's Lives* (May to November 1762): "As the use of biography, and the duty of a biographer, are so excellently set forth in the *Rambler,* by Mr. *Samuel Johnson,* who, from his great knowledge of the human mind, has the art of exhausting every argument, and of seeing, as it were, at one view, every thing that can be said on any subject" (V, 227).

11. Preface to Charles Wiseman's *A Complete English Grammar* (V, 311).

12. Edward Young, *Conjectures on Original Composition, in a Letter to the Author of Sir Charles Grandison* (1759; rpt. Leeds, England: Scolar Press, 1966). Young writes, "An *Original* may be said to be of a *vegetable* nature; it rises spontaneously from the vital root of Genius; it *grows,* it is not *made*" (12).

13. Eustace Budgell's magazine, the *Bee, or Universal Weekly Pamphlet* (1733–35) suffered similar complaints of plagiarism from Budgell's contemporaries, who failed to accept the notion of a magazine as a compilation of essays from previously published sources. For a fascinating account of the reception of Budgell's *Bee,* see Harold Herd's chapter "The Decline and Fall of Eustace Budgell" in his *Seven Editors* (London: George Allen & Unwin, 1955), 9–25.

14. James M. Kuist, *The Nichols File of the "Gentleman's Magazine"* (Madison: University of Wisconsin Press, 1982), 3.

15. William Cooke, "Table Talk," *European Magazine* 24 (December 1793): 419.

16. Wardle, 103.

17. Oliver W. Ferguson praises the "attractive" persona Goldsmith displayed in the *Bee:* "There is something appealing about a writer who can positively celebrate his obscurity . . ." ("Oliver Goldsmith: The Personality of the Essayist," *Philological Quarterly* 61 [Fall 1982]: 181).

18. See, for example, William Rider, *An Historical and Critical Account of the Lives and Writings of the Living Authors of Great-Britain* (1762; rpt. Los Angeles: Augustan Reprint Society, 1794), 5–7.

19. Spector, *"The Connoisseur:* A Study of the Functions of a Persona," in *English Writers of the Eighteenth Century,* ed. John H. Middendorf (New York: Columbia University Press, 1971), 110.

20. Anon., Review of the *Prater, Monthly Review* 6 (May 1757): 458.

21. Johnson, *Idler* No. 1 (15 April 1758): 3.

22. Graham, 163.

23. George S. Marr, *The Periodical Essayists of the Eighteenth Century* (New York: D. Appleton, 1924), 155–56.

24. Anon., Review of the *Bee, Critical Review* 8 (December 1759): 499.

25. Wardle, 106.

26. Cibber was reviewing dramatic productions for Griffiths when Goldsmith joined the *Monthly,* and the two may have been acquainted (Nangle, 9). Ginger notes that "Colley Cibber's boorish son" shared with Goldsmith the task of writing the Monthly Catalogue for Griffiths in May 1757. He speculates: "The newcomer [Goldsmith] seems to have been fascinated by the unrelieved disreputability of this man who was estranged from a beautiful and talented wife, the singer and actress Susanna Arne" (102).

27. Eddy, *Samuel Johnson, Book Reviewer,* 3–6.

28. Ibid., 3.

29. Crane, *New Essays,* xxxiii.

30. Percy, "The Life of Dr. Goldsmith," in *The Miscellaneous Works of Oliver Goldsmith, M.B.,* 4 vols. (London: J. Johnson et al., 1801), I, 64.

31. Arthur Murphy, *An Essay on the Life and Genius of Dr. Johnson* (1792), in *The Lives of Henry Fielding and Samuel Johnson, Together with Essays from the "Gray's-Inn Journal,"* intro. by Matthew Grace (Gainesville, Florida: Scholars' Facsimiles & Reprints, 1968), 364.

Chapter 6. "The Philanthropic Bookseller": Goldsmith's Work for Newbery

1. Basker, 195.

2. Ibid., 194.

3. Graham, 177–78.

4. Eddy, *Johnson, Book Reviewer,* 4.

5. S. Roscoe, *John Newbery and His Successors, 1740–1814: A Bibliography* (Wormley, Hertfordshire: Five Owls Press, 1973), 10.

6. Kent, *Goldsmith and His Booksellers,* 58.

7. Roscoe, 405.

8. Newbery, "Introduction," *Newtonian System of Philosophy,* 1761; quoted in Roscoe, 9.

9. Mayo, *The English Novel in the Magazines,* 274–88.

10. Ibid., 276–77.

11. Spector, *ELP,* 283–88.

12. Prior, I, 350.

13. Dobson, 77.

14. Prior, I, 350.

15. Anon. [William Rose], Review of *A Letter from Xo Ho, a Chinese Philosopher at London, to His Friend Lien Chi at Pekin, Monthly Review* 16 (May 1757): 469.

16. Haig, 44.

17. Prior, I, 356.

18. Anon., Review of *The Citizen, Critical Review* 13 (May 1762): 397–400.

19. Anon., Review of *The Citizen, Monthly Review* 26 (June 1762): 477.

20. Rider, 13–14.

21. One of the most convincing studies of *The Citizen* is Wayne Booth's "The Self-Portraiture of Genius: *The Citizen of the World* and Critical Method," *Modern Philology* 73 (May 1976, Part 2: A Supplement to Honor Arthur Friedman): S85–S96. Booth makes an intriguing case for *The Citizen* as Goldsmith's most important work.

22. *Letters*, 39–40.

23. John Langhorne, *The Effusions of Friendship and Fancy*, 2 vols. (1766; rpt. New York: Garland, 1970), I, 38.

24. Charlotte Lennox, *The Female Quixote, or The Adventures of Arabella* (1752; New York: Oxford University Press, 1989), 3.

25. Nangle effectively refutes this misconception in the preface to his index (v–xiv).

26. Clara M. Kirk, *Oliver Goldsmith* (New York: Twayne, 1967), 33.

Chapter 7. Defining a Self: The Essayist and His Readers

1. Vincent Carretta, *George III and the Satirists from Hogarth to Byron* (Athens: The University of Georgia Press, 1990), 49.

2. Wolfgang Iser, *The Implied Reader: Patterns of Communication in Prose Fiction from Bunyan to Beckett* (Baltimore: The Johns Hopkins University Press, 1974), xiii.

3. Iser, 46, 62–63.

4. Michael McKeon, *The Origins of the English Novel, 1600–1740* (Baltimore: The Johns Hopkins University Press, 1987), 63.

5. Quintana, 16.

6. George Rudé, *Hanoverian London: 1714–1808* (Berkeley: University of California Press, 1971), 78.

7. Ibid., 79.

8. Bryant Lillywhite, *London Coffee Houses: A Reference Book of Coffee Houses of the Seventeenth, Eighteenth and Nineteenth Centuries* (London: George Allen and Unwin, 1963), 24.

9. Spector, *ELP*, 14.

10. Anon., advertisement for the *Humanist, London Evening Post* (19–22 March 1757): 3.

11. Jeremy Black, *The English Press in the Eighteenth Century* (London: Croom Helm, 1987), 20.

12. Johnson, *Idler*, 23.

13. Michael Harris, "Periodicals and the Book Trade," in *Development of the English Book Trade, 1700–1899*, ed. Robin Myers and Michael Harris (Oxford: Oxford Polytechnic Press, 1981), 77.

14. Kernan, 59.

15. Statistics quoted in Black, *English Press*, 105.

16. Harris, "Periodicals and the Book Trade," 66.

17. Haig, 36.

18. Kernan, 54.

19. *London Chronicle, or Universal Evening Post* 1 (1 January 1757): 1.

20. Black, *English Press*, 203.

21. Giles Barber, "Book Imports and Exports in the Eighteenth Century," in *Sale and Distribution of Books from 1700*, ed. Robin Myers and Michael Harris (Oxford: Oxford Polytechnic Press, 1982), 77–105.

22. For a discussion of Israel Mauduit's pamphlet *Considerations on the Present German War*, and the battle between Pitt and Bute over English policy toward the Germans, see Robert R. Rea, *The English Press in Politics, 1760–1774* (Lincoln: University of Nebraska Press, 1963), 1–27.

23. Brewer, 96–136; Spector, *ELP*, 34–49.

24. *Letters*, 28.

25. Seitz, "The Irish Background of Goldsmith's Social and Political Thought," *PMLA* 52 (June 1937): 405–11.

26. Richard R. Madden, *The History of Irish Periodical Literature,* 2 vols. (London: T. C. Newby, 1867), II, 42.

27. A. J. Barnouw, "Goldsmith's Indebtedness to Justus Van Effen," *Modern Language Review,* 8 (July 1913): 314–24.

28. Brewer, 29.

29. Wardle, 70.

30. Sullivan, I, 30–33.

31. Spector, *ELP,* 284.

32. Anon., *Busy Body,* No. 4 (16 October 1759): 19–20.

33. Ibid., 24.

34. Cooke, "Table Talk," *European Magazine* 24 (November 1793): 339.

35. Spector, *ELP,* 273.

36. John Vladimir Price takes issue with Goldsmith's calling the English a race of philosophers. He argues that in 1760 "the epicentre of philosophical writing in Britain was surely in Scotland." Price provides useful observations on contemporary responses to philosophical texts in his "The Reading of Philosophical Literature," in *Books and Their Readers in Eighteenth-Century England,* ed. Isabel Rivers (Leicester, U.K.: Leicester University Press, 1982), 173.

37. Hopkins, 96–137; for a contrasting view, see Wardle, 110–14.

38. Prior, I, 367–68.

39. Ibid., 368.

40. Percy, "The Life of Dr. Goldsmith," I, 62.

41. Boswell wrote to Johnson: "You remember poor Goldsmith, when he grew important, and wished to appear *Doctor Major,* could not bear your calling him *Goldy*" (*Life of Johnson,* III, 101). For Hester Thrale's anecdote on the "Doctor Minor" insult, see *Thraliana,* I, 80.

42. *Life of Johnson,* I, 408.

43. Prior, I, 383.

44. Crane, *New Essays,* xxxiii.

45. Friedman misdates this issue as 1760, when it should be 1762 (III, 181n).

46. Goldsmith had published a pamphlet on the Cock Lane Ghost entitled *The Mystery Revealed* on 23 February 1762 (IV, 415–41).

47. Crane, "The 'Deserted Village' in Prose (1762)," *Times Literary Supplement* (8 September 1927): 607.

48. Friedman's discussion of the evidence concerning the date of composition reveals that *The Vicar* was probably written "during the period 1760 or 1761 to 1762" (IV, 5).

Chapter 8. "Arrant Tories" and "Soure Whigs": The Political Context of Goldsmith's Journalism

1. Parts of this chapter first appeared as "The Politics of Goldsmith's Journalism," *Philological Quarterly* 69 (Winter 1990): 71–89, and have been reproduced with permission of the editor.

2. Donald Davie, "Notes on Goldsmith's Politics," in *The Art of Oliver Goldsmith,* ed. Andrew Swarbrick (London: Vision Press, 1984), 81.

3. R. W. Seitz, "The Irish Background," 405–41.

4. See, for example, Francis Godwin James, *Ireland in the Empire, 1688–1770* (Cambridge: Harvard University Press, 1973), 240–45.

5. For a discussion of Tory and Irish opposition to the Militia Bill, see James, 260–61,

and J. C. D. Clark, *The Dynamics of Change: The Crisis of the 1750s and English Party Systems* (Cambridge: Cambridge Press, 1976), 234–37.

6. Letters, 105–6.

7. Ibid., 105n; Wardle, 219–20.

8. Davie, 79–89.

9. See, for example, Robert Hopkins, "Matrimony in *The Vicar of Wakefield* and the Marriage Act of 1753," *Studies in Philology* 74 (July 1977): 322–39. Hopkins argues that Goldsmith's disapproval of the Marriage Act and his concerns over erosion of ecclesiastical authority over marriage were central political concerns in *The Vicar.* See also Morris Golden, "Goldsmith, *The Vicar of Wakefield,* and the Periodicals," *Journal of English and Germanic Philology* 76 (October 1977): 525–36. As Golden demonstrates, periodicals such as *Lloyd's Evening Post* and the *London Chronicle* excerpted scenes in the novel relevant to topical and political issues such as judicial reform.

10. Burke, *Correspondence,* I, 134.

11. Namier demonstrates the extent to which the politics of the 1760s was determined by family and regional alliances, rather than by definable "parties" *(The Structure of Politics).* The terms *Whig* and *Tory* were, indeed, shifting during the Seven Years' War period, but were nonetheless applied frequently. *Whigs,* generally, were supporters of Newcastle and, later, opponents of Bute, who favored strong parliamentary control of government. Supporters of Bute, the new king's favorite, were often designated *Tories:* they were supporters of strong royal prerogative and opponents of the sort of "liberty" Wilkes, Burke, and others professed.

12. Rea, 17.

13. Percy, *Correspondence,* VII, 171.

14. Brewer, 29.

15. Ibid., 4.

16. Nobbe, 18.

17. Brewer, 45.

18. Eveline Cruickshanks, *Political Untouchables: The Tories and the '45* (London: Duckworth, 1979), 113.

19. Fielding, *The History of Tom Jones, a Foundling* (1749), ed. Martin C. Battestin and Fredson Bowers (Middletown, Conn.: Wesleyan University Press, 1975), bk. 6, ch. 14, 321–22.

20. Anon., *Monitor* 5 (16 August 1755): 12.

21. Rea, 2. J. Steven Watson refers to Oxford in 1760 as "comically 'tory' " and argues that its " 'toryism' under analysis turns out to be merely a cant phrase to express its hatred of royal interference" *(The Reign of George III, 1760–1815* [Oxford: Clarendon Press, 1960], 56).

22. Brewer, 219.

23. Spector, *ELP,* 20–22.

24. Ibid., 33–34.

25. Brewer, 17.

26. Quintana, 188.

27. For an excellent contextual discussion of "luxury," the great moral bugbear of Tory social philosophers, see John Sekora, *Luxury: The Concept in Western Thought, Eden to Smollett* (Baltimore: Johns Hopkins University Press, 1977).

28. Davie sees in *The Traveller* a solution to the problems of depopulation: more royal authority. He sees the poem as "a fervent apologia for the monarchical form of government" (84). In his article "Conventional Ethics in Goldsmith's *The Traveller,*" *Studies in English Literature* 17 (Summer 1977): 463–76, Leo Storm claims that the poem is an attempt to restore balance and harmony to a nation disrupted by Wilkes and his followers.

29. Seitz, "Some of Goldsmith's Second Thoughts on English History," *Modern Philology,* 35 (1938): 279–88.

30. *Life of Johnson,* I, 372.

31. Boswell relates that Goldsmith accused Johnson of being one "who can now shelter [himself] behind the corner of a pension" (*Life of Johnson,* IV, 113). If the quotation is accurate, Goldsmith may have been envious of Johnson's having been pensioned, and may have felt some lingering disappointment about not being so honored himself.

32. Seitz, "The Irish Background," passim.

33. Wardle, 117.

34. Greene, *The Age of Exuberance: Backgrounds to Eighteenth-Century Literature* (New York: Random House, 1970), 81.

35. Goldsmith, "A Parallel between the Gracchi and the Greatest Man of the present Age," *British Magazine* 1 (January 1760): 14.

36. Greene, "Introduction," *Johnson: Political Writings,* xvii.

37. *The Political Journal of George Bubb Dodington* (1784), ed. John Carswell and Lewis Arnold Dralle (Oxford: Clarendon Press, 1965), 394.

38. Cruickshanks, 113.

39. Linda Colley, *In Defiance of Oligarchy: The Tory Party, 1714–60* (Cambridge: Cambridge University Press, 1982), 282.

40. John Mitchell, *The Contest in America Between Great Britain and France, With Its Consequences and Importance* (London: Millar, 1757), 52.

41. Ibid., 56.

42. First printed by Prior in 1837 from a manuscript entitled *Preface and Introduction to the History of the Seven Years' War,* the work was included by J. W. M. Gibbs in his edition of 1886, probably the most valuable of the collected editions before Friedman's (see Gibbs, V, 7–59). This work is part of the original in Goldsmith's autograph entitled *The Political View of the Result of the Present War with America upon Great Britain, France, Prussia, Germany, and Holland.* John W. Oliver, in "Johnson, Goldsmith, and 'The History of the Seven Years' War,'" *Times Literary Supplement* (18 May 1921): 324, points out that Goldsmith apparently recast articles in the *Literary Magazine* (May 1756 and August 1756) which have been attributed to Johnson. He presents evidence suggesting a Goldsmith-Johnson collaboration on *The History.* R. W. Seitz, in "Goldsmith and the *Literary Magazine*" (412), shows Goldsmith's borrowing from another article in the *Literary* ("Of the Constitution of the German Empire," September 1756) in his compilation, and he argues against Goldsmith's authorship of articles in the *Literary.* Even if Goldsmith was not principally responsible for writing *The History,* his involvement in the compilation and selection of previously written articles supplies some evidence about his political leanings during the war.

43. Gibbs, V, 7–8.

44. Ibid., 33.

45. Ibid., 42.

46. John Sainsbury, *Disaffected Patriots: London Supporters of Revolutionary America, 1769–1782* (Kingston, Ont. and Montreal: McGill-Queen's University Press, 1987), 3–16.

47. Greene, "Johnson and the Great War for Empire," in *English Writers of the Eighteenth Century,* ed. John H. Middendorf (New York: Columbia University Press, 1971), 43.

48. Greene, "Johnson and the Great War for Empire," 44.

49. Spector, *ELP,* 76.

50. Bertelsen, 174.

51. Ian Watt, *The Rise of the Novel* (Berkeley: University of California Press, 1957).

52. Goldsmith's sister, Mrs. Hodson, suggested that the "Man in Black" represented Goldsmith himself (*Letters,* 169–70). The character's background also resembles that of Goldsmith's father (*Percy's Memoir,* 13).

53. Sekora, 102.

54. Walter J. Shelton, *English Hunger and Industrial Disorders: A Study of Social Conflict during the First Decade of George III's Reign* (Toronto: University of Toronto Press, 1973), 109–10.

55. Brewer, 9.

56. Spector, *ELP*, 86–87.

57. Clark, 40.

58. Brewer, 221–22.

59. Stevick, "Introduction," *The Case of Authors*, ix–x.

60. Anon., Review of *The Case of Authors, Monthly Review* 8 (1758): 354.

61. Ralph, 30.

62. Clark, 39–40.

63. First noticed by R. W. Seitz, "Goldsmith and the *Literary Magazine*," 418–20.

64. Spector, *Arthur Murphy*, 32.

65. Abbott, 105.

66. Note Hume's tongue-in-cheek response to accusations of his "partiality" in a letter to John Clephane, 3 September 1757: "I always knew you to be a good friend, though I was afraid that I had lost you, and that you had joined that great multitude who abused me, and reproached me with Paganism, and Jacobitism, and many other wretched *isms*, of which I am only guilty in part" (Hume, *Letters* I, 263). In defending his *Compleat History*, Smollett wrote to John Moore (2 January 1758): "Whatever may be its defects, I protest before God I have, as far as in me lay, adhered to Truth without espousing any faction" (Smollett, *Letters,* 65).

67. See Wardle, 217–20, for a discussion of Goldsmith's publication of his *History of England from the Earliest Times to the Death of George II* (1771) and public accusations of his party bias.

68. Greene, headnote to *The False Alarm, Johnson: Political Writings,* 313–17.

69. Greene, "Introduction," *Johnson: Political Writings,* xxx.

70. *Life of Johnson,* I, 363.

71. Greene, "Introduction," *Johnson: Political Writings,* xxv.

72. Ibid., xxiii.

73. Gibbs, V, 169.

74. Ibid.

75. Spector, *Arthur Murphy,* 33.

76. *Lloyd's Evening Post,* to which Goldsmith contributed in 1762, was one of several journals that published attacks on Murphy (Spector, *Arthur Murphy,* 36).

77. Prior, I, 344.

78. Smollett, *Letters,* 87.

79. Spector, *ELP,* 95–96.

80. Smollett, *Letters,* 69.

81. Prior, II, 99.

Chapter 9. "Paternoster Row is Not Parnassus"

1. Stephen Bann, "The Sense of the Past: Image, Text, and Object in the Formation of Historical Consciousness in Nineteenth-Century Britain," in *The New Historicism*, ed. H. Aram Veeser (New York: Routledge, 1989), 103.

2. Frank Lentricchia, "Foucault's Legacy—A New Historicism?" in *The New Historicism*, 231.

3. Anon. [Hugh Kelly?], "The Motives for Writing: A Dream," *Court Magazine* 1 (December 1761): 167–69.

4. Rider, 15, 17.

5. Ibid., 16.

6. Prior, II, 17. Crane, in *New Essays*, remarks: "I know of no positive evidence that Goldsmith wrote for this [*Christian's*] magazine" (140).

7. Golden, "Goldsmith and the *Universal Museum*," 339–48.

8. Cooke, "Table Talk," *European Magazine* 24 (September 1793): 171.

9. Forster, II, 138.

10. Wardle, 234.

11. Robert D. Hume, "Goldsmith and Sheridan and the Supposed Revolution of 'Laughing' against 'Sentimental' Comedy," in *Studies in Change and Revolution: Aspects of English Intellectual History, 1640–1800,* ed. Paul J. Korshin (Menston, U.K.: Scolar Press, 1972), 238.

12. For another possible connection between Colman and *She Stoops to Conquer,* see Taylor, "A Source for Goldsmith's Tony Lumpkin in *The Connoisseur,"* *English Language Notes* 26 (March 1989): 30–36.

13. Robert D. Hume, "Goldsmith and Sheridan," passim.

14. Joshua Reynolds, *Portraits,* ed. Frederick W. Hilles (London: William Heinemann, 1952), 44.

15. Graham, 127.

16. Anon. [John Hawkesworth], Review of *The Traveller, Gentleman's Magazine* 34 (December 1764): 594.

17. Graham, 119.

18. Abbott, 86.

19. Sullivan, I, 140.

20. Clifford, 170.

21. Abbott, 86–111.

22. For treatment of Goldsmith as a lighthearted humorist, see Stuart M. Tave, *The Amiable Humorist: A Study in the Comic Theory and Criticism of the Eighteenth and Nineteenth Centuries* (Chicago: University of Chicago Press, 1960).

23. What little information is available concerning Kelly's life is largely derived from Cooke's three-part "Table Talk" column, *European Magazine* 24 (November 1793): 337–40; 24 (December 1793): 419–22; 25 (January 1794): 42–48.

24. Cooke provides an account of this episode, as well as others relating to Goldsmith's dramatic career, in his "Table Talk," *European Magazine* 24 (August 1793): 91–95; 24 (September 1793): 170–74; 24 (October 1793): 258–64.

25. Cooke, "Table Talk," *European Magazine* 24 (September 1793): 171. Cooke reports that the journal, edited by Goldsmith, employed Irish playwright Isaac Bickerstaffe, Kenrick, and Kelly. Cooke quotes Goldsmith as saying that it "died of too many doctors" (171).

26. Forster, II, 93–94.

27. The best modern presentation of evidence concerning Kelly's periodical career is by Robert R. Bataille, "Hugh Kelly's Journalism: Facts and Conjectures," *Journal of Newspaper and Periodical History* 1 (Summer 1985): 2–10.

28. Prior, II, 176.

29. Cooke, "Table Talk," *European Magazine* 24 (November 1793): 338.

30. "The Motives for Writing: A Dream," *Court Magazine* 1 (December 1761): 167–69.

31. Bataille, 3–4.

32. Haig, 70–74.

33. Bataille, 5. For such an enduring column, the *Babler* has received remarkably little attention. Graham fails to mention it, as does Spector, who mentions Kelly only in connection with the *Lady's Museum* and with "probable editorship" of the *Prater* (1756)—a false assumption, as Kelly first arrived in London in 1760 (Spector, 160, 66n; Bataille, 2).

34. Cooke, "Table Talk," *European Magazine* 24 (November 1793): 340.

35. In "An Address to the Public," which was published with the text of his comedy *A Word to the Wise* (1770), Kelly complained that his well-known association with the *Public Ledger,* and the paper's reputation for opposing Wilkes, caused the failure of his comedy.

36. Young, *Conjectures on Original Composition,* 4–6.

37. Ibid., 7.

38. Cumberland, I, 353.

39. Young, 12.

40. Anon., "To the Authors of the *Court Magazine*," 1 (November 1761): 122.

41. Stuart M. Tave, *The Amiable Humorist* (Chicago: University of Chicago Press, 1960).

42. Greene, "Samuel Johnson and the Great War for Empire," 39.

43. Thomas Touchit [pseud.], "Advantages from Political Writing," *Literary Magazine* 3 (15 July–15 August 1758): 317–19.

44. Reprinted as "His Majesty's Most Gracious Speech to Both Houses of Parliament, on Monday the 4th Day of July 1757," *Literary Magazine* 2 (15 June–15 July 1757): 307.

45. Jenyns, 141.

46. Alexander Andrews, *The History of British Journalism, from the Foundation of the Newspaper Press in England to the Repeal of the Stamp Act in 1855, with Sketches of Press Celebrities*, 2 vols. (1859; rpt. Grosse Pointe, Mich.: Scholarly Press, 1968), I, 180.

47. Smollett, *Letters*, 65.

48. Cumberland, I, 353.

49. *Life of Johnson*, I, 412.

Select Bibliography

Bibliographies and Guides

Balderston, Katharine C. *A Census of the Manuscripts of Oliver Goldsmith.* New York: Brick Row Book Shop, 1926.

Bond, Richmond, ed. *Studies in the Early English Periodical.* Chapel Hill: University of North Carolina Press, 1957.

Crane, R. S., and F. B. Kaye. *A Census of British Newspapers and Periodicals, 1620–1800.* Chapel Hill: University of North Carolina Press, 1927.

Eddy, Donald D. *A Bibliography of John Brown.* New York: Bibliographical Society of America, 1971.

Kuist, James M. *The Nichols File of the "Gentleman's Magazine."* Madison: University of Wisconsin Press, 1982.

Lillywhite, Bryant. *London Coffee Houses: A Reference Book of Coffee Houses of the Seventeenth, Eighteenth, and Nineteenth Centuries.* London: George Allen and Unwin, 1963.

Nangle, Benjamin Christie. *The Monthly Review, First Series, 1749–1789: Indexes of Contributors and Articles.* Oxford: Clarendon Press, 1934.

Raven, James. *British Fiction, 1750–1770: A Chronological Check-List of Prose Fiction Printed in Britain and Ireland.* Newark: University of Delaware Press, 1987.

Roscoe, S. *John Newbery and His Successors, 1740–1814: A Bibliography.* Wormley, Hertfordshire: Five Owls Press, 1973.

Scott, Temple. *Oliver Goldsmith Bibliographically and Biographically Considered.* New York: Bowling Green Press, 1928.

Stone, George Winchester, Jr., ed. *The London Stage, 1660–1800.* Part 4, 1747–1776, 3 vols. Carbondale: Southern Illinois University Press, 1962.

Sullivan, Alvin, ed. *British Literary Magazines.* Vol. 1, *The Augustan Age and the Age of Johnson, 1698–1788.* Westport, Conn.: Greenwood Press, 1983.

Tierney, James E. "The Study of the Eighteenth-Century Periodical: Problems and Progress." *Papers of the Bibliographical Society of America* 69 (1975): 165–86.

Weed, Katherine K., and Richmond Bond. *Studies of British Newspapers and Periodicals from Their Beginning to 1800.* Chapel Hill: University of North Carolina Press, 1946.

Williams, Ioan, ed. *Novel and Romance, 1700–1800: A Documentary Record.* New York: Barnes & Noble, 1970.

Williams, Joseph B. *Tercentenary Handlist of English & Welsh Newspapers, Magazines & Reviews.* London: London *Times,* 1920.

Woods, Samuel H., Jr. *Oliver Goldsmith: A Reference Guide.* Boston: G. K. Hall, 1982.

Periodicals

References to Goldsmith's periodical writing are to Friedman's *Collected Works*. Other references, unless otherwise noted, are to bound volumes of the original or microfilm copies in the Early English Newspaper or English Literary Periodical Series from University Microfilms (Ann Arbor, 1948 to present).

Adventurer (1752–54) Johnson's essays: Yale ed., 1963)

Annual Register (1759 [for 1758]–1820?)

Auditor (1762–63)

Babler (1763–67)

Bee, or Universal Weekly Pamphlet (1733–35)

Bee (1759)

Bee Revived (1750)

British Magazine, or Monthly Repository for Gentlemen and Ladies (1760–67)

Briton (1762–63)

Busy Body (1759)

Centinel (1757)

Christian's Magazine (1760–63?)

Connoisseur (1754–56) (3d ed., London, 1757)

Con-Test (1756–57)

Court Magazine (1761–65)

Covent-Garden Journal (1752)

Crab-Tree (1757)

Critical Review, or Annals of Literature (1756–1817)

Entertainer (1754)

European Magazine (1782–1826)

Gazetteer and London Daily Advertiser (1735–97)

Gentleman's Magazine (1731–1907)

Gray's Inn Journal (1752–54)

Humanist (1757)

Impartial Review (1759)

Lady's Magazine (1760–63)

Lady's Museum (1760–61)

Literary Journal (1730–31)

Literary Magazine (1756–58)

Lloyd's Evening Post, and British Chronicle (1757–85?)

London Chronicle, or Universal Evening Post (1757–1800?)

London Evening Post (1727–80?)

London Magazine (1732–85)

London Packet (1770–99?)

Memoirs of Literature (1710–17)

Monitor (1755–65)

Monthly Catalogue (1724–32)

Monthly Chronicle (1728)

Monthly Review, or Literary Journal (1749–1844)

New Memoirs of Literature (1725–27)

North Briton (1762–63)

Old Maid (1756)

Patriot (1762)

Prater (1756)

Rambler (1750–52) (Yale ed., 1969)

Public Ledger, or Daily Register of Commerce and Intelligence (1760–1945)

Royal Magazine, or Gentleman's Monthly Companion (1759–61?)

Spectator (1711–15) (Bond ed., 1965)

Tatler (1709–11) (Bond ed., 1987)

Test (1756–57)

Universal Chronicle, or Weekly Gazette (1758–60) ("Idler" essays: Yale ed., 1963)

Universal Magazine (1747–1815)

Universal Museum (1762–1772)

Universal Visiter (1756)

Weekly Magazine, or Gentleman and Lady's Polite Companion (1759–60)

Westminster Magazine (1773–85)

World (1753–56)

Other Primary Sources

Addison, Joseph, and Richard Steele. *The Spectator*, ed. Donald F. Bond. 5 vols. Oxford: Clarendon Press, 1965.

Anon. ["Miss Cassandra"]. *An Address to the Gentlemen under the Denomination of Old Batchelors*. London: "Printed for the Author," 1757.

Anon. *The Battle of the Reviews*. London: R. Marriner, 1760.

Anon. *The Bubbled Knights; or, Successful Contrivances*. London: Francis Noble, 1757.

Anon. *A Critical Essay on the "Epigoniad", Wherein the Author's horrid Abuse of Milton is Examined*. Edinburgh, 1757.

Anon. *The History of Miss Katty N——*. London: Francis Noble, 1757.

Anon. *Memoirs of B—— Tracey*. London: J. King, 1757.

Anon. *Memoirs of Sir Thomas Hughson and Mr. Joseph Williams, With the Remarkable History, Travels, and Distresses, of Telemachus Lovet. The whole calculated for the Improvement of the Mind and Manners, and a becoming and useful Entertainment for the Youth of both Sexes*. London: "Printed for the Author," 1757.

Anon. *A New Battledore for Miss in her Teens, For the Use of Boarding Schools*. London: M. Cooper, 1757.

Anon. *The Prostitutes of Quality: or, Adultery À-La-Mode*. London: J. Cooke and J. Coote, 1757.

Anon. *True Merit, True Happiness: Exemplified in the Entertaining and Instructive Memoirs of Mr. S——*. London: Francis Noble, 1757.

Bellmour, Charlotte. *The Fair Citizen: or The Real Adventures of Miss Charlotte Bellmour*. London: T. Lownds, 1757.

Boswell, James. *The Life of Samuel Johnson, LL.D.* (1791), ed. George Birkbeck Hill and L. F. Powell. 6 vols. Oxford: Clarendon Press, 1934–50.

————. *Boswell's London Journal, 1762–1763,* ed. Frederick A. Pottle. New York: McGraw-Hill, 1950.

Brown, John. *An Estimate of the Manners and Principles of the Times,* 2d ed., 2 vols. London: Davis and Reymers, 1757.

————. *An Additional Dialogue of the Dead, between Pericles and Aristides.* London: Davis and Reymers, 1760.

Burke, Edmund. *A Philosophical Enquiry into the Origin of Our Ideas of the Sublime and Beautiful* (1757), ed. J. T. Boulton. New York: Columbia University Press, 1958.

————. *The Correspondence of Edmund Burke,* ed. Thomas W. Copeland. 9 vols. Cambridge: Cambridge University Press, 1958–70.

Burney, Fanny. *Cecilia.* 1782; London: Virago Press, 1986.

Colman, George, and Robert Lloyd. *Two Odes.* London: H. Payne, 1760.

Cumberland, Richard. *Memoirs of Richard Cumberland.* London: Lackington, Allen & Co., 1807.

Disraeli, Isaac. *The Calamities and Quarrels of Authors,* ed. Benjamin Disraeli. 1812–14; London: Frederick Warne, 1867.

Dodington, George Bubb. *The Political Journal of George Bubb Dodington* (1784), ed. John Carswell and Lewis Arnold Dralle. Oxford: Clarendon Press, 1965.

Dunkin, William. *An Epistle to the Right Honourable Philip, Earl of Chesterfield. To which is added Lawson's Obsequies: An Eclogue.* Dublin: Faulkner, 1759.

Fielding, Henry. *The History of Tom Jones, a Foundling* (1749), ed. Martin C. Battestin and Fredson Bowers. Middletown, Conn.: Wesleyan University Press, 1975.

————. *Amelia* (1751), ed. Martin C. Battestin. Middletown, Conn.: Wesleyan University Press, 1983.

Foote, Samuel. *The Plays of Samuel Foote,* ed. Paula R. Backscheider and Douglas Howard. New York: Garland, 1983.

Goldsmith, Oliver. *The Collected Letters of Oliver Goldsmith,* ed. Katharine C. Balderston. Cambridge: Cambridge University Press, 1928.

————. *Collected Works of Oliver Goldsmith,* ed. Arthur Friedman. 5 vols. Oxford: Clarendon Press, 1966.

————. *Essays and Criticism,* ed. Isaac Reed and Thomas Wright. 2 vols. London: J. Johnson, 1798.

————. *The Miscellaneous Works of Oliver Goldsmith, M.B.* 4 vols. London: J. Johnson, 1801.

————. *The Works of Oliver Goldsmith,* ed. J. W. M. Gibbs. 5 vols. London: George Bell & Sons, 1884–86.

Gray, Thomas. *Correspondence of Thomas Gray,* ed. Paget Toynbee and Leonard Whibley. 3 vols. Oxford: Clarendon Press, 1935; rpt. 1971.

————. *Odes by Mr. Gray.* Strawberry-Hill, Pall-Mall: Dodsley, 1757.

Hume, David. *The Letters of David Hume,* ed. J. Y. T. Greig. 2 vols. Oxford: Clarendon Press, 1932.

Jenyns, Soame. *A Free Inquiry into the Nature and Origin of Evil,* 2d ed. London: Dodsley, 1757.

Johnson, Samuel. *Political Writings,* ed. Donald J. Greene. Vol. 10, Yale Edition of the Works of Samuel Johnson. New Haven: Yale University Press, 1977.

————. *The Rambler,* ed. W. J. Bate and Albrecht B. Strauss. Vols. 3–5, Yale Edition of the Works of Samuel Johnson. New Haven: Yale University Press, 1969.

————. *The Idler and The Adventurer,* ed. W. J. Bate and Albrecht B. Strauss. Vol. 2, Yale Edition of the Works of Samuel Johnson. New Haven: Yale University Press, 1963.

Knox, Vicesimus. *Essays Moral and Literary.* 2 vols. London: Dilly, 1779.

Langhorne, John. *The Effusions of Friendship and Fancy.* 2 vols. 1766; rpt. New York: Garland, 1970.

Leake, John. *A Dissertation on the Properties and Efficacy of the Lisbon Diet-Drink; A Medicine, for many Years, successfully used in Portugal, in the cure of the Venereal Disease and Scurvy.* London: Clarke, 1757.

Lennox, Charlotte. *The Female Quixote; or, The Adventures of Arabella.* 2 vols. 1752; rpt. New York: Garland, 1974.

————. *Memories for the History of Madame de Maintenon, and of the last Age.* London: Millar, 1757.

Lyttleton, George. *Dialogues of the Dead.* 1760; rpt. New York: Garland, 1970.

Marriott, Thomas. *Female Conduct: Being an Essay on the Art of Pleasing. To be practiced by the Fair Sex, Before, and After Marriage.* London: W. Owen, 1759.

Medley, Thomas [pseud.]. *The Shandymonian: Containing a Conclamation of Original Pieces, a Higgledy-Piggledy of Controversies and Opinions on Various interesting Subjects. . . .* London: W. Nicoll, 1779.

Mitchell, John. *The Contest in America Between Great Britain and France, With Its Consequences and Importance.* London: Millar, 1757.

Murphy, Arthur. *The Plays of Arthur Murphy,* intro. Richard B. Schwartz. 4 vols. New York: Garland, 1979.

————. "An Essay on the Life and Genius of Dr. Johnson" (1792). In *The Lives of Henry Fielding and Samuel Johnson, Together with Essays from the "Gray's-Inn Journal,"* introduced by Matthew Grace. Gainesville, Florida: Scholars' Facsimiles & Reprints, 1968.

Percy, Thomas. "The Life of Dr. Goldsmith." In *The Miscellaneous Works of Oliver Goldsmith, M.B.* 4 vols. London, J. Johnson, 1801.

————. *The Percy Letters,* gen. eds. David Nichol Smith and Cleanth Brooks. 7 vols. Vols. 1–5, New Orleans: Lousiana State University Press; Vols. 6–7, New Haven: Yale University Press, 1944–77.

————. *History and Sources of Percy's Memoir of Goldsmith,* ed. Katharine C. Balderston. Cambridge: Cambridge University Press, 1926.

Rabener, G. W. *Satirical Letters.* 2 vols. London: Linde, 1757.

Ralph, James, *The Case of Authors by Profession or Trade.* 1758; rpt. ed. Philip Stevick. Gainesville, Fla.: Scholars' Facsimiles & Reprints, 1966.

Reynolds, Joshua. *Portraits by Sir Joshua Reynolds,* ed. Frederick W. Hilles. London: William Heinemann, 1952.

Rider, William. *An Historical and Critical Account of the Lives and Writings of the Living Authors of Great-Britain.* 1762; rpt. Los Angeles: Augustan Reprint Society, 1974.

Smollett, Tobias. *The Letters of Tobias Smollett,* ed. Lewis M. Knapp. Oxford: Clarendon Press, 1970.

St. Pierre, William. *The History of two Persons of Quality, taken from memoirs written in the reign of Edward IV.* London: Francis Noble, 1757.

Steele, Richard. *The Tatler,* ed. Donald F. Bond. 3 vols. Oxford: Clarendon Press, 1987.

Thornton, Bonnell, and George Colman. *The Connoisseur.* 3d ed. London: Baldwin, 1757.

Thrale, Hester Lynch. *Thraliana: The Diary of Mrs. Hester Lynch Thrale (Later Mrs. Piozzi): 1776–1809,* ed. Katharine C. Balderston. 2 vols. Oxford: Clarendon Press, 1942.

Wilkie, William. *The Epigoniad* (1757). London: J. Murray, 1759.

Witherspoon, John. *The History of a Corporation of Servants*. Glasgow: Gilmour, 1765.

Young, Edward. *Conjectures on Original Composition* (1759). Rpt. Leeds, U.K.: Scolar Press, 1966.

Secondary Souces

Abbott, John Lawrence. *John Hawkesworth, Eighteenth-Century Man of Letters*. Madison: University of Wisconsin Press, 1982.

Andrews, Alexander, *The History of British Journalism, from the Foundation of the Newspaper Press in England, to the Repeal of the Stamp Act in 1855, with Sketches of Press Celebrities*. 2 vols. 1859; rpt. Grosse Pointe, Mich.: Scholarly Press, 1968.

Bäckman, Sven. *This Singular Tale: A Study of "The Vicar of Wakefield" and Its Literary Background*. Lund, Sweden: C. W. K. Gleerup, 1971.

Balderston, Katharine C. "The Birth of Goldsmith." *Times Literary Supplement* (7 March 1929): 185–86.

———. *History and Sources of Percy's Memoir of Goldsmith*. Cambridge: Cambridge University Press, 1926.

Bann, Stephen. "The Sense of the Past: Image, Text, and Object in the Formation of Historical Consciousness in Nineteenth-Century Britain." In *The New Historicism*, ed. H. Aram Veeser. New York: Routledge, 1989.

Barber, Giles. "Book Imports and Exports in the Eighteenth Century." In *Sale and Distribution of Books from 1700*, ed. Robin Myers and Michael Harris. Oxford: Oxford Polytechnic Press, 1982, 77–105.

Barnouw, A. J. "Goldsmith's Indebtedness to Justus Van Effen." *Modern Language Review* 8 (July 1913): 314–24.

Basker, James. *Tobias Smollett: Critic and Journalist*. Newark: University of Delaware Press, 1988.

Bataille, Robert R. "Hugh Kelly's Journalism: Facts and Conjectures." *Journal of Newspaper and Periodical History* 1 (Summer 1985): 2–10.

Bertelsen, Lance. *The Nonsense Club: Literature and Popular Culture, 1749–1764*. Oxford: Clarendon Press, 1986.

Black, Jeremy. *The English Press in the Eighteenth Century.* London: Croom Helm, 1987.

Black, William. *Goldsmith*. London: Macmillan & Co., 1909.

Booth, Wayne. "The Self-Portraiture of Genius: *The Citizen of the World* and Critical Method." *Modern Philology* 73 (May 1976, Part 2: A Supplement to Honor Arthur Friedman): S85–S96.

Brewer, John. *Party Ideology and Popular Politics at the Accession of George III*. Cambridge: Cambridge University Press, 1976.

Carretta, Vincent. *George III and the Satirists from Hogarth to Byron*. Athens: The University of Georgia Press, 1990.

Clark, J. C. D. *The Dynamics of Change: The Crisis of the 1750s and English Party Systems*. Cambridge: Cambridge University Press, 1982.

Clifford, James. *Dictionary Johnson: Samuel Johnson's Middle Years*. New York: McGraw-Hill, 1979.

Colley, Linda. *In Defiance of Oligarchy: The Tory Party, 1714–60.* Cambridge: Cambridge University Press, 1982.

Crane, Ronald S. *New Essays by Oliver Goldsmith.* Chicago: University of Chicago Press, 1927.

———. Review of Balderston, "The Birth of Goldsmith." *Philological Quarterly* 9 (1930): 190–91.

———. Review of Seitz, "Goldsmith and the *Literary Magazine.*" *Philological Quarterly* 9 (1930): 192.

———. "The 'Deserted Village' in Prose (1762)." *Times Literary Supplement* (8 September 1927): 607.

Cruickshanks, Eveline. *Political Untouchables: The Tories and the '45.* London: Duckworth, 1979.

Davie, Donald. "Notes on Goldsmith's Politics." In *The Art of Oliver Goldsmith,* ed. Andrew Swarbrick. London: Vision Press, 1984.

Davis, Bertram H. *Thomas Percy.* Boston: Twayne, 1981.

DeMaria, Robert, Jr. *Johnson's "Dictionary" and the Language of Learning.* Chapel Hill: University of North Carolina Press, 1986.

Dobson, Austin. *Life of Oliver Goldsmith.* London: Walter Scott, 1888.

Eddy, Donald D. *Samuel Johnson: Book Reviewer in the "Literary Magazine, or Universal Review," 1756–1758.* New York: Garland, 1979.

Emery, John Pike. *Arthur Murphy: An Eminent English Dramatist of the Eighteenth Century.* Philadelphia: University of Pennsylvania Press, 1946.

Ferguson, Oliver. "Oliver Goldsmith: The Personality of the Essayist." *Philological Quarterly* 61 (Spring 1982): 179–91.

Forster, Antonia. "From 'Tasters to the Public' To 'Beadles of Parnassus': Reviewers, Authors, and the Reading Public, 1749–1774." Dissertation, University of Melbourne, 1986.

Forster, John. *The Life and Times of Oliver Goldsmith.* 2 vols. London: Bickers & Son, 1877.

Friedman, Arthur. "Goldsmith and the *Weekly Magazine.*" *Modern Philology* 32 (February 1935): 281–99.

———. "Goldsmith's Contributions to the *Critical Review,*" *Modern Philology* 44 (1946): 23–52.

Fussell, Paul. *Samuel Johnson and the Life of Writing.* New York: Harcourt Brace Jovanovich, 1971.

Ginger, John. *The Notable Man: The Life and Times of Oliver Goldsmith.* London: Hamish Hamilton, 1977.

Golden, Morris. "Goldsmith, *The Vicar of Wakefield,* and the Periodicals." *Journal of English and Germanic Philology* 76 (October 1977): 525–36.

———. "Goldsmith's Attributions in the *Literary Magazine.*" *Notes & Queries* 201 (October 1956): 432–35.

———. "Goldsmith and the *Universal Museum and Complete Magazine.*" *Notes & Queries* 202 (August 1957): 339–48.

———. "Goldsmith and 'The Distresses of an Hired Writer.'" *Notes & Queries* 200 (April 1955): 165.

Graham, Walter. *English Literary Periodicals.* New York: Thomas Nelson & Sons, 1930.

Gray, Charles H. *Theatrical Criticism in London to 1795.* New York: Columbia University Press, 1931.

Greene, Donald J. "Samuel Johnson and the Great War for Empire." In *English Writers of the*

Eighteenth Century, ed. John H. Middendorf. New York: Columbia University Press, 1971, pp. 37–65.

————. *The Age of Exuberance: Backgrounds to Eighteenth-Century Literature.* New York: Random House, 1970.

Gwynn, Stephen. *Oliver Goldsmith.* New York: Henry Holt, 1935.

Haig, Robert L. *The "Gazetteer," 1735–1797: A Study in the Eighteenth-Century English Newspaper.* Carbondale: Southern Illinois University Press, 1960.

Harris, Michael. "Periodicals and the Book Trade." In *Development of the English Book Trade, 1700–1899,* ed. Robin Myers and Michael Harris. Oxford: Oxford Polytechnic Press, 1981, pp. 66–94.

Hawkins, Aubrey. "Some Writers on *The Monthly Review.*" *Review of English Studies* 7 (April 1931): 168–81.

Hazen, Allen T. "New Styles in Typography." In *The Age of Johnson: Essays Presented to Chauncey Brewster Tinker,* ed. Frederick W. Hilles. New Haven: Yale University Press, 1949, pp. 403–9.

Herd, Harold. *Seven Editors.* London: George Allen & Unwin, 1955.

Hopkins, Robert H. *The True Genius of Oliver Goldsmith.* Baltimore: Johns Hopkins Press, 1969.

————. "Matrimony in *The Vicar of Wakefield* and the Marriage Act of 1753." *Studies in Philology* 74 (July 1977): 322–39.

Hume, Robert D. "Goldsmith and Sheridan and the Supposed Revolution of 'Laughing' Against 'Sentimental' Comedy." In *Studies in Change and Revolution: Aspects of English Intellectual History, 1640–1800,* ed. Paul J. Korshin. Menston, U.K.: Scolar Press, 1972, pp. 237–76.

Irving, Washington. *Oliver Goldsmith: A Biography* (1849), ed. Elsie Lee West. Vol. 17, *The Complete Works of Washington Irving.* Boston: Twayne, 1978.

Iser, Wolfgang. *The Implied Reader: Patterns of Communication in Prose Fiction from Bunyan to Beckett.* Baltimore: The Johns Hopkins University Press, 1987.

James, Francis Godwin. *Ireland in the Empire, 1688–1770: A History of Ireland from the Williamite Wars to the Eve of the American Revolution.* Cambridge: Harvard University Press, 1973.

Jones, Claude E. "Contributors to the *Critical Review,* 1756–1785." *Modern Language Notes* 61 (November 1946): 433–41.

————. "The *Critical Review*'s First Thirty Years (1756–1785)." *Notes and Queries* n.s. 3 (1956): 78–80.

Jones, W. Powell. "The Contemporary Reception of Gray's *Odes.*" *Modern Philology* 28 (August 1930): 61–82.

Kaminski, Thomas. *The Early Career of Samuel Johnson.* New York: Oxford University Press, 1987.

Kent, Elizabeth Eaton. *Goldsmith and His Booksellers.* Ithaca: Cornell University Press, 1933.

Kenny, Robert W. "Ralph's *Case of Authors:* Its Influence on Goldsmith and Isaac D'Israeli." *PMLA* 52 (March 1937): 104–13.

Kernan, Alvin. *Printing Technology, Letters & Samuel Johnson.* Princeton: Princeton University Press, 1987.

Kirk, Clara M. *Oliver Goldsmith.* New York: Twayne, 1967.

Knapp, Lewis M. "Ralph Griffiths, Author and Publisher." *The Library* 20 (September 1939): 197–213.

————. "Dr. John Armstrong, Littérateur, and Associate of Smollett, Thomson, Wilkes, and Other Celebrities." *PMLA* 59 (December 1944): 1019–58.

Larson, Magali S. *The Rise of Professionalism: A Sociological Analysis.* Berkeley: University of California Press, 1977.

Lentricchia, Frank. "Foucault's Legacy—A New Historicism?" In *The New Historicism,* ed. H. Aram Veeser. New York: Routledge, 1989.

Lucas, F. L. *The Search for Good Sense: Four Eighteenth-Century Characters.* London: Cassell, 1958.

Madden, Richard R. *The History of Irish Periodical Literature.* 2 vols. London: T. C. Newby, 1867.

Marr, George S. *The Periodical Essayists of the Eighteenth Century.* London: J. Clarke, 1923.

Mayo, Robert D. *The English Novel in the Magazines, 1740–1815.* Evanston, Ill.: North-western University Press, 1962.

McKeon, Michael. *The Origins of the English Novel, 1600–1740.* Baltimore: The Johns Hopkins University Press, 1987.

Melville, Lewis. *The Life and Letters of Tobias Smollett.* Boston: Houghton Mifflin, 1927.

Middendorf, John H., ed. *English Writers of the Eighteenth Century.* New York: Columbia University Press, 1971.

Mossner, Ernest Campbell, and Harry Ransom. "Hume and 'The Conspiracy of the Book-sellers': The Publication and Early Fortunes of the *History of England.*" *University of Texas Studies in English* 29 (1950): 162–82.

Namier, L. B. *The Structure of Politics at the Accession of George III.* 2 vols. London: Macmillan and Co., 1929.

Nobbe, George. *The "North Briton": A Study in Political Propaganda.* 1939; rpt. New York: AMS Press, 1966.

Nussbaum, Felicity A. *The Autobiographical Subject: Gender and Ideology in Eighteenth-Century England.* Baltimore: The Johns Hopkins University Press, 1989.

————. "Introduction," *The Plays of David Mallet.* New York: Garland, 1980.

Oakes, Norman. "Ralph Griffiths and the *Monthly Review.*" Dissertation, Columbia University, 1961.

Oliver, John W. "Johnson, Goldsmith and 'The History of the Seven Years' War.'" *Times Literary Supplement* (18 May 1922): 324.

Price, John Vladimir. "The Reading of Philosophical Literature." In *Books and Their Readers in Eighteenth-Century England,* ed. Isabel Rivers. Leicester, U.K.: Leicester University Press, 1982.

Prior, James. *The Life of Oliver Goldsmith, M.B., from a Variety of Original Sources.* 2 vols. London: John Murray, 1837.

Quintana, Ricardo. *Oliver Goldsmith: A Georgian Study.* New York: Macmillan Company, 1967.

Rea, Robert R. *The English Press in Politics: 1760–1774.* Lincoln: University of Nebraska Press, 1963.

Roper, Derek. *Reviewing Before the "Edinburgh": 1788–1802.* Newark: University of Delaware Press, 1978.

————. "The Politics of the *Critical Review,* 1756–1817." *Durham University Journal* n.s. 22 (March 1961): 117–22.

————. "Smollett's 'Four Gentlemen': The First Contributors to the *Critical Review.*" *Review of English Studies* n.s. 10 (February 1959): 38–44.

Rudé, George. *Hanoverian London: 1714–1808.* Berkeley: University of California Press, 1971.

Sainsbury, John. *Disaffected Patriots: London Supporters of Revolutionary America, 1769–1782.* Kingston, Ont.: McGill-Queen's University Press, 1987.

Sarason, Bertram D. "Edmund Burke and the Two *Annual Registers.*" *PMLA* 68 (June 1953): 496–508.

Seitz, R. W. "Goldsmith and the *Literary Magazine.*" *Review of English Studies* 5 (1929): 410–30.

———. "The Irish Background of Goldsmith's Social and Political Thought." *PMLA* 52 (June 1937): 405–11.

———. "Some of Goldsmith's Second Thoughts on English History." *Modern Philology* 35 (February 1938): 279–88.

Sekora, John. *Luxury: The Concept in Western Thought, Eden to Smollett.* Baltimore: Johns Hopkins University Press, 1977.

Sells, A. L. Lytton. *Thomas Gray: His Life and Works.* London: George Allen & Unwin, 1980.

Shelton, Walter J. *English Hunger and Industrial Disorders: A Study of Social Conflict During the First Decade of George III's Reign.* Toronto: University of Toronto Press, 1973.

Sherbo, Arthur. *New Essays by Arthur Murphy.* East Lansing: Michigan State University Press, 1963.

Sitter, John. *Literary Loneliness in Mid-Eighteenth Century England.* Ithaca: Cornell University Press, 1982.

Smith, J. H. "Tony Lumpkin and the Country Booby Type in Antecedent English Comedy." *PMLA* (1943): 1038–49.

Spector, Robert D. *English Literary Periodicals and the Climate of Opinion During the Seven Years' War.* The Hague: Mouton, 1966.

———. "*The Connoisseur:* A Study of the Functions of a Persona." In *English Writers of the Eighteenth Century,* ed. John H. Middendorf. New York: Columbia University Press, 1971, pp. 109–121.

———. *Arthur Murphy.* Boston: Twayne, 1979.

Storm, Leo. "Conventional Ethics in Goldsmith's *The Traveller.*" *Studies in English Literature* 17 (Summer 1977): 463–76.

Tave, Stuart M. *The Amiable Humorist: A Study in the Comic Theory and Criticism of the Eighteenth and Nineteenth Centuries.* Chicago: University of Chicago Press, 1960.

Taylor, Richard C. "Goldsmith's First Vicar." *Review of English Studies* 41 (March 1990): 191–99.

———. "The Politics of Goldsmith's Journalism." *Philological Quarterly* 69 (Winter 1990): 71–89.

———. "A Source for Goldsmith's Tony Lumpkin in *The Connoisseur.*" *English Language Notes* 26 (March 1989): 30–36.

Tupper, Caroline F. "Oliver Goldsmith and 'The Gentleman Who Signs D.'" *Modern Language Notes* 45 (February 1930): 71–77.

Veeser, Aram, ed. *The New Historicism.* New York: Routledge, 1989.

Wardle, Ralph M. *Oliver Goldsmith.* Lawrence: University of Kansas Press, 1957.

Watson, J. Steven. *The Reign of George III: 1760–1815.* Oxford: Clarendon Press, 1960.

Watt, Ian. *The Rise of the Novel.* Berkeley: University of California Press, 1957.

Wichelns, Herbert A. "Burke's Essay on the Sublime and Its Reviewers." *Journal of English and Germanic Philology* 21 (1922): 645–61.

Woods, Samuel H. "The Goldsmith Problem." *Studies in Burke and His Time* 19 (Winter 1978): 47–60.

Index